SHADOW OF THE ALMIGHTY

The life and testimony of
JIM ELLIOT
By
ELISABETH ELLIOT

OM Publishing
PO Box 48, Bromley, Kent, England

NCU:PA

ELL

© 1958 Elisabeth Elliot

First published in the United Kingdom by Hodder & Stoughton Ltd

First STL edition 1979
This edition 1988
Reprinted 1990

STL ISBN 1 85078 035 8

OM Publishing is an imprint of Send The Light
(Operation Mobilisation),
PO Box 48, Bromley, Kent, England, BR1 3JH

Production and Printing in England by
Nuprint Ltd, Station Road, Harpenden, Herts, AL5 4SE

To Valerie

I think the writings of your father, whom you do not remember, will one day help you to know him in a way which my descriptions of him can never do. And I pray that as you know him, you will learn to love the One he loved, and to follow Him as faithfully.

CONTENTS

Part Four   Ecuador, 1952–1956

ACKNOWLEDGEMENTS

ONE AFTERNOON about two months before Jim's death I was reading some of his letters and diaries. I turned to him and said, 'I'm glad I have these. I'm going to need them when I write your biography.' He made a remark about the absurdity of some of my ideas, and went on reading his *Time* magazine.

Shortly after his death I began putting together the writings which he left behind. Marilou McCully, Olive Fleming, Barbara Youderian, and Marj Saint have been my friends in the truest sense, and my strong supporters in this task from its very beginning. When they asked me to interrupt the writing of the biography in order to write *Through Gates of Splendour*, I flew to New York, and it was there that Melvin Arnold of Harper & Brothers read the first draft of this book. His encouragement then and his continued editorial advice have been a very great help.

For their help in supplying material on Jim's background and early years, and for their generously allowing me to use all of the letters Jim wrote to them, I am very grateful to Jim's family: his father and mother, the Fred Elliots of Portland; his brothers Bob, also of Portland, and Bert of Yurimaguas, Peru; and his sister Jane Hawthorne of Wheaton, Illinois. I would like to thank also Jim's friends Werner

Durtschi and Wayne McCroskey of Portland for their recollections of Jim's school days; Dick Fisher of Astoria, Oregon, for his vivid descriptions of Jim's early years, and for the use of a letter which Jim wrote to him; Olive Fleming for a letter Jim wrote to her husband Pete; Evelyn Corkum of Seattle for her testimony of Jim's influence on her life during her high school days; Ron Harris for his account of Jim's visit to his home in Mexico; Eleanor Vandevort of the Sudan and Bill Cathers of Ecuador for letters Jim wrote to them; and my brother Dave Howard of Costa Rica for his memories of college days. Sam Saint of New Jersey was kind enough to read the manuscript and give me some valuable suggestions. Mardelle Senseney and Ruth Keenan of Shell Mera, Ecuador, assisted greatly by checking the many Scripture references.

I should like to thank the Dohnavur Fellowship for their permission to quote from the work of Amy Carmichael.

Special thanks are due to Bill and Irene Cathers for assuming virtually all responsibility here on the jungle station so that I could be free to write.

ELISABETH ELLIOT

Shandia, Ecuador
April, 1958

PREFACE

It is only when we obey God's laws that we can be quite sure that we really know Him. The man who claims to know God but does not obey His laws is not only a liar, he lives in self-delusion. In practice, the more a man learns to obey God's laws, the more truly and fully does he express his love for Him. Obedience is the test of whether we really live "in God" or not. The life of a man who professes to be living in God must bear the stamp of Christ.[1]

THESE WORDS, written about AD 90 in the first epistle of John, embody the radicals of Jim Elliot's life. Obedience leads to knowledge. Obedience is the expression of love to God. Obedience means that we live in God. And if we live in Him, our lives bear the stamp of Christ.

Some who pick up this book may make no claim to know God. Others may make the claim but be victims of the self-delusion that John observes. Yet others may know Him, and obey Him, but wonder sometimes at the value of this knowledge and this obedience. I think that this book will have something to say to all three. If those in the first category *want* to know God, they may perhaps learn how. Those in the second group may find that they are missing a great deal by not backing their claims with action. And those in the third category may be encouraged to pursue their course.

Jim's aim was to know God. His course, obedience — the only course that could lead to the fulfilment of his aim. His end was what some would call an extraordinary death, although in facing death he had quietly pointed out that many have died because of obedience to God.

He and the other men with whom he died were hailed as heroes, 'martyrs'. I do not approve. Nor would they have approved.

Is the distinction between living for Christ and dying for Him, after all, so great? Is not the second the logical conclusion of the first? Furthermore, to live for God *is* to die, 'daily', as the apostle Paul put it. It is to lose everything that we may gain Christ. It is in thus laying down our lives that we find them.

The relationship between man and God is a very practical one. It finds its sphere of operation in the common life. Let us not forget that any relationship whatever between God and man rests today on the fact that *God* lived the life of a common man — was born in a stable, sweated in a carpenter shop, preached from a little fishing-boat, sat down tired beside a well and conversed with a courtesan, ate and drank and walked with ordinary men, and submitted to an ignoble death — in order that we could recognise Him. Nobody called Him a hero or a martyr. He was simply doing what His Father told Him to do, and doing it with *delight*.

Those who want to know Him must walk the same path with Him. *These* are the 'martyrs' in the Scriptural sense of the word, which means simply 'witnesses'. In life, as well as in death, we are called to be 'witnesses' — to 'bear the stamp of Christ'.

I believe that Jim Elliot was one of these. His letters and journals are the tangible ground for my belief. They are not mine to withhold. They are a part of the human story, the story of a man in his relation to the Almighty. They are facts.

'I write like I talk—without thinking much beforehand —and sometimes spiel stuff that were better left in the ink bottle,' Jim wrote to me in 1948. 'I think it was Browning who, having been queried on something he wrote in early life, said, "When I wrote that, two people knew what it meant, God and I. Now only God knows." So with anything perplexing, throw it out, discounted as an abortion sprung from a mind that is at times over-productive to its own hurt.'

Once in 1952 I mentioned to Jim that I had sent an excerpt from one of his letters to a friend. He replied:

> I'm not too excited about your sending my letters to others. I don't like to write a page knowing that perhaps a not-as-sympathetic reader as yourself may scan it. This is a confession that I am not trying to impress you with my letters. I barely reread them, pay little attention to grammar and punctuation, and know that my handwriting has suffered. I guess I will have to trust you to be choosy in sending representations of me to folks whose impression-factors should be delicately censored.

In the task of selection I have not 'delicately censored' anything at all which I felt would contribute to the faithful portrayal of the whole man as I knew him. The reader will notice the repetition of certain ideas throughout his writings. He will also wonder if perhaps in certain chapters I have included only those portions of his writings which indicate the growth of his soul, to the exclusion of those which would show a more 'human' side of his personality. Of both of these—the repetition, the long passages dealing with soul-exercise—I would say this: I have taken pains to let my choices represent the tone of Jim's writings as a whole, so that the number of excerpts on a given subject, or during a given period, are in direct proportion to the total content of the letters and diaries. There were periods when his writing was occupied almost exclusively with the metaphysical. There were others when it dealt with the mundane.

When Jim was twenty years old he prayed, 'Lord, make my way prosperous, not that I achieve high station, but that my life may be an exhibit to the value of knowing God.' His life was that to me, who shared it more intimately than any other. Was it extraordinary? I offer these pages so that the reader may decide for himself. If his answer is yes—if he finds herein the 'stamp of Christ', and decides that this is extraordinary—what shall we say of the state of Christendom?

Notes

1. 1 John 2:3–6, JBP.

PROLOGUE

WHEN JIM was a college student in 1949 he wrote these words:

He is no fool who gives what he cannot keep to gain what he cannot lose.

Seven years later, on a hot Sunday afternoon, far from the dormitory room where those lines were written, he and four other young men were finishing a dinner of baked beans and carrot-sticks. They sat together on a strip of white sand on the Curaray River, deep in Ecuador's rain forest, waiting for the arrival of a group of men whom they loved, but had never met—savage Stone Age killers, known to all the world now as Aucas.

Two days before, the hope of years had been partially fulfilled. Three of these Indians had met them on the beach where they now sat. The first friendly contact, long anticipated and carefully prepared for, had been completely successful. The young man and his two women companions stepped off the jungle green on the other side of the river and, after slight hesitation, accepted the hand of Jim Elliot, who led them across the river to the other white men. At first the naked tribespeople were distrustful and with reason. They had known of white men who flew in great birds similar to that which now stood beside them on the sand, who had proved that they could not be trusted. But somehow they had sensed, throughout the long weeks when these five men had attempted to show them their friendship, that there was no 'catch' here.

The white men had at first dropped gifts to the Aucas, similar to those they had received in other years—machetes, cooking-pots, ribbons, cloth. These things were most welcome, and the Indians began to wait for the sound of that yellow *ayamu* which appeared with regularity (though whether a people who cannot count beyond three would recognise the seven-day rhythm is questionable). When the sound of the motor was heard, they would run from their manioc patches, from inside the great, oval-shaped, leaf-thatched houses, or from downriver where they had been fishing in their dugout canoes. There they were again—those strange, white-faced men, waving and shouting, then lowering a bucket on a rope, from which the Indians could grab all manner of delights. And what was that? Suddenly a voice boomed through the air—in their own language! The man was speaking to them.

'Come! We are your friends. We like you. We are your friends.'

Could it be that they did not intend to take away the Indians' land, to destroy their crops, to kill their people, as others had done? There were some who began to believe. An idea came to them. Why not encourage these men? Would it not be worth while to find out what their true intentions were? Might there not be greater gains for the Indians if they played along with the strangers?

The following week they returned the airborne gift. A beautiful feather crown, carefully woven, with a palm-splinter facing, was placed in the basket which was slowly circling at their feet. Later an extraordinarily enterprising Auca made a little model plane, as much like the Piper Family Cruiser as he could make it, and set it up on the roof of his house. Had he been secretly spying on the house in Arajuno, which was the base of operations, where a model plane had been hung on a pole for just such an inspection? Or was it entirely his own idea to construct a model?

When the plane circled over one day, the Aucas heard one

16

of the men call, 'We are on the Curaray. Come. Come and see us.' This was too much for some of them. Still torn by doubts and long-held fears of these white men, they hesitated two days—possibly spying out the situation from the thick growth of jungle into which they know how to vanish as effectively as the dappled ocelot of their forest. But on the third day their curiosity—or who can say what motives—overcame their fears, and, answering the calls of the five men who strode up and down the beach, three young Indians made their appearance.

Who were these white men? Brothers of the monkey that swung in the vines, with their hairy faces and arms? Brothers of the armadillo who wears what must be an uncomfortable covering and never walks naked? Sons, perhaps, of the Sun-Maker, since they came from the skies? Yet they laughed, they spoke words which the Indians could understand, they offered gifts of food. Food, was it? It must be—it tasted good, though totally different from anything they knew (hamburgers, bread, lemonade, mustard; these could hardly be compared to the dry, heavy manioc root, tapir meat, and peanuts which formed part of their diet).

And that wonderful water! One of the men poured some into an Indian's hand (they called him 'George' among themselves), and when he rubbed it on his body the flies as if by magic stopped their biting.

The white men were constantly making strange marks with a black-tipped stick on a smooth white leaf. Then they would look hard at those marks, and speak the words the Indians had spoken. But to one another they made weird sounds—not words, surely? Yes, they must be words—they seemed to understand one another, to be talking. But it was not 'hearable'. And why did they not answer the Indians when they spoke to them?

The young girl discovered that the surface of the great *ayamu* was smooth. It was like—but it was not like anything she knew. How would she describe it to the others when she got home? Like a plantain leaf? But then, that is not broad and resistant. She rubbed her body against it ecstatically.

And just how did that creature fly? 'George' had to know. He peered into its crop, then into its belly. Those wings wouldn't flap. How did it work? Gesticulating and jabbering, he convinced the pilot that he was not afraid, that he wanted to fly. Up, up over the trees with a frightening roar they rose. How strange the world looked to his near-sighted eyes—for the forest Indian knows nothing of wide spaces, distant horizons. He knows only the brown mud at his feet, the height of a tree, the short reach of a river as far as the next curve. Perhaps he has climbed a tree and looked out over the greenness in search of the smoke which tells him of a house, but he has seen nothing like this which spread out beneath 'George' now.

Suddenly his eyes focused on a change in the scene below—people, tiny people, were running about. They looked the same size as the white men looked before, when they flew over his head. Yes, they must be *his* people. The plane circled lower. Ah, yes—there was his brother, his father, his old grandmother. He shouted wildly and they watched with astonishment. Now the plane circled up higher again. He was so overcome with glee that he shouted all the way back to the beach, where the white sand suddenly spread out huge and bright and rose to meet the plane. With a teeth-chattering grinding they bounced along the ground, and the trees finally stood still. There were the two women again. How describe to them what he had seen?

Late in the afternoon the young girl decided it was time to leave these strange people, who seemed to have no desire for her. She ran down the sand strip. 'George' called after her, but no, she was resolute. At last, as she disappeared into the forest, he followed. Later the older woman joined them, and they raced over the steep hills and through the mud to their village, breathless to tell of their experiences. But there were old matted heads of black hair back in the shadows which silently shook as they heard the tale. Between those cylinders of balsa stuck in their ear-lobes, dark plans were taking shape.

Back at the beach on the Curaray, the five men waited eagerly the next day for the return of their friends. Pacing the beach as before, they shouted the few phrases they had learned of the Auca language, phrases elicited from an escaped member of the tribe who lived on an hacienda near one of the mission stations. But their calls were answered only by the stillness of the virgin jungle on both sides of the winding river. Once a tree fell, alerting them all to tense expectancy. Nothing happened. Finally Jim Elliot looked at his watch.

'Okay, boys—I give them five minutes. If they don't show up, I'm going over!'

Wisdom prevented his carrying out this threat, but the long afternoon brought no reward for their vigil.

The 'neighbours' were apparently in conference—should they return and invite the white men to their village? Who should go? They could not know with what eagerness and longing they were awaited.

Sunday morning dawned clear. Again God had answered prayer. The river had not risen to obliterate the little landing-strip, and the skies were good for flying. Nate, the pilot, took off. After circling the Indian village, he spotted about ten Aucas making their way along the beach in the direction of the four foreigners.

'This is it, guys!' he shouted as the Piper bounced on to the beach. 'They're on their way!'

Nate's wife was informed by radio of the expected contact and was asked to stand by again at 4.30 pm.

Lunch over, the men busied themselves fixing up a minia-ture 'jungle' and model house in the sand, with the intention of demonstrating to the savages how to build an airstrip, should they be interested enough to want the white men to come and live among them. Then the five missionaries sang together, as they had so often done, spontaneously and joyously:

> 'We rest on Thee, our Shield and our Defender,
> We go not forth alone against the foe.
> Strong in Thy Strength, safe in Thy keeping tender,
> We rest on Thee, and in Thy name we go.

> 'Yea, in Thy name, O Captain of Salvation,
> In Thy blest name, all other names above,
> Jesus our Righteousness, our sure Foundation,
> Our Prince of Glory, and our King of Love.

> 'We go in faith, our own great weakness feeling,
> And needing more each day Thy grace to know,
> Yet from our hearts a song of triumph pealing,
> We rest on Thee, and in Thy name we go.

> 'We rest on Thee, our Shield and our Defender,
> Thine is the battle, Thine shall be the praise
> When passing through the gates of pearly splendour,
> Victors, we rest with Thee through endless days.'[1]

Committing themselves and all their carefully laid plans to Him who had so unmistakably brought them thus far, they waited for the Aucas.

Before four-thirty that afternoon the quiet waters of the Curaray flowed over the bodies of the five comrades, slain by the men they had come to win for Christ, whose banner they had borne. The world called it a nightmare of tragedy. The world did not recognise the truth of the second clause in Jim Elliot's credo: 'He is no fool who gives what he cannot keep to gain what he cannot lose.'

Note
1. Hymn by Edith G. Cherry in *Golden Bells Hymnal* 547.

PART ONE

Portland, Oregon,

1927 — 1945

— I —

Strong Roots

Those that be planted in the house of the Lord shall flourish in the courts of our God.[1]

TOWARDS THE MIDDLE of the nineteenth century the hardwood bush country of Ontario between Lake Huron and Lake Erie was still semi-frontier. Among the many who were attracted there by the promise of good cheap land were the Elliots, from a clan of the southern border of Scotland. They settled a hundred miles west of Toronto, near Molesworth, a tiny country village comprising two general stores, a schoolhouse, lodge hall, two blacksmith shops, and two churches. Of these last, the Elliots naturally chose the Presbyterian kirk. The choice was an auspicious one, for it was here that they encountered the MacAllisters, a family from the north of Scotland. Sunday after Sunday the eight Elliot children associated with the eleven MacAllister children. These friendships eventually led to four Elliot-MacAllister marriages, which in turn produced thirty-six double cousins.

One of the four couples, John and Margaret Elliot, owned a small frame house on a hill, surrounded by orchards and grazing land. John was a hard-working stock-trader, respected for his square dealing, eager that his eight children should learn the value of honest labour. Opportunity for this was not lacking. There was stock to feed in the barns during the long winter from September to May, a large wood-house to keep filled behind the kitchen, crops to plant and hoe, reap and store, maple sap to collect and boil down, and of course cows to milk and chickens to feed. Often added to these were household chores, for the children's mother was subject to frequent violents attacks of asthma, and these finally necessitated the oldest son Fred's being taken out of school to help at home. Denied the remainder of his formal education, he became an avid reader, and learned many practical skills while helping his father with carpentry and the care of machinery.

When he reached teen-age, Fred went with his younger brother Will to work in the harvest-fields of Saskatchewan, and from there to British Columbia. Fred had been converted at the age of thirteen when he was taught that the Lord's return was imminent, but it was in British Columbia, under the teaching of Harry Ironside, that he recognised that life was worth living only if given over completely to God. He decided to surrender his life, and later began travelling with Mr Ironside as he went about preaching in rural communities of the north-west.

At about the same time that John and Margaret Elliot were married in Ontario, the call 'Go West!' lured a young man from Berne, Switzerland, where his father was civil engineer of that city. Emil Luginbuhl's money got him as far as Colorado, where he went to work in a smelter until he saved enough to take a homestead in the State of Washington. One day word came that a ribbon-maker's daughter, who had sung in the choir with him back home in Switzerland, had reached America. He lost no time in writing to her, and as soon as he could persuade her to come west, Emil Luginbuhl and Emma Maurer were married on a Methodist preacher's homestead two miles from what is now Roosevelt, Washington.

In the midst of the vast grassland of eastern Washington, Emil created a beautiful oasis by irrigation, producing in time apples, pears, plums, peaches, cherries, apricots, grapes, and strawberries, as well as vegetables and flowers. There was such an abundance that he was able to supply not only his own family but also the neighbouring dryland farmers, who came in wagons and helped themselves to boxes-full of produce.

The acreage that was not planted in gardens or grain-fields was grazing land for sheep—wide, rolling hills stretching away as far as the foothills of Mt Adams, over which hung a blue-purple haze in the evening. The two Luginbuhl children, Jim and Clara, had only an hour a day for play. The chores of the barn and corrals for Jim, the baking of bread, housework, and occasional sheep-herding for Clara filled the remainder of the day.

It was to this ranch, with its large frame house set among tall poplar trees, that Mr Ironside, the travelling preacher, came one day with his young friend, Fred Elliot. Clara Luginbuhl was eighteen, and very much in love, she thought, with her uncle's foreman at that time. But three years later, while she was a student in chiropractic college in Portland, Oregon, she attended meetings in a little Baptist church where Fred—who had been encouraged by Mr Ironside to speak in public—was preaching, taking with her each night a different boy-friend. Fred noticed the pretty, blue-eyed girl on Monday night, and assumed her escort was the Elect. On Tuesday, however, he brightened to note a different one at her side. Seeing a third on Wednesday, he decided there was hope for him, and asked if he could see her home on Thursday. After that they saw each other daily. At Easter Fred sent her a lily, and a correspondence began which lasted two years, at the end of which time they were married, following Clara's graduation in 1918.

They made their home in Seattle for four years, where Clara practised chiropractic and Fred worked as an evangelist in the Puget Sound area. Their first child, Robert, was born there in 1921. The next year they moved to Portland, Oregon, to a small house which Clara's father had purchased years before as a summer home. Here three more children were born, Herbert in 1924, Jim in 1927, and Jane in 1932.

Clara had her professional office off the living-room of her home so that she could keep her fingers on the family pulse, for she considered the children her first responsibility. The idea of hiring baby-sitters never occurred to her. What the family could not do together, they simply did not do. The Elliot children went to worship meetings and Sunday School from the time they were six weeks old. 'I don't think it hurts any child to sit quiet through an adult meeting,' Clara declared; 'it's good for his nerves.' And as for any foolishness about 'forcing religion down their throats', the parents had not the slightest worry. They wanted the best for their children ('except money, which can become a curse,' they said) and gave it to them—spiritual as well as physical care, and all the other good things they could offer. If the child failed to appreciate the need for spiritual guidance, he probably failed, too, to see the need of physical rest when bedtime came around, but the parents guided him just the same, to God as well as to bed.

Fred Elliot read the Scriptures daily to his children, seeking to show them the glory of Christ above all else, striving always to avoid legalisms or a list of 'don'ts'. 'I prayed *with* them as well as for them,' he says. And each of the children at an early age heard the call of Jesus and set his face to follow.

Jim was only about six when he said to his mother one night as they returned home from a meeting. 'Now, mama, the Lord Jesus can come whenever He wants. He could take our whole family, because I'm saved now, and Janie is too young to know about Him yet.'

He began telling his small friends what he believed about salvation, 'preaching' to them from the lawn swing.

The Elliot home was always wide open to friends, including missionaries from many parts of the world. The impression this made on the four children was deep, teaching them the grace of hospitality as well as giving them priceless opportunities to know many kinds of people. 'The children loved to have company, even though it meant giving up their beds,' said Jim's mother, 'and because they met new acquaintances so often at home they were cheerful and free and uninhibited in public.'

Obedience and honesty were stressed above all else in the discipline of the children, while mischief was sometimes winked at and sometimes reproved with a brief scolding. The parents made an issue of nothing unless they intended to carry it through, believing that empty threats were dishonest and ruinous to a child's sense of justice. Fred Elliot administered the more serious punishments, occasionally postponing a spanking in order to give it in private. When the children reached the age of fourteen, they were told that from then on they were responsible to the Lord for their actions, since they had accepted Him as Saviour and Lord of their lives. 'And don't ever think you'll get by with something because we don't know about it,' their mother told them. 'God knows, and has His own way of punishing.'

They learned to appreciate the outdoors, tobogganing on Mt Hood in winter, picnicking on the rugged Oregon coast in summer or visiting the old Luginbuhl homestead in Washington, where they raced on the grass-covered hills, tumbled in the haymow, and were occasionally permitted to help care for the sheep and feed the new lambs. Their parents took them to stock shows, taught them to raise fruits, vegetables, and animals, and shared in their good times. Each child had his own hobbies, Jim's being the building of model sailing-ships and airplanes, collecting stamps and reading. His love for beauty was demonstrated in unexpected ways. His mother recalls how one afternoon, coming home tired from a shopping trip, she found a huge bouquet of autumn leaves which Jim had arranged for her on the dining-room table. He took a keen interest in the home and garden, in the colour of the breakfast-nook curtains or the rug in the living-room, as well as in the holly trees and roses outside. In grammar school the teacher was so pleased with his early efforts to draw that she lined the room with his pictures.

His interest in art was not, however, what his schoolmate Dick Fisher remembers. His most vivid recollection:

> I was a playground monitor, which meant that I locked the bicycles in the rack after everyone had arrived. I always had to wait for Jim. I can remember him tearing down 80th Street every day as the bell would sound, sliding on the gravel in front of the Gable Funeral Home as he rounded the fenced section of the pathway through the Seventh Day Adventist Church yard, and finally wide open across the school yard, until, in a big cloud of dust, he would brake to a stop at the rack, jump off the bike, mutter something about being late and thanks, and disappear into the school building. For one whole year that was my complete acquaintance with this picture of speed, fury, and recklessness.

Note

1. Psalm 92:13.

— 2 —

Orator and Garbage Collector

Whatsoever thy hand findeth to do, do it with thy might.[1]

JIM CHOSE architectural drawing as his major when he entered Benson Polytechnic High School in 1941. The *Tech Pep*, his high school newspaper, was sprinkled with his editorials, as well as with news items describing his performance as star in several school plays. Said a teacher who directed one of these, 'I have never had so talented an amateur. After the play, other teachers urged me to encourage Jim to enter the professional theatre.'

He had a reputation, too, as the 'oratorical king' of Benson. On the occasion of President Roosevelt's death, toward the end of Jim's high school days, he was given a few hours' notice to prepare a speech for a special assembly called for that afternoon. His coach commented, 'He gave the finest speech I've ever heard from a schoolboy—in fact, one of the finest speeches I've ever heard.'

Jim's grammar school pal, Dick Fisher, went on to Benson also. He continues with his impressions of Jim:

I was tall and skinny. Jim was a little shorter but had a real "build", brown hair and rugged good looks—the girls always looked at him twice. The thing I admired above all was his keen mind. He comprehended things and understood instructions

28

very fast, while I was always about a mile back. He would try to explain things to me in real simple terms. . . .

When we got out of plumbing class, our next was drawing, which was about five city blocks away. To navigate through the middle of school, in crowded corridors, all in the five minutes between bells, was no simple feat. I can still see Jim bowling and pushing his way, his chin out, a picture of forward motion on the loose.

He usually carried a small Bible on top of his textbooks, and an audience of one or two was all he required to open it and start talking. He always said grace before he ate his lunch, and never missed an opportunity to talk to me about Jesus Christ, about whether I believed in Heaven, Hell, the Hereafter, et cetera. When he would have to prepare a talk for a meeting, he would get me alone, deliver his speech and ask for my criticism. At first I would laugh so hard he would get mad, but as time went on he developed the Hellfire-and-Brimstone, fist-pounding type of delivery (very effective in keeping the audience awake).

As wartime gas rationing began to have its effect on mass transportation, and as the weather got better, Jim and I started hitchhiking home from school. This not only saved us a nickel a day, but it gave us more time to talk and ponder the great things of the world. One night, Jim told me about his intention to become president of our country—an idea he earnestly worked on for a while.

One afternoon Jim took me home to meet his family. I especially noticed on that first visit the number of chores Jim had to do, and his methodical system of doing them. He had chickens, rabbits and goats to feed, the furnace to stoke, and the yard to keep up, with an errand or two to run. In no time at all, a portion of these jobs was allotted to me, and Jim's leadership ability advanced.

Jim and Dutch (Werner Durtschi) went out for football, and, after a lot of talking, they got me to join them. Jim played guard. I always thought he was about the funniest thing I ever saw in a football uniform. He reminded me of a big knock-kneed moose, out of water. His only bid for fame on the team was in getting more mud on his face than anyone else.

Jim was hot to get Dutch and me on a camping expedition, so after a few visits to the hock shops down on the waterfront to get some good buys in equipment, we started hitchhiking one Friday afternoon after school. You can see us, Dutch, Jim and I, all with pack sacks and rifle barrels with tin cans over them to keep out the rain—a tough looking bunch for any motorist. We always had a prayer meeting before we left on a camping trip, and I often thought if we had a guardian angel, he was kept on his toes and didn't get much sleep either.

No one would pick up the three of us, so while two of us hid in the brush, one did the "thumbing". Once when a car stopped, the three of us ran over to it, and the driver said, "How many are there, anyway?" and we said that there were only three and that we were very small—we managed to squeeze in along with the four already in the car.

Next day as we moved along the edge of a golf course we heard a duck quacking. We started across the fairway. Jim was in the lead, and when he saw the duck he pumped a shell into the breech, and then his rifle jammed. Dutch fired from behind me, his shell passing over the duck's back. I got off the next shot, and hit the duck on the fly, landing him in the lake about fifteen feet from shore. Jim took a stick and was trying to fish him out when he heard a yell from behind and turned to see a woman waving her arms frantically, yelling something about a pet duck. We felt panicky, but Jim was determined to get our prize, and finally succeeded, getting pretty wet in the operation. The woman was pretty close before we got moving, and was quite upset, yelling "murderers" and crying, so we didn't waste much time crossing the course and heading for a high ridge. We felt a little cruel, but we figured any duck that could fly was wild, and therefore fair game for us, although we regretted the lady's sorrow and asked the Lord to comfort her.

On another week-end we went to Louterelle Falls on the Columbia River. We climbed to the top, held hands, and peered over the edge. When it was Jim's turn he said, "It's the most terrific thing I've ever seen—just like looking from a cloud." We took the path in behind the falls to the rear edge of the pool at the foot of the cliff, and Jim assumed one of his Man of Destiny poses and peered up through the falling mist and meditated. He said if all this was the handiwork of God, what would eternity hold?

Another time, while attempting to get over a barbed-wire fence to examine a buzzard I'd shot, I accidentally pulled the trigger on my rifle. The shot went through Jim's hair. This had quite a sobering effect on us for a while.

Jim's older brother Bert had a lucrative garbage-collecting business in which Jim and Dick Fisher joined him on Saturdays. Bert drove the truck, while the two younger boys rode on top of the load, trying to swat sea-gulls out of the air with discarded fluorescent tubes, or picking through their collection of the morning. In this way they accumulated enough bricks to build themselves an outdoor barbecue, enough bottles to trade in for a goodly number of pies at the supermarket, and assorted useful objects which included several stoves, a bed, chairs, a bear rug complete with head, and even a set of autopsy tools, which inspired Jim to take taxidermy lessons. One of his first stuffed trophies was a sea-gull captured on the garbage route.

When the two entered the supermarket to trade in their armloads of bottles, the line at the cashier's booth simply melted away. In cold weather Jim dressed in a helmet-type hat with wool earmuffs dangling at the sides, sheepskin jacket with wool collar, coveralls, and an ancient pair of shoes worn down at the heels — all of this redolent of their cargo on the truck.

'We generally went in there twice a day on Saturdays,' says Fisher. 'Those poor girls hated to see us coming.'

Fisher continues:

We got interested later on in the slavery question in Africa. While I thought the use of force to break slavery chains was the answer, Jim was more interested in a missionary approach. However, I was quick to point out the dangers of cannibal soup

31

(an old-fashioned recipe consisting of one part missionary to a hundred parts of water); Jim's rebuttal to this was his faith in the Lord who, he said, had delivered many more men in their time than guns had ever done.

Somebody gave Jim a book of poetry, and he began to memorise passages from well-known works. Whenever I was in town I'd go to see him in the evening. He'd be sitting at his desk, and when I'd walk in the door, he'd start in on "Quoth the Raven, Nevermore". I'd sit there, wide-mouthed and awed, while he went through the whole thing with gestures and fanfare.

Jim was extremely wary of women, fearing that they only intended to lure a man from his goals. "Domesticated males aren't much use for adventure," he warned me. Whenever a young lady got a bit too friendly at a social function and I appeared to be taking the hook, I'd hear a voice in my ear saying, "Beware, Fisher, beware."

After I left Portland, and I was working in the Pentagon in Washington, Jim suggested that we correspond in poetry. His object was to make for better diction and sentence structure. I couldn't write nearly as good poetry as Jim, nor did I have his vocabulary, but I learned from him what I could. Then I determined to teach him something instead of always being on the receiving end. I got a book on the Chinook Indian language and sent Jim a copy. We started writing to each other in Chinook. This got our letters by the censor.

While they were in Portland, Dutch, Fisher, and Jim took many trips together and occasionally were away for weeks at a time without their parents knowing their whereabouts. On one occasion of which Dutch tells they hopped the gondola car of a freight train, which later stopped in a tunnel, and for a short time the boys wondered whether they would be asphyxiated. On another attempt to get a free ride Jim threw his fishing-pole into the freight car, reached for the handle to swing himself up, and was flung to the ground by the speed of the train. He had to continue the journey minus the fishing-pole.

Jim could not always be persuaded to join in these escapades, however, especially if the trip was to be over a weekend, because he was conscientious about his responsibilities at the Gospel Hall. When his father and Bert were away on an evangelistic trip in Arizona, Jim felt that he should be at home to help, as well as be present in the Sunday meetings. During this trip his father wrote to him frequently—letters which so impressed Jim that he read them to Fisher, remarking on his father's knowledge of the Scriptures and adding, 'The effectual, fervent prayer of a righteous man availeth much.'[2] Fisher relates this incident:

> One Friday night as Jim and I hitchhiked home together after school we had a little trouble getting a ride. Since it was raining we stood in the doorway of a store and ran out whenever a car came. There were "stop" signs on the corner, and every car stopped. After a couple of false alarms and a little embarrassment on our part, an elderly gentleman drove up. As he looked to the left to check approaching traffic before proceeding across the highway, Jim opened the door and we were in and had the door closed before he could figure out what had happened. Jim said, with a big grin, "How far you going?" The driver stuttered, "Sixtieth". "That's good enough for us," said Jim and we rode with him to Sixtieth Street, where he stopped and let us out. "Thanks for the ride," said Jim, but the driver looked as if he were the one who had been taken for a ride. Jim and I were almost hysterical with laughter, but we didn't try that trick again.

High school escapades did not divert Jim's attention from his goal of serving God. The third member of the Benson threesome, Werner Durtschi, recalls:

> One day near Jim's last year in high school I saw him running around the outdoor track, training. I asked him what he was doing that for. He said, "Bodily exercise is profitable for a little."[3] He was building his body for the rigours of missionary life.

Another high school classmate, Wayne McCroskey, tells of an occasion when there was to be a big school dance.

Jim and I were eating lunch in the cafeteria when the student body officers came through selling tickets. I shook in my boots when I saw that none other than the student-body president himself was taking our table. He was a six-foot-three athlete, all-city baseball and basketball star, popular in the school. When he asked me to buy a ticket to the dance I stammered out some alibi about being too busy. Next he tackled Jim and was told "no sale". He knew Jim pretty well and, recognizing Jim's influence among the students, knew too that losing this sale would make others more bold to refuse, so he turned the heat on. He wound up his argument with, "Jim, you're in this student body as much as I am, and ought to support it." I won't forget the answer:

"Yes," Jim said, "I'm in the student body, but not the way you are. I'm a Christian and the Bible says that I'm *in* the world but not *of* it. That's why I'm not going to the dance."

The student-body president began to wilt, and tried to stop Jim's little sermon by saying, "Yeah, Jim, I understand...that's fine, fella.... OK, sorry I mentioned it...you bet...." He forgot his ticket-selling and slunk out of the cafeteria.

Jim and I were members of the public-speaking club, whose constitution stated that failure to complete an assignment would be penalised by expulsion from the club. The club president assigned us a political speech during the Roosevelt-Dewey campaign, but when Jim was called on, he replied that he had no speech. The president looked worried, because Jim was the backbone of the club.

"Jim," he said, "you know the rules. If you don't give a speech I'll have no choice but to expel you. Now come on up here. You don't need any preparation. Give us an ex-temp on your favourite candidate."

Jim looked right back at him and said, "I have no favourite candidate and I have no speech," and, rising out of his seat, "but I'll be happy to take three minutes to tell you why, if you wish."

The light suddenly dawned on the president's face. Jim had told him of his position as he understood the Bible—that a follower of Jesus could not participate in war or politics. With a face flushed with embarrassment, he said, "That won't be necessary, Jim. I believe we all understand your reasons, and I waive the rules. You are excused."

Although I shared Jim's views, it had never occurred to me to risk my club membership for so seemingly small an issue. Jim's attitude was Esther's: "If I perish, I perish."[4]

World War II was in progress during Jim's high school days, and although Jim was never forced, by a draft call, to take a public stand as a conscientious objector, his convictions on the question were settled. He believed that the Church of Christ, in contrast to the community of Israel in Old Testament times, has abandoned national and political ties. In the words of the writer of Hebrews: 'But we are citizens of Heaven.' 'Our outlook goes beyond this world to the hopeful expectation of the Saviour who will come from Heaven, the Lord, Jesus Christ.'[5] The principle of non-resistance which Jesus demonstrated once and for all on the Cross was one which Jim felt must be obeyed, in public life as well as in personal.

The war question, however, was one which he discussed at length with class-mates and teachers, and his views naturally enough diminished his popularity. So did his inviting a young Chinese, Mun Hope, to the school assembly. This young preacher gave a straight Gospel sermon on sin and judgment before the entire faculty and student body. These two factors, in Fisher's judgment, cut down Jim's chances (considered high) of becoming class president. However, he was given the position of vice-president of his class for his senior year.

Notes

1. 1 Ecclesiastes 9:10.
2. James 5:16.
3. 1 Timothy 4:8, ASV.
4. Esther 4:16.
5. Philippians 3:20, JBP.

PART TWO

Wheaton, Illinois,

1945 – 1949

— 3 —

Degree of A.U.G.

We should remember that while knowledge may make a man look big, it is only love that can make him grow to his full stature. For whatever a man may know, he still has a lot to learn, but if he loves God, he is opening his whole life to the Spirit of God.[1]

MANY A FRESHMAN entering college has no clear idea of what he is there for. Vaguely, it is to 'get an education', but many have done this without going to college, and many have gone to college without getting educated. The idea of an education presents itself to the freshman in a bewilderingly vast variety of forms—the orientation programme, with its lectures, examinations, and faculty receptions; the confusion of registration day, with its lines of frantic students trying to sign up for the course they have chosen before the loud-speaker crackles to announce that Section B of History 115 has closed; catalogues, listing professors who are only names to him so far, and courses elective and requisite; the booths representing organizations; athletic fees, chem-lab fees, dining-hall tickets, room keys— all these things are somehow included in that broad term 'education', and the student whose value scale places social acceptance and reputation high may be sucked into a whirl of extracurricular activity from which he finds it difficult to extricate himself.

38

When Jim Elliot entered Wheaton College in Illinois in the fall of 1945, his goal was clear. First of all, he had committed himself entirely to God and recognised the discipline that this commitment would involve. 'No man that warreth entangleth himself with the affairs of this life, that he may please Him who hath chosen him to be a soldier.'[2] This automatically eliminated many problems, and many 'good' things, in order to give place to those which furthered his purpose. Other students, however, lacking a defined primary aim, often pursued too many of the secondary ones presented to them.

It was this singleness of purpose which his fellow students noticed especially. If some thought he had a 'one-track mind' because he talked so freely about Christ, there were others who, for the same reason, regarded him as especially 'spiritual' and wanted him to be 'prayer chairman' of the freshman class. Neither opinion moved him. A frequent prayer of his was, 'O God, my heart is fixed.'[3]

One student recalls how Jim would stand in the tearing wind on the railroad station platform, head thrown back, fists jammed into his pockets, feet apart, as he waited for the 'Roarin' Elgin' (Aurora and Elgin)—a 'face-to-the-wind' personality.

Another remembers waiting in the dining-hall line reading her New Testament, when she heard a hearty voice behind her: 'Put up your sword, Van!' and turned to see Jim's friendly grin. In the dining-hall he would greet the girls behind the steam tables, the cashier, the bus-boys, as he shoved his tray along. He chose his food carefully: fresh fruits and vegetables, preferably raw; few starches, few desserts. He ate too rapidly, but in moderate quantity, in accord with the rules for wrestling training, as well as with his own ideas about preserving a rugged body for missionary work in the future.

Jim was sure that God had led him to Wheaton. He had

not come simply because father had sent him. Nobody was 'putting him through'. In fact, he did not know where the money would come from. God honoured this faith, however, and funds were supplied, through a friend, through a scholarship, and through part-time employment, so that in November he was able to write:

This schooling experience is one wherein I can perpetually celebrate that all has been supplied by His ever-tender loving-kindness. To Him be all the glory and thanks.

The only record we have of his freshman and sophomore years is in his letters to his family which, aside from very brief notes on what he was doing, were heavily sprinkled with thoughts on eternity, and occasionally a bit of advice to a brother or sister, of which the following is a sample, written to his sister Jane early that fall:

Begin each day with private reading of the Word and prayer. Bunyan has well said, "Sin will keep you from this Book, or this Book will keep you from sin." From the very first, as you begin high school, give out gospel tracts to those you meet. Make a bold start—it's easier that way, rather than trying to begin half-way through. Memorise Scripture on the street car. Buy up the time! It's costly because it's so fleeting. These are terse remarks, and trite, but I wish someone had said them to me about Labour Day, 1941. 'Do your best to present yourself to God as one approved, a workman who has no need to be ashamed, rightly handling the Word of Truth.'[4]

Jim set his alarm every night to waken him in time for prayer and study of the Bible. He wrote:

None of it gets to be "old" stuff, for it is Christ in print, the Living Word: We wouldn't think of rising in the morning without a face-wash, but we often neglect that purgative cleansing of the Word of the Lord. It wakes us up to our responsibility.

A new appreciation of his home and parents was one of the fruits of that first year of college. In May he wrote:

> This is the spring of my nineteenth year. Slowly I have come to realise that my arrival at this point is not of my own efforts, nor merely by the sure ticking of this winged racer called Time, but by the quiet, unfelt guidance of a faithful mother and a father-preacher who has not spent so much time rearing other people's children that he hasn't had time for his own.
>
> My calendar says "Mother's Day", with Father's not far off. And so the people will pause for a few hours to honour those for whom Children's Day comes 365 days a year, those who dare not interrupt their labour of love to seek that honour. The florist shops will bustle, there will be a flurry of carnations, and the following Thursday it will all be forgotten until another May rolls around. I, too, pause, though not with flowers, for such are fast-fading sentiments for the immutable devotion of true parental care. I am grateful to you and to our mutual Father, who has loved us all with a love unknowable.

He wrote at the close of his freshman year:

> It has been a profitable year, drawing closer to my Saviour and discovering gems in His Word. How wonderful to know that Christianity is more than a padded pew or a dim cathedral, but that it is a real, living, daily experience which goes on from grace to grace. And its goal—sometimes seemingly distant, but bright and unfading, lit up and glowing with the beauties of the Sun of Righteousness.

Jim hitchhiked home that summer, and told his brother of the experience in a letter:

> Monday night I was walking a hard stretch of pavement at Cedar Rapids, Iowa, when a new Studebaker pick-up lived up to its name. "Where you goin'?" I queried. "California," retorted a tough marine sergeant. That word had a good effect, kinda warming and cheery, and I thought of God's word to Moses,

"My presence shall go with thee, and I will give thee rest."[5] Amen, said my spirit. We slept three hours Tuesday morning in the truck, pushing on through Nebraska and taking a good hunk out of Wyoming by midnight. At Caspar, Wyoming, the marine's ex-father-in-law owns a tavern. I slept in my clothes on a smelly couch in the back room. Two eggs and black coffee for breakfast. Mid-afternoon, at the junction of Routes 30N and 30S, a coal-truck found me and took me to Cokeville. The Lord is consistently good. Surely with Him there is no "shadow of turning".[6] An ancient Buick stopped, whose driver was a sailor with a throat like the one described in Romans 3, an "open sepulchre". He had a cracked head—that is, his auto did—and we were forced to stop frequently for gas, water, and oil. I was driving while the sailor slept, and within three miles of Boise there suddenly came a grinding crack from up front. I woke the sepulchre-throated gob. "What," said I, "is that noise?" "——," said he, "if I know." We slept till 6 am when a wrecker towed us into Boise. The sailor stuck with his car; I stuck with Highway 30. Got to Portland at 12.20. Total 20 rides, 70 hours, $1.32 in my pocket, and I beat the slow train! Haven't we a wonderful Lord? He says, "Command ye me concerning the work of my hands,"[7] and as we begin to mumble something about getting a ride, bang! there it is. "Before they call, I will answer."[8] I didn't wait over 15 minutes for any ride. That was a faith-strengthening experience.

Jim spent the summer at home, returning to Wheaton in September. In one of the first letters to the family he wrote:

The acquisition of academic knowledge (the "pride of life")[9] is a wearing process and I wonder now if it is all worth while. The shiny paint laid on by curiosity's hand has worn off. What thing better can a man know than the love of Christ, which passes knowledge? Oh to be revelling in the knowledge of Him, rather than wallowing in the quagmire of inscrutable philosophy! My philosophy prof says I can't expect to learn much in his class— all he wants to do is to develop an inquiring mind in order to "make explicit and critically examine philosophical problems of the wider generality." Ho hum.

A few days later he wrote home:

Another Sunday gone, taking with it its joys, privileges, and opportunities, leaving a little good stored in memory's house, and an almost imperceptible amount of growth which every day of walk down here gives to our maturing process in the family of God. "And they shall see His face."[10] In hope of that event we rest, are purified and comforted.

Jim had made it a practice to stay in on Saturday nights ('Saves my mind for the breaking of bread on Sunday morning'), but a football game in the afternoon was not excluded.

He wrote on October 5:

Attended my first social event of the year, a football game. Seems strange to be in crowds, and even stranger to find myself worked up by so small a thing as a ball game. The shouting seems a useless process—far better to be shouting God's praises. I feel that being alone is far more conducive to fellowship with my Father who daily grows more precious as I slowly learn His ways. Looking on His face with the eye of faith, we are changed into the same image, from glory to what? Asceticism? Bless God, more glory! Show a little faith to Him, and He gives more faith.

October 26. They've asked me to take over the position of business manager of the *Tower* next year. It would mean that I would get six grade points, free tuition for a year, and a $12,000 responsibility—but it would also mean late hours, a reduced class schedule, and participation in a lot of formal foolishness which I find difficult to reconcile with my non-conformist attitudes.

His rejection of the offer brought protests from the family, to which he replied on November 2:

Your letter arrived too late to dissuade me from my decision regarding the post on the *Tower* staff. Last week-end I was quite upset about the whole matter, but after a long session of prayer my mind became settled, and I found peace in believing that it was not the Lord's will that I take it. Yet I still cannot set down reasons for the decision, save this, that the Lord showed the psalmist the path of life, evidently by his simply lingering in His presence. Psalm 16:11. I waited on Him and somehow the answer came—I trust it was of the Spirit. "A man's heart deviseth his way," said Solomon, "but the Lord directeth his steps."[11] My heart has devised to serve Him. I must leave the next step to Him.

Perhaps in the preparation of a young soul who has thus committed himself to serve Him, the Lord finds it necessary sometimes to narrow that one's vision until it is clearly focused. Before Jim graduated from college, he learned to appreciate the wider vision which it opened to him, but in these first two years he was not quick to accept the college programme as an unmixed blessing. His father, whose education had of necessity been curtailed, was anxious that Jim should fully apprehend the privileges that were his, and wrote to Jim in praise of education. Jim's reply:

You speak of it as "rounding out one's manhood". It rounds it out, all right, but I'm afraid sometimes it's more in the style of 1 Corinthians 8:1, "knowledge puffs up". "Culture", philosophy, disputes, drama in its weaker forms, concerts and opera, politics—anything that can occupy the intellect seems to turn aside the hearts of many here on campus from a humble life in the steps of the Master, though we sing about this most delicately! No, education is dangerous, and, personally, I am beginning to question its value in a Christian life. I do not disparage *wisdom*—that comes from God, not from PhD's.

Excerpts from further letters to his parents:

December 6. I'm finding my study load heavy just now, and it's almost impossible to split the sheets before 11 pm. I would much appreciate your prayers here, for it's difficult to keep from becoming drowsy in 7.30 Greek class in the morning, much more to keep one's mind in sincere morning prayer and study before that time. This, though, is what Paul meant when speaking of the rigour which must be sustained if one is to be a good soldier of Jesus Christ, enduring hardness.

January 3, 1947. I have felt the impact of your prayers in these past weeks. I am certain now that nothing has had a more powerful influence on this life of mine than your prayers. I was thinking today, Dad, how you used to read Proverbs to us. I can't remember much of what you read in the breakfast nook, but find that the experience has left in my mind a profound respect and love for the old wise man's words. Thank God you took the time—the value of such is inestimable.

January 27. My prayers have been much for the high school group lately as I realise more and more the guidance I needed in those reckless, golden days of glory and of grieving, when every problem was so monstrous and every detail loaded full of meaning. I think the "problem boys" would be less of a problem if we only would think back a few years to the time when our most common grief was a broken window, and our highest glory an apple war. A year's patient, prayerful shepherding will bring most of that flock home with Little Bo Peep's lambs, "dragging [*sic*] their tails behind them". It takes a while for revelry to turn to reverence, and much repetition of truth to eventually turn young zeal into habitual channels for good. Take care that well-doing does not become a weariness. It is "after ye have done the will of God" that you have most need of patience.[12]

Jim had gone out for wrestling during his freshman year, believing that participation in some sport contributed to his training as a soldier of Jesus Christ. As the apostle Paul wrote, 'But I pommel my body and subdue it, lest after preaching to others I myself should be disqualified."[13] Jim had no background in high school wrestling, but made the varsity squad his first year, and was known on the mat as tricky and daring. His ability to tie himself into knots led to the nickname 'India Rubber Man'. Often an opponent, sure that Jim's arm or leg would soon snap, was baffled to note the casual unconcern on his face.

Jim had written his mother:

> It's sure a good feeling not to be water-logged and flabby while one is studying. I think it definitely stimulates the entire body process, including thinking, to be physically alert. Like the horse in Job, one can rejoice in his strength.

Mother, however, was unconvinced, and continued writing to warn him of the dangers of the sport, so 'unnecessary', as sports often seem to mothers. It was during Jim's second season on the squad that he wrote:

> My first evil effect from this "ungodly" thing, as Granny [an elderly friend in Wheaton] calls it, showed up on Saturday. It is a puffing of the inner flanges of the ear, commonly called "cauliflower". Not considered very serious in wrestler's circles. Granny thought it was terrible for me to go off to the match singing hymns, and when I afterward told her that we always had prayer before a fight, it nearly shattered her faith.

He soon returned to the subject of education and of God's purposes:

> *February 8.* No, Dad, I have no chance at Darby's books, and if I had would have no time to read them. It is because of this that I begrudge myself an education, for at a time when my mind still functions quickly it is forced to work on subjects like René Descartes' rational epistemology or Laplace's nebular hypothesis, while I would so much more enjoy study on the things of God. Be that as it may, my Father knows best, and I'm confident that He has placed me here; my task is to labour quietly until the pillar-cloud removes and leads farther, working out God's purposes in God's time.
>
> *February 22.* Several of my housemates and I have begun prayer together here in our "den", and such times we do have! The first fruits of Glory itself. It's the sort of fest I'd call a

"consecrated bull session", where as soon as we hit a subject that has a need God can fill, we dive for our knees and tell Him about it. These are times I'll remember about college when all the philosophy has slipped out memory's back gate. God is still on His throne, we're still on His footstool, and there's only a knee's distance between!

My grades came through this week, and were, as expected, lower than last semester. However, I make no apologies, and admit I've let them drag a bit for study of the Bible, in which I seek the degree A.U.G., "approved unto God".[14]

March 15. The Student Foreign Missions Fellowship is paying visits to all of the Inter-Varsity groups in this area. Yesterday was my first time. Don't know when I've had so much joy. Left about 3 pm in a team member's car; started the meeting about 7.45. Six of us went, one as song leader, the other five to speak about ten minutes each. One spoke on the need — giving statistics on population, death rates, low numbers — of male missionary applicants (18 women to one man), presenting the logical challenge of the distribution of God's servants. I spoke on the Holy Spirit in missions. Another took methods: radio, translation, medicine, teaching, business, movies, air transport, building, etc. A fellow from Africa took the practical side — being able to resist temptation and disease, knowing something about building and digging, etc. Finally there was a question period — questions were varied and stimulating. Coming home we stopped for a bite to eat, and ran into a confused waitress. Had a heart-rending time trying to speak the Words of Life to her, and as I think of all this country now, many just as confused, and more so, I realised that the 39th Street bus is as much a mission field as Africa ever was.

March 22. I lack the fervency, vitality, *life* in prayer which I long for. I know that many consider it fanaticism when they hear anything which does not conform to the conventional, sleep-inducing eulogies so often rising from Laodicean lips; but I know too that these same people can acquiescently tolerate sin in their lives and in the church without so much as tilting one hair of their eyebrows. Cold prayers, like cold suitors, are seldom effective in their aims.

March 29. Only two more days, and another month will have marched quickly by to take its place in the ranks of past months—and as it does, I would say "thank God for those 31 days". By God's grace I have been able to sing two songs honestly, as I never sang them before. One is that thoughtlessly sung chorus, "Every day with Jesus is sweeter than the day before". These past two weeks have been of such progressive joy that I can say nightly of my Saviour's goodness, "it's sweeter today than yesterday". And the other is that hymn "Sweet Hour of Prayer". Nightly we have gathered here and usually it runs past the hour before we again rise from our knees, feeling as if our faces should be veiled for the small glimpse of Glory the Lord has given us. This, to me, is *real* Christianity, when fellows pray and see miracles worked on campus the following day. Each day becomes a time of wrought wonders.

From the last letter of his sophomore year:

What a brutish master sin is, taking the joy from one's life, stealing money and health, giving promise of tomorrow's pleasures and finally leading one onto the rotten planking that overlies the mouth of the pit. It is with honest praise to God I can look up tonight and rejoice in His loving-kindness in delivering me from a life of useless frustration and the ultimate agonies of the gnawing, undying worms of remorse and regret.

It was sometime during these first two years at college that Jim became conscious of the direct, personal implications of the Lord Jesus' command to go and preach the gospel. He decided that the command was directed to him. There is no record of the exact time when this decision was made, but a small black loose-leaf notebook, his companion in college days, contains evidence of his concern for the millions who had not had the chance to hear what God had done to bring man to Himself. This notebook was found on the Curaray beach after Jim's death, its pages scattered along the sand, some washed clean of ink, others stained with mud and rain but still legible. Besides the names of hundreds of people for whom Jim prayed, the notes contained also a recipe for soap-making (doubtless jotted down in anticipation of pioneer life on some mission field); notes for his own sermons preached in English, Spanish, and Quichua; notes on the Auca language, and several pages of mission statistics written while in college, of which the following is an excerpt:

1,700 languages have not a word of the Bible translated.

90% of the people who volunteer for the mission field never get there. It takes more than a "Lord, I'm willing!"

64% of the world have never heard of Christ.

5,000 people die every hour.

The population of India equals that of North America, Africa, and South America combined. There is one missionary for every 71,000 people there.

There is one Christian worker for every 50,000 people in foreign lands, while there is one to every 500 in the United States.

In view of the unequivocal command of Christ, coupled with these staggering facts, Jim believed that if he stayed in the United States the burden of proof would lie with him to show that he was justified in so doing.

He began planning to go to the foreign mission field, wherever God might lead, and took the first practical step in that direction in the summer of 1947, when he hitchhiked to Mexico with a college friend, Ron Harris, whose parents were missionaries there. Of his early impressions he wrote to his parents on June 23:

Ron took me to the Panteon (cemetery) and we wandered around there reading tombstones and looking for bones. When a person has been buried long, and they need more space, they just dig in all over again and let the femurs fall where they may. Decomposition is rapid here. Soon the funeral procession of a brother who died yesterday arrived, and we went over to observe. The hole was a little short, but the hand-carved coffin fit OK on an angle. It was let down on ropes and another box marked "gunpowder" was thrown in on top. They told me it held the bones of the dead man's wife, just dug up from another section of the cemetery. Both were buried in the grave of their grandmother who died thirty-five years ago!

When the preaching was over everyone who knew the man picked up a handful of dirt and chucked it on the coffin, then stood back while the diggers finished off the job. Then came the flowers. Everyone brings some and they are stacked like cordwood all over—beautiful glads, daisies, calla lilies, and more I can't name. What a place!

Mexico has stolen my heart. We've been here a fortnight (as Ron's folks say; they are very English) and they have invited me to stay as long as I wish. Right now I almost wish it were for life. . . . The Lord has been good to me in bringing me here and giving this brief opportunity to see the field and hear the language a bit. Missionaries are very human folks, just doing what they are asked. Simply a bunch of nobodies trying to exalt Somebody.

Jim was with the Harrises for six weeks, beginning the study of Spanish, observing the principles on which they worked, receiving counsel from them, and making notes about everything he noticed, even to Spanish names for birds, flowers, and mountains.

Towards the end of his stay in Mexico he was asked to speak in a children's meeting. With exactly one month's Spanish tucked behind him, he decided to attempt it without an interpreter.

Ron Harris recalls:

The subject was Noah's ark and the rainbow of promise. About 150 kids were very quiet and attentive while he spoke for over half an hour. There was a blackboard behind him, and every time he needed a word he didn't know, he would draw on the board and get someone to tell him the word needed. His enthusiasm and willingness to use what he learned made him get ahead rapidly with Spanish in so short a time.

There was little doubt in Jim's mind, as he hitchhiked back towards Oregon, that it was Latin America to which God was calling him. He knew then that he could never be satisfied with the "usual". His face was set towards those who had never heard.

Notes

1. 1 Corinthians 8:1–3, JBP.
2. 2 Timothy 2:4.
3. Psalm 108:1.
4. 2 Timothy 2:15, RSV.
5. Exodus 33:14.
6. James 1:17.
7. Isaiah 45:11, para.
8. Isaiah 65:24.
9. 1 John 2:16.
10. Revelation 22:4.
11. Proverbs 16:9.
12. Hebrews 10:36.
13. 1 Corinthians 9:27, RSV.
14. 2 Timothy 2:15.

— 4 —

Straight for the Goal

I do not consider myself to have "arrived" spiritually . . . but I do concentrate on this: I leave the past behind and with hands outstretched to whatever lies ahead I go straight for the goal, my reward the honour of being called by God in Christ.[1]

WHEN JIM ARRIVED at Wheaton in 1945 he thought that perhaps his stay would be just two years. But by the fall of 1947, after a few weeks at home on his return from Mexico, funds were available for him to continue, and he accepted this as God's signal to return. His first letter home was dated September 15:

Dr Brooks asked me to speak for a few minutes to the freshmen on Saturday, and the Lord gave strength to exhort and encourage. The subject was "What I as a Junior Wish Someone had Told Me When I was a Freshman". I mentioned that beyond "believing" and "behaving" in the Christian life, there is also "being", and I brought in New Testament exhortations such as

> *"Be not ignorant."*
> *"Be not deceived."*
> *"Be sober."*
> *"Be vigilant."*
> *"Be mindful of the Word."*
> *"Be steadfast,"* etc.

May the Lord give me power to live as His Word demands.

In accord with his thinking of the previous year, Jim decided on a Greek major. Besides wanting to get to the bottom of the original language of the New Testament in order to gain a thorough grasp of its meaning for his own instruction, he believed that a knowledge of Greek would greatly aid him in translating the Bible into a primitive tongue.

For the same reasons, I too had chosen Greek as my major, and our schedule of classes that year was almost identical — rather a rare coincidence in a college of fifteen hundred students with so wide a choice of courses. It dawned on me one day that the Jim Elliot who appeared in Thucydides class, in Herodotus, the Septuagint, ancient history, and in the seminars on poets and dramatists, must be the same Elliot my brother had been talking about for two years, a buddy of his on the wrestling squad, whom Dave thought I should meet.

Jim sat across the aisle from me in ancient history class. Yes, I thought, he looks like a wrestler all right. Just under six feet tall, he had the bull neck and barrel chest I would have expected. Grey-blue eyes looked blue with the sky-coloured sweater he wore most of the time, accompanied by grey flannel trousers and slightly shabby gabardine jacket. Socks and bow ties usually matched, and I noted that he fell into the no-rubbers-or-briefcase category, a minor point in his favour in my eyes.

We talked occasionally after classes, and one day in October Jim asked me for a date, which on the spur of the moment I accepted but later broke. This, I was informed by my friends, was a poor move. Didn't I know that Jim Elliot was a woman-hater? I had rejected a unique opportunity.

Jim had gained for himself this reputation because of his determination to eliminate the non-essentials from his schedule. Dating he regarded as one thing he might well do without. Furthermore, during those early months of his junior year God had spoken to him through the word of Matthew 19:12, 'There are eunuchs who have made themselves eunuchs for the sake of the kingdom of heaven. He who is able to receive this let him receive it.'[2] No ascetic, Jim enjoyed to the full all that he believed God had given him to enjoy, but he felt it wisest to exclude from the sphere of activity anything which had the power to distract him from the pursuit of the Will. The precepts of 1 Corinthians 7 were inescapable to him, and it was not without reason that the Trainer of Souls set these lessons before him at this particular time. Whether God were actually giving him what he called the 'gift of single life' (an expression that Jim took from 1 Corinthians 7:7):[3] 'each has his own special gift from God'— he did not yet know; neither did he try to rationalise himself out of that possibility. He believed Christ to be utterly sufficient for the entire fulfilment of the personality, and was ready to trust Him literally for this.

Jim wrote in his journal:

> To that soul which has tasted of Christ, the jaunty laugh, the tempting music of mingled voices, the haunting appeal of smiling eyes—all these lack flavour. And I would drink deeply of Him. Fill me, O Spirit of Christ, with all the fullness of God.

In studying the separation of the Levites in Deuteronomy 9 and 10, and of their having 'no inheritance', he wrote, 'Lord, if Thou wilt but allow me to take this set-apart place, by Thy grace, I shall covet no inheritance. NOTHING BUT CHRIST.'

When my brother Dave asked Jim to spend Christmas vacation at 'Birdsong', our home in Moorestown, New Jersey, Jim accepted with alacrity, thinking (he revealed later) that it would be a good opportunity to get acquainted with me—a reason which at the time he kept entirely to himself. No one could have guessed the struggle he had during those two weeks because of the lessons he had been learning with regard to the dangers of getting himself 'attached', while at the same time he recognised a growing interest in me. However, I suspected nothing during those weeks.

He wrote to his family on December 21 from my home:

> What God's way is in bringing me here I cannot now say, nor perhaps ever can while the ticking of clocks assails the ear, but that He is leading and that His purpose shall not fail, I know without doubt.... Here I am in the midst of a fine family: a fellow Bob's age and his wife (Phil and Margaret); Betty, who is twenty-one today and a senior at Wheaton, is next followed by brother Dave. Below him are Ginny, a bobby-soxer of fifteen who closes her eyes like Jane when she grins, which she does much; and Tommy, thirteen; with Jimmy, seven, who combine to keep the rest of us in fine spirits and good humour. Again I find God's people very good and these particularly godly. I went to "church" this morning and find myself appallingly ignorant of the form we so vigorously condemn (yet at times unwittingly follow) in the assembly.[4] I cannot repeat the Apostles' Creed or sing the proper Presbyterian tunes to the Doxology. Pray for me. I need constancy of spirit and mind.

My family was enchanted with Jim. As staid Easterners of Philadelphia and New England stock, we found his sudden wide smile and strong handclasp, his complete ingenuousness, refreshing. He fixed everything that needed fixing around the ageing place that had been home for eight of us for a number of years. He wiped dishes for a little old lady who was then a kitchen helper for my mother. 'That young man,' said the lady, 'will go places. When he finds a fork that is not well washed, he washes it again himself, instead of asking me to.' In spite of her deafness the old lady was able to hear Jim's singing. He knew hundreds of hymns by heart, and was quite uninhibited about breaking forth at any moment in his hearty, unmodulated baritone.

He went sledding and ice skating with my teen-age brother and sister, and shovelled snow for my father. I don't recall his doing very much for me except keeping me awake talking, long after the rest of the family had retired. We discussed a broad range of topics — his views on the war question (when my mother had innocently asked if he had been in the service, he said 'No, *ma'am*' with such vehemence she was taken aback), New Testament principles of the conduct of the Church, women, poetry, and many other subjects on which his views were, I thought, out of the ordinary. I enjoyed these sessions partly because at that time I disagreed with him on so many things. At any rate, I decided Jim Elliot was a 'character', and I liked him.

When we got back to Wheaton, Jim found that I always did my Thucydides assignment at a certain table in the hall of East Blanchard. He started joining me there quite regularly. There were moments when I was a little suspicious that I was doing most of the work, but I was totally unaware of motives other than the purely utilitarian on his part. We found it an efficient way to get through pages of the Greek classic.

When, months later, he told me that his interest in me had begun before Christmas vacation, I was surprised. I learned that his personal feelings had been held in check by a principle of which he once wrote to his parents:

No one warns young people to follow Adam's example. He waited till God saw his need. Then God made Adam sleep, prepared for his mate, and brought her to him. We need more of this "being asleep" in the will of God. Then we can receive what He brings us in His own time, if at all. Instead we are set as bloodhounds after a partner, considering everyone we see until our minds are so concerned with the sex problem that we can talk of nothing else when bull-session time comes around. It is true that a fellow cannot *ignore* women — but he can think of them as he ought — as sisters, not as sparring partners!

As is often the case, despite a heavier schedule than ever

before, Jim found that his time alone with his Bible was even more vitally necessary. He began spending an hour before breakfast in the Old Testament, a few minutes at noon in the Psalms, and evenings in the New Testament. On January 18, 1948, he began recording in a notebook what he was learning:

What is written in these pages I suppose will some day be read by others than myself. For this reason I cannot hope to be absolutely honest in what is herein recorded, for the hypocrisy of this shamming heart will ever be putting on a front and dares not write what is actually found in its abysmal depths. Yet, I pray Lord, that you will make these notations to be as nearly true to fact as is possible, that I may know my own heart and be able to definitely pray regarding my gross, though often unrecognised, inconsistencies. I do this because I have been aware that my quiet time with God is not what it should be. These remarks are to be written from fresh, daily thoughts given from God, in meditation on His Word.

Genesis 23—Abraham calls himself a stranger and sojourner in a land he believed God was going to give to him. This is the first time he shows any real inclination to make a home on earth, and how slight it is—only a field, some trees, and a cave in which he can bury his dead. Lord, show me that I must be a stranger, unconcerned and unconnected with affairs below, as Abraham "looked for a city".[5] It was when he owned his strangerhood that the sons of Heth called him a "prince of God" among them. Abraham made no attempt to be a prince of men, as had Lot, and they all recognised his character and inheritance (qualities of a prince) as being not of men but of God. Oh to be known as Israel, a prince with God; no longer as Jacob of the carnal mind!

Help me, Lord, not to mourn and weep for those things, once precious, which you teach me are but dead (whether desires, pleasures, or whatever may be precious to my soul now), but give me a willingness to put them away out of my sight (verse 14). Burying-places are costly, but I would own a Machpelah where corpses (dead things in my life) can be put away.

Such commentaries on his daily reading filled many pages of notebooks, which he called 'museums of pressed flowers, picked with Him, where He is leading me to "feed among the lilies".'[6]

It was during this year that Jim discontinued his practice of making notes in his Bible, or underlining verses. He bought himself a new version, and, though it was thoroughly thumbed and dog-eared within a year, it was without any markings. This practice, he felt, helped to keep him seeking new truth and allowed the Spirit of God, rather than a red pencil, to emphasise the particular words that he needed.

Jim was not always successful, however, in gleaning something 'fresh' from the Word. One morning not long after he began recording, he wrote:

> Yesterday though I had plenty of time for study and read the chapter faithfully, and earnestly sought truth that would be fresh, I cannot say that I found any. Perhaps I sought too hard. Perhaps I strove with the Spirit and frightened the Heavenly Dove in my eagerness. Teach me, Lord, how to listen and not always to seek to squeeze truth out of Scriptures which Thou dost not yet choose to open. My study and prayer time is not yet what I would have it.

After reading, digesting, and recording, Jim set himself to praying. He had lists of people to pray for, a list for each day of the week, and if time alone in his room was limited, he prayed as he walked up to breakfast on campus, or as he stood in line at the dining-hall. An odd moment here and there in the day was given to prayer for those names, or to memorization of Bible verses which he carried, written on small cards, in his pocket. These cards were kept till they were ragged, and occasionally were the cause of his being called antisocial, for there were times when they or the prayer-list notebook took precedence over small talk.

The sessions in the Psalms were sometimes shared with another. He wrote:

Happy time in Psalm 119 and in prayer with Dave at noon today. Oh what love God has led me into for them—Bob, Bill, and now Dave. What times we shall have, now and in His presence beyond, where looms no shade of terror! "Fear dissolved in blood." But still He waits, well knowing the Spirit's cry, and the Bride's and creation's groan.

It was Marcus Aurelius who said, 'A man's thoughts dye his soul.' Constant dwelling in the words of the Lord dyed Jim's soul, and its colour was not hidden from fellow students. 'His life had an impact on me,' wrote his room-mate. 'I remember the time he spent in prayer, and I remember with conviction, for he was walking closer to his Lord than his room-mate.'

To those accustomed to the shibboleths of 'Fundamentalism' Jim's ideas sometimes seemed startling. Often in dining-hall bull sessions someone would say, 'Where in the world did you get an idea like that, Elliot?' The answer is found in his notebook:

2 Timothy 2:9 says, "The word of God is not bound." Systematic theology—be careful how you tie down the Word to fit your set and final creeds, systems, dogmas, and organised theistic philosophies! The Word of God is not bound! It's free to say what it will to the individual, and no one can outline it into dispensations which cannot be broken. Don't get it down "cold", but let it live—fresh, warm, and vibrant—so that the world is not binding ponderous books about it, but rather is shackling you for having allowed it to have free course in your life. That's the apostolic pattern.... And those who are arguing about foreknowledge, election, and such: read those verses 14–26, and then look how the apostle is willing to leave it a paradox. "God gives repentance", and "they recover themselves". Yes, yes, I'm naïve, and glad to be so in such a case.

Jim studied the Word for himself, and if what he understood it to mean was not in conformity with what is commonly understood, his standard did not shift. He wrote:

> The pattern of my behaviour is not set in the activities of those about me. Don't follow the example of those you left in the world, nor those you find in the Church. Rather, the law of God, found in His Word, shall be my standard, and as I see it, there are few examples of this sort of living anywhere.

About a month after the Christmas holiday interrupted his college studies he wrote in his journal:

> Genesis 28: God's promise to Abraham was that his seed should be as the dust of the earth and as the stars of heaven. Stars suggest those children of Abraham which are so by faith, a heavenly people with a heavenly purpose and with heavenly promises. "In Isaac shall thy seed be called."[7] Jacob—later Israel—gives his name to the earthly people whose promises, purposes, and character were earthly. The differences of these destinations mark peoples so entirely different that to argue similarities in law, warfare, or inheritance is to be careless in the reading of the Scripture.

Thus Jim's views on warfare and law, theology and philosophy, while regarded as iconoclastic by some, had their basis in his simple, literal interpretation of Scripture and application of it to daily life. Even his birthday greetings were not run-of-the mill, as this to his brother Bert illustrates:

> For you, brother, I pray that the Lord might crown this year with His goodness and in the coming one give you a hallowed dare-devil spirit in lifting the biting sword of Truth, consuming you with a passion that is called by the cultured citizen of Christendom "fanaticism", but known to God as that saintly madness that led His Son through bloody sweat and hot tears to agony on a rude Cross—and Glory!

To his fifteen-year-old sister Jane, Jim wrote:

Fix your eyes on the rising Morning Star. Don't be disappointed at anything or over-elated, either. Live every day as if the Son of Man were at the door, and gear your thinking to the fleeting moment. Just how can it be redeemed? Walk as if the next step would carry you across the threshold of Heaven. Pray. That saint who advances on his knees never retreats.

Jim was doing a great deal of praying in these days concerning the mission field. He wrote, quoting Paul:

"Some have not the knowledge of God—I speak this to your shame."[8] And they must hear. The Lord is bearing hard upon me the need of the unreached millions in Central Asia. Why does not the Church awake? What a high calling is offered any who will pray, "Send me."[9]

Our young men are going into the professional fields because they don't "feel called" to the mission field. We don't need a call; we need a kick in the pants. We must begin thinking in terms of "going out", and stop our weeping because "they won't come in". Who wants to step into an igloo? The tombs themselves are not colder than the churches. May God send us forth.

He was a member of the Student Foreign Missions Fellowship, and attended its prayer meetings in the early morning. He often worked late at night, making up packages for relief in Europe. But his vision of world need included those at his own doorstep as well, and Sunday afternoon found him travelling into Chicago to talk of Christ to those waiting for trains in the large railroad stations. He wrote:

No fruit yet. Why is it I'm so unproductive? I cannot recall leading more than one or two into the kingdom. Surely this is not the manifestation of the power of the Resurrection. I feel as Rachel, "Give me children, or else I die."[10]

Love for God, Jim believed, must be manifested in love, not only for those who do not know Him, but also for those

ll themselves by His name. 'If anyone says, "I love
wrote John in his First Epistle, "and hates his brother,
he is a liar."[11] There was a small group of Christians in a
near-by town, who met regularly on simple New Testament
lines. Jim jointed them, with the hope of being of some help.
His diary shows that he felt something of the same discouragement there that he felt in the railroad-station effort in
Chicago:

> "The rod of the man I shall choose shall bud."[12] If Thou has
> chosen me, Father, then I should be budding, blossoming,
> bearing fruit for Thee.

His desire does not seem to have been visibly fulfilled, but
the exercise of soul that it cost Jim did something at least to
preserve him from what, for the average college student, is
often a life of unmitigated selfishness.

He sought the help of older Christians in learning to live
for God, and there were occasions when he asked them to pray
with him. Of one of these he wrote:

> Had fellowship in prayer with brother Harper, and discussion of
> the things of God. A happy experience. God, I pray Thee, light
> these idle sticks of my life and may I burn up for Thee. Consume
> my life, my God, for it is Thine. I seek not a long life but a full
> one, like you, Lord Jesus.

Further excerpts from the notebook of that junior year
show his relentless pursuit of God:

> *February 3.* O God, save me from a life of barrenness, following a
> formal pattern of ethics, and give instead that vital contact of
> soul with Thy divine life that fruit may be produced, and
> Life—abundant living—may be known again as the final proof
> for Christ's message and work.
>
> *March 10.* Saviour, I know Thou hast allowed me absolute

liberty, to serve Thee, or to go my own way. I would serve Thee forever, for I love my Master. I will not go out free. Mark my ear, Lord, that it might respond only to Thy voice.

April 16. O Lamb of God, what a Sacrifice Thou art! Whose blood could avail like Thine? Goat's blood could not cleanse, for animals are amoral. My own would not avail for I am immoral. Only Thou art perfectly moral, and only Thy blood could be of any effect.

It was on this day that Jim and several other students were travelling as a gospel team. As they crossed a railroad track, the car stalled, and was wrecked by an oncoming freight only a few seconds after they leaped to safety. Jim sent a clipping from the newspaper to his parents with the following comment:

> The details are fairly accurate, but newspapermen know nothing about the ministering spirits sent by the Ruler of the Universe to be ministers for them who are to be heirs of salvation. It sobered me considerably to think that the Lord kept me from harm in this. Certainly He has a work that He wants me in somewhere. Oh that I might "apprehend that for which also I am apprehended".[13]

So Jim escaped accidental death for at least the second time—the first having been the bullet through his hair—and he was led on, for a few more years, to a very different kind of death, which seemed strangely prophesied in his journal entry of the second day after the railroad accident:

> (Leviticus 17:10): He who consumes blood will ever have the face of God set against him. So with me. If I would save my life-blood, and forbear to pour it out as a sacrifice—thus opposing the example of my Lord—then must I know the flint of the face of God set against my purpose. Father, take my life, yea, my blood if Thou wilt, and consume it with Thine enveloping fire. I would not save it, for it is not mine to save.

63

Have it, Lord, have it all. Pour out my life as an oblation for the world. Blood is only of value as it flows before Thine altar.

The school year was nearly over when Jim stopped me in the hall one day between classes. He handed me a small black leather-bound book, which I took back to the dormitory and found to be a hymnal. In the flyleaf he had written, first in his distinctive, flowing hand, and then in small, clear printing, a few words, a Scripture verse in Greek, and the notation 'Hymn number 46'. Turning quickly to the number, I found these words:

> "Have I an object, Lord, below
> Which would divide my heart with Thee?
> Which would divert its even flow
> In answer to Thy constancy?
> O teach me quickly to return,
> And cause my heart afresh to burn.
>
> Have I a hope, however dear,
> Which would defer Thy coming, Lord—
> Which would detain my spirit here
> Where naught can lasting joy afford?
> From it, my Saviour, set me free
> To look and long and wait for Thee.
>
> Be Thou the object bright and fair
> To fill and satisfy the heart,
> My hope to meet Thee in the air,
> And nevermore from Thee to part;
> That I may undistracted be
> To follow, serve, and wait for Thee."
>
> —G. W. FRAZER

It had only been in the last few weeks before he gave me this booklet that I had had any idea that Jim was interested in me. Had I, however, entertained any hopes, the choice was clear to both of us now. It had to be Christ—alone.

We took a walk one evening, discussing what seemed to us a strange path in which the Lord had led us. We had dated only once—a missionary meeting in Chicago a month before. We had spent much time in study and conversation together, but neither had acknowledged anything beyond a very worthwhile friendship. Now we faced the simple truth—we loved each other.

Hardly aware of our direction, we wandered into a gateway and found ourselves in a cemetery. Seated on a stone slab, Jim told me that he had committed me to God, much as Abraham had done his son, Isaac. This came almost as a shock—for it was exactly the figure which had been in my mind for several days as I had pondered our relationship. We agreed that God was directing. Our lives belonged wholly to Him, and should He choose to accept the 'sacrifice' and consume it, we determined not to lay a hand on it to retrieve it for ourselves. There was nothing more to be said.

We sat in silence. Suddenly we were aware that the moon, which had risen behind us, was casting the shadow of a great stone cross between us.

The date of that night is marked in Jim's hymn-book, beside the following lines:

> *"If Thou shouldst call me to resign*
> *What most I prize, it ne'er was mine:*
> *I only yield Thee what is Thine:*
> *Thy will be done!"*
>
> —CHARLOTTE ELLIOTT

After my graduation Jim spent the first few days of the summer alone in his aunt's home in Glen Ellyn, a small town near Wheaton. During this time Jim thought over the decision God had brought him to. There was no question in his mind as to the rightness of it, but something of the conflict of his soul is revealed in the following journal entry:

> *June 18.* Joshua 5 and 6. "Devoted things." Here is something for my soul as regards Betty. As far as we both are concerned she was "devoted"—not to destruction as was Jericho, but to God, as a burnt living sacrifice. Now I agreed to this with God, allowing that He should have her and me both, wholly His, devoted. But the subtle danger was in retaining hopes ("nice things", gold and silver) that He would give her to me eventually, that our decision to go separately for God would be ultimately revoked by Him and on such fare I survived. But this was just as if I had never really "devoted" her at all, for there was still a future claim on her. Now comes this word: "... keep yourselves from the devoted thing and become ... troubled" (verse 18). Ah, how like again—hidden in the tent in secret were those secret longings for something I may not have, gloated over in lonely moments. But the Cross is final. There is no turning now, nor half-way stopping place. I must go on, asleep until God sees my need of Eve—if such need ever arises. Fix my heart wholly, Lord, to follow Thee, in no detail to touch what is not mine.

Notes

1. Philippians 3:12−14, JBP.
2. RSV.
3. RSV.
4. This is a term that will appear frequently in the pages to follow. It is used in the New Testament sense of a local group of believers. It is the central meaning of the Greek word *ekklesia*.
5. Hebrews 11:10.
6. Song 4:5.
7. Genesis 21:12.
8. 1 Corinthians 15:34.

9. Isaiah 6:8.
10. Genesis 30:1.
11. 1 John 4:20, RSV.
12. Numbers 17:5, ASV.
13. Philippians 3:12.

— 5 —

Flame of Fire

Then flew one of the seraphims unto me, having a live coal in his hand, which he had taken with the tongs from off the altar: and he laid it upon my mouth, and said, Lo, this hath touched thy lips; and thine iniquity is taken away, and thy sin purged.[1]

IRECTION WAS GIVEN in answer to Jim's prayer for guidance for the summer, which he had recorded several months earlier:

Guidance for Israel in their wanderings was unquestionable (Numbers 9). There could be no doubt if God wished them to move. Shall my Father be less definite with me? I cannot believe so. Often I doubt, for I cannot see, but surely the Spirit will lead as definitely as the pillar of cloud. I must be as willing to remain as to go, for the presence of God determines the whereabouts of His people. "Where I am, there shall also My servant be."[2] Very well, Lord—what of this summer?

In July, 1948, Jim and three other Wheaton students, Dave Howard, Roger Lewis, and Verd Holsteen, travelled together as a gospel team, representing the Foreign Missions Fellowship. The itinerary took them through the Midwestern states, from Michigan to Montana, where they spoke in churches, Bible conferences, camps, and schools, presenting to young people the need of a life given wholly to the Lord. They emphasised the responsibility of the Church to the tribes who have never heard of Christ. Jim did not want this trip to be just another 'junket'.[3] He wrote:

> [He makes] His ministers a flame of fire. Am I ignitible? God deliver me from the dread asbestos of "other things". Saturate me with the oil of the Spirit, that I may be aflame. But flame is transient, often short-lived. Canst thou bear this, my soul— short life? In me there dwells the Spirit of the Great Short-Lived, whose zeal for God's house consumed Him. And He has promised baptism with the Spirit and with Fire. "Make me Thy fuel, Flame of God."[4]

That prayer was answered immediately and also ultimately. Dave writes:

> During those weeks the Lord did a work in our own hearts, and to this day I can hear Jim preaching with a passion which I have seldom seen in anyone else. Several years later, when I was representing missions among students, more than once I ran into young people in colleges or Bible schools around the country who had originally responded to God's claims as a result of Jim's preaching on the FMF trip, and who are now preparing for missionary service.

The following are excerpts from his journal of that trip:

> Father, let me be weak that I might loose my clutch on everything temporal. My life, my reputation, my possessions, Lord, let me loose the tension of the grasping hand. Even, Father, would I lose the love of *fondling*. How often I have released a grasp only to retain what I prized by "harmless" longing, the fondling touch. Rather, open my hand to receive the nail of Calvary, as Christ's was opened—that I, releasing all, might be released, unleashed from all that binds me now. He thought Heaven, yea, equality with God, not a thing to be clutched at.

So let me release my grasp.

Have had much struggle of soul lately—doubts as to the truth of God's care for the world, springing I think from so little evidence of His power in the gospel. Comforted mightily yesterday morning by realizing that the rest of faith is upon fact, and that especially in the Resurrection of Christ. If he be not raised from the dead, my faith is vain.

Father, make of me a crisis man. Bring those I contact to decision. Let me not be a milepost on a single road; make me a fork, that men must turn one way or another on facing Christ in me.

And a letter to his mother, dated August 16, 1948, typical in its occupation with Christ of so many which he wrote over the years, I quote in full:

Beloved Mother *et al*: This will likely be my last letter home before I get there, I hope. It seems hard to write of news on the road somehow. We have been held up all afternoon getting repairs on the brake, so that we are now late for a meeting in an Indian reservation up in Red Lake, Minnesota. I type while we travel because it is exceedingly difficult to find time to write while we are staying in homes. Dave is reading Hudson Taylor's *Life* while I am trying to get the gist of his reading while I write.

I simply cannot explain what God is doing for us in this trip. I now begin to see why the Lord led me on this fresh experience of nightly ministering . . . [to see] the secrets of His working "in me mightily",[5] as Paul puts it. More when I get home. How unworthy a servant I have been, how absolutely insufficient to be given the Word of Reconciliation. But God is so very wise, I dare not ask, "Why hast Thou made me thus?"[6] The boys have stopped reading and Roj has burst into his powerful baritone with "Beyond the Sunset", inspired by the blazing throes of the dying sun which sprawls bloody riot in the western sky. Beautiful. I think I have never so enjoyed a sunset as the one we saw last evening. We are quite far north here and saw the northern lights the other night. Yesterday we had four services and a radio broadcast this morning. What glory to be weary in the work of the Kingdom!

From the last few letters I discover that all mention your physical condition, Madre. I do hope I can be of some encouragement. What have we down here, "unclothed",[7] anyhow? Oh, that we might be clothed upon with the glory of the Son of God. We *shall* be changed! Doesn't that grip you? I wish it were possible to transmit the inner flow of peace and power, the comfort the thought of translation has become to me. Of the flesh and its false emotions I have quite had my fill. Of Jesus I cannot seem to get enough. Thank God, though, He does not thwart the soul's desire for Himself, but only whets the desire, intensifying, sublimating. Oh, Mother, in patience possess your soul. He is on the threshold, waiting for His lovers to rouse themselves to answer His knock. Maranatha! Hallelujah! Lift up your heads. Soon shall the cup of glory wash down earth's bitterest woes. The dawn of Heaven breaks. There is balm in Gilead.

We are nearing our destination again. Oh that the power of God would again give us assurance of His working in us mightily. I have trouble keeping the prophet's spirit subject to the prophet.[8] The spirit is liquid and easily flows and surges, sinking and boiling with the currents of circumstances. Bringing every thought into the obedience of Christ is no easy-chair job.

Tuesday morning—Glad to get the opportunity to preach the gospel of the matchless grace of our God to stoical pagan Indians. Oh what a privilege to be made a minister of the things of the "happy God". I only hope that He will let me preach to those who have never heard that name Jesus. What else is worth while in this life? I have heard of nothing better. "Lord, send me!"[9]

> "Let us our feebleness recline
> On that eternal love of Thine,
> And human thoughts forget:
> Childlike attend what Thou wilt say,
> Nor leave our sweet retreat."[10]

—Love, Jimmy.

71

The journal continues on August 23:

I write on board the train, having just finished *The Growth of a Soul*, the life of Hudson Taylor. The month's trip is over and I trust Eternity will reveal fruit for the effort. I have not known before such freedom in ministering. Surely prayer has been heard and answered. What a mystery of Grace that God should allow me to take up the Sword to battle, being such a child. And this childishness today's soul-twistings well demonstrate. Boarded at Billings about 5.30 am and slept fitfully till nine. Woke with the realization that I am in Satan's realm still. One woman near me seemed to encourage the red-eyed imp Desire, and oh, how base and hateful I think of myself now having prayed and read some of the Word. What *will* Hell be like, enraged by unslaked Lust and made seven times hotter with the vengeance of an outraged God? Oh to think of these men and women, these happy boys and girls going there. Father, save them, I pray; grace only makes me differ. When will the Spirit's power make me a witness of the things which I have seen and heard?

Slept through the Continental Divide and awoke to find streams running west instead of east. Now a friendly river is ruffled by playful winds. The beauty of the West cannot be written, so high is it, it can hardly be enjoyed in its fullness. The battling of trees for foothold among castle crags, the thunder wars in distant mountains, the casual meadows, and the great rock laminations twisted weirdly and left clutching at the heavens—who can know these but the one who knows the Forger of the Lion and Enfolder of the Lamb?

Was sensitively touched at reading of H. Taylor's love victory. I cannot understand man, even a godly man. Having been conquered by a power unseen and willingly owning the sway of the Absolute, thus "finding himself" and satiating the ultimate longings of his breast, he can ache with a perfect fury to be subjugated still further to the rule of a woman's love. Or perhaps it is his desire to possess, having been strangely dispossessed by owning Christ as Lord. And within I feel the very same. Oh that Christ were All and Enough for me. He is supposed to be,...but oh, to be swept away in a flood of consuming passion for Jesus, that all desire might be sublimated to Him.

Copied out a few lines from Maxwell's *Born Crucified* yesterday, which I must learn:

> *"The Cross falls like a two-edged sword*
> *Of heavenly temper keen,*
> *And double were the wounds it made*
> *Where'er it glanced between.*
> *'Twas death to sin, 'twas life*
> *To all who mourned for sin.*
> *It kindled and it silenced strife,*
> *Made war and peace within."*[11]

Jim arrived home in Portland on the 24th, and was there only a few days before going to a Bible conference in California, and from there back to Wheaton. On August 28 he wrote this letter to his brother:

Dear brother Bert: Saturday is at its peak here at 7272.[12] The girls are arguing in the kitchen over where they will each bake their cookies so that they will not be in each other's way. This pastry feud arises from an undefined idea which has led to much food being served at "sings" at the Elliot house. I cannot say that I understand just why so much worry is expended over such menials, but the women say that eats are an absolute essential, so there is no use talking. How I wish we could enter into the Saviour's meaning when He spoke of meat which they knew not of. Notice, He was actually *refusing* food which they brought from the city because he had an opportunity to do His Father's will. But this, of course, if carried to any sort of conclusion would make us all very hungry for meat which perishes, and the discomfort would doubtless stumble some. I have come to believe a little in the apostolic principle of fasting, though I cannot say that I have entered into it with much fervour. But we must remember that "good eating" is as much taught against in the New Testament as is idolatry or physical violence. Ministry of this sort would bring a man into disrepute and gain for him the term "fanatic" so we can shy away from preaching it, I suppose! Oh, what vacillating, half-way slovens, dolts, and boors we are when it comes to careful and practical application of the more delicate demands of our Christianity. I have found that fasting is a tool for use as a "pry" on the Great Inscrutable's heart; when He sees one earnest enough in his pursuit of holiness that he neglects his daily food for prayer, He must be amazed and cannot help but honour such simple sacrifice. Hmmm— long enough on this—and all from cookies in the kitchen, too.

I could not help but be disappointed somewhat to learn of your remaining in Arkansas for a time yet. However, the Lord is teaching me to say with the psalmist, "I delight to do Thy will,"[13] instead of the usual, "Well, I suppose it's the Lord's will so we'll just have to put up with it." Oh the delirium of consciously being in the will of the Master: what joy, brother! And this brings a knowledge of His presence and this affords rest. "My presence shall go with thee, and I will give thee *rest*."[14]

Last night was the crowning event of Patricia's girlhood dreams. And like dream-fulfilment it did indeed appear! Not even the finery of the wildest Poe's fantasies could have been more gratifying to the aesthetic sensibilities. Glows and sparkles, pastels and flowing mesh veils with hats as delicate as the wings of dragon-flies, candle-glimmer and shuddering organ-strains, smiles and laughter and a sweeping spirit of affability upon every handclasp. Amalek assumes some subtle attitudes. I would have no complaints were I not dreadfully jealous for the person in whose name all this is carried on. Power we lack; paint we have in abundance. Somehow, I have not learned the poor simple Galilean to take on such airs. Well, one benefit I found was that everyone was in a mood to talk, and this afforded some good opportunities for quiet ministration. I pray that the sweetness of the Spirit will purge out the pride I sense arising as I write these comments. Oh, for grace in the inward parts, holiness unto the Lord.

Colleen [Bert's fiancée] was imposing as a Roman matron. She has a great soul and I sense in her a rising above these paltry and beggarly things of the seen world. Deal cautiously with her, Bert, she is as a railroadman's watch—great gold, and somewhat cumbersome, but full of good works, honest and well-regulated. She is all woman, and will doubtless emit some yet unforeseen eccentricities as well as some deep-buried beauties. Eve's daughters are as flowers and none can ever say they are through unfolding. And what man can predict the consummate end of such a life when its ultimate centre is Sharon's Rose?

Your exercise for Peru intrigues me no end. It is this I wanted most to discuss with you as I have felt a shifting burden from Latin American interests to Oriental fields, more particularly India. I cannot say why, but only that the sad neglect of the North American assemblies weighs heavily upon me. We have, to date, TWO brethren from North America, in a country of 400,000,000! More than all the people in North and South America and Africa combined!

And then, too, I wanted to fellowship with you before the Throne and in "holy discourse", as Wesley used to put it. . . .

I am not at all sure of the movements of the next two weeks. Dad wants to go to the Oakland conference and I should be in Wheaton to register for the draft again by September 12. If you have any plans please let me know. Perhaps you could come to Wheaton for a brief visit. This shall be before the Lord.

Must get into the Book for a little defrosting. God make us

> ". . . lone like the Tishbite, like the Baptist, bold,
> Cast in a rare and apostolic mold".

In the clutches of the Cross,
Jim.

Notes

1. Isaiah 6:6,7.
2. John 12:26.
3. Hebrews 1:7, ASV.
4. Poem by Amy Carmichael, 'Make Me Thy Fuel'.
5. Colossians 1:29.

6. Romans 9:20.
7. 2 Corinthians 5:4.
8. 1 Corinthians 14:32.
9. Isaiah 6:8.
10. Hymn by Gambold, *Little Flock Hymnal*, 1856.
11. Quoted in *Born Crucified* by L. E. Maxwell (Chicago: Moody Press).
12. The street number of the Elliot house.
13. Psalm 40:8.
14. Exodus 33:14.

– 6 –

Behold Obscurity

I called upon the Lord...
He heard my voice...
He made darkness His covering...
He delivered me...
Yea, Thou dost light my lamp,
My God lightens darkness.[1]

BACK AT COLLEGE by the second week of September, 1948, Jim Elliot wrote to his parents describing registration and his room situation:

Arrived safely though three hours late, and was not able to register at all on Monday, so began with the Class of '50 on Tuesday morning. My courses are eight hours of Greek (Church Fathers, Xenophon, Advanced Grammar, which is a terrific course from Tenney with a $14 textbook), elementary Hebrew, and two hours of textual criticism.

My room is nice, though a little small. I have it a good deal to myself as my room-mate is nephew of the house-mother and studies and eats his meals downstairs. I lack sheets, however. Blankets are plentiful and towels I have in sufficiency. Pillows are extravagant. Send three sheets when it is convenient, they are lending me those I'm using now.

I'm certainly glad I was able to get home when I did. What I learned while there I don't think I can express, concerning the centrality of Christ in the home, in the assembly and in individual life. Oh, He is enough, satiating every cell. May we learn to give Him the deserved place, and allow Him to preside....

Time is gone, with space (as in Eternity) so I must get to my first Hebrew lesson. — Lovingly to each, Jim.

A week later I stopped in Wheaton for a few days on my way to Canada, having graduated from college the previous spring. Jim and I had agreed not to correspond during the summer, but when we saw one another again in September, we knew that the three months of silence had been a good test. Our love for one another had grown, but as to God's purpose in it, there was no further sign. As Jim said, in the words of Isaiah, 'We wait for light, but behold obscurity; for brightness, but we walk in darkness.'[2]

One evening Jim allowed me to read his first journal, a notebook begun in January, 1948, and filled by September of that year. With it he handed me this note:

There are a few things I should say about all of this, I suppose. Please excuse the form. I was at no time that I can recall writing for an audience, particularly *your* probings, so you will find abundant misspellings, horrors of punctuation, and some of the thoughts are so poorly expressed that they will be meaningless. Remember, too, that I usually wrote with some portion of the Word fresh in my thoughts giving a background to the entries which a reader cannot fill in without searching every little reference, and this, I think, you will not have time to do. In spite of what I entered as a prologue [see page 57] regarding the possibility of others reading this, I find on glancing over it that I have been more honest in places than I intended. You will know me as no one else does in reading this. Most of it is heart-cry from a little child to a Father whom I have struggled to get to know. Other is purely academic and will do you no good at all. I might say that you were more in my thoughts than these pages suggest. It is not written as a diary of my experiences or feelings, but more as a "book of remembrance"[3] to enable me to ask definitely by forcing myself to put yearnings into words. This I have failed miserably to do, but I don't apologise now. All I have asked has not been given, and the Father's withholding has served only to intensify my desires. He knows that the "hungrier" one is, the more appreciative he becomes of food, and if I have gotten nothing else from this year's experience He has given me a hunger for Himself I never experienced before. He only promises water to the thirsty, satiation to the unsatisfied (I do not say *dis*satisfied), filling to those famished for righteousness. So He has, by His concealing of Himself, given me longings that can only be slaked when Psalm 17:15 is realised. Betty, we shall behold Him face to face, much as you and I have looked with longing on one another. And He will tell us of His love in those looks as we have never known it here. "Thine eyes shall see the king in his beauty: they shall behold the land that is very far off."[4]

> *"There the Red Rose of Sharon*
> *Unfolds its heartsome bloom,*
> *And fills the air of Heaven*
> *With ravishing perfume:—*
> *Oh, to behold it blossom,*
> *While by its fragrance fann'd,*
> *Where glory—glory dwelleth*
> *In Immanuel's land!"*[5]

He knows our love, and is touched from a sympathy within, and I feel He holds us from each other that He might draw us to Himself. Let us pray individually, "Draw me..." and it may be that then we will be allowed to say together, "...we will run after Thee."[6]

"And I will wait upon the Lord, that hideth His face from the house of Jacob, and I will look for Him" (Isaiah 8:17).

"Our eyes are upon Thee" (2 Chronicles 20:12).

Jim had told his parents very little about me, but wrote to them on September 26:

I have just come in from a long talk with Betty Howard. I don't know what I have written of her, nor what impressions I have given, but somehow she is deliciously satisfying company—and this, strangely enough, is not on account of a fine-featured face, a shapely form, nor even on account of rare conversational powers. Of the former two she possesses little of appeal. Of the latter, though she has decided gifts of expression, she does not at all strike one as startling. This is what amazes me, for objectively she has practically nothing that would centre my interests. We find, however, that our thought-patterns coincide in a myriad of minutiae as well as in a great many major issues. There is a thought-bond that I have known with few others, and a huge thirst for God that may surpass my own in many respects. Both of us sense the kindred interests in one another, but are a little awed to speak of it, fearing it may lead to relationships neither of us intended.

I can hear Ruby [Jim's sister-in-law] laughing, but the Lord led us both to feel last spring that we were to go through life unmarried—she from Isaiah 54, I from Matthew 19:12 and I Corinthians 7. She is not playing a game.... I have said "Begone" to this feeling often, and even now wish it did not obscure my thinking, but it persists, not as something cumbersome, a "weight", but more as soul-pressure, almost as a prayer-burden persists, only in my emotions more distinctly. She leaves Tuesday, for which I'm thankful, as I must think clearly if I'm to understand Hebrew and Greek.

The Lord knows how I surrendered this "love-life" business to Him long ago, and the assurance that He will eventually lead into His way is strong tonight. Beloved, if you ever prayed for Jim, redouble your earnestness. I seek His will alone. Enough for now. All questions will be answered as honestly as a hypocrite of my experience can answer them.

During those few days together, one verse in particular of a hymn whose nineteen verses Jim had memorised was especially meaningful to us:

> *"But flowers need night's cold darkness,*
> *The moonlight and the dew.*

> *So Christ, from one who loved it,*
>   *His shining oft withdrew;*
> *And then for cause of absence*
>   *My troubled soul I scann'd—*
> *But Glory shadeless shineth*
>   *In Immanuel's land."*[7]

Jim decided that we should begin a correspondence when I left for Canada. His first letter to me is dated October 2, 1948, and shows that his purpose before God remained the same:

It's hard to pull out of the nebulae that have collected in thinking about this letter, some clever point with which to impress you right off. So I won't attempt it, but proceed as though I had been writing in my present capacity for a good long time. Got your card Wednesday afternoon: clever, devastatingly so. I wish I had here a "feel-o-meter" to transcribe what has been going on inside for the last few days. I began with that word I think I spoke to you of when we were together in chapel that last morning: trembling.

And what should a tuffy like me be trembling about? Three things: you, me, and God. I tremble to think that forwardness in declaring my feeling to you is actually affecting your entire life. I have an idea that it will be almost impossible for you to discern the Lord's mind for you without struggling through a maze of thought and feeling about me. What if, in the real test, your feeling should overcome your faith? Whose then the responsibility? Not entirely yours. For this I fear—that I, stepping out of the path of the Lord for just a moment, should draw you with me and thus be accountable for the "loss" of two lives.

There is within a hunger after God, given of God, filled by God. I can be happy when I am conscious that He is doing what He wills to do within. What makes me tremble is that I might allow something else (you, for example) to take the place my God should have.... I tremble lest in any way I offend my

Eternal Lover. Whatever passes between you and me, let us take note of this: all shall be revoked at His command. . . . Above all else I will that He might find in me the travail of His soul and be satisfied. Reading in Nehemiah these days—are we willing to build with a trowel in one hand while the other grasps a sword?

Our letters were very infrequent. 'Did I not sense,' Jim wrote, 'the value of discipline, I would counsel you to give way to any urges to communicate. However, we best learn patience by practising it.'

Excerpts from the journal of this time show that the state of his soul was not constant:

September 28. "He *hath* led me, and brought me into darkness, and not into light."[8] Because I cannot see, nor even assuredly feel, His satisfaction with me, I cannot doubt the leading simply because of the dark. The leading is nonetheless real, the pathway has simply been into a place I didn't expect or ask for.

September 29. Woke this morning with thoughts from Acts 5, about holding back part of the price. Ananias and Sapphira were not slain for not giving, but for not giving everything they said they had given. Holy Ghost, forbid that I should lie against Thee, not against man, but God. How can I know my heart as regards Bets? I cannot. Thou dost, my Father. Reveal myself to me, that I may see what Thou dost see.

> *"My soul is night, my heart is steel,*
> *I cannot see, I cannot feel.*
> *For Light, for Life, I must appeal*
> *   In simple faith to Jesus."*[9]

October 1. Flood of peace within this morning as I seek God's face. "He came and preached peace to you which were afar off."[10] Lord Jesus, I thank Thee that Thou didst banish the very principle of distance on that Cross. Thou wast forsaken, thrust away from God, that Thou shouldst bring me near. GRACE! All grace.

October 3. Heavy and sorrowful because of my coldness, insincerity, and fruitlessness. Oh, how needy, what emptiness I feel. I am not ready to see the King in His beauty. I should be ashamed to meet Him this night. The Saviour's words come tenderly: "Blessed are those who feel their spiritual need";[11] πτωχοὶ —"crouching, cringing" becomes μακάριοι—happy. How is this possible? Yea, God looks at the end!

A letter to his parents on October 8 mentions two other issues which were before him then: the possibility of being drafted, and his urgent desire to get to the mission field. Excerpts from this letter:

Fellow-heirs: Mom's birthday letter just arrived with the five dollars, and has proved already a source of comfort. Somehow I've had trouble resting in His love the last couple of days but find afresh the truth of Romans 15:13, "in believing" we find joy and peace. I've found it hard to do just that, doubting in darkness what God made lucidly clear in the light. But the soul is built for struggle and the Spirit given to comfort and sustain. What a wretched ingrate I am for all the blessings He has laid to me, signs that He is designing my life. Faith is to be the life-blood of the just, but my spirit's circulating system is a little sluggish, I fear.

This is my twenty-first birthday. I suppose I should borrow seraphic fire and wax poetic, but I don't feel quite up to it. The sweater Werner sent fits beautifully. I expect the package will arrive this afternoon. Thanks for it all in advance. And to Auntie for the five dollars, many thanksgivings. I know these gifts are backed by your prayers, for (as one brother applied it) "where your treasure is, there will your heart be also"![12] Thanks for Neil's address. I wait still for a snap of the family. The sheets are in use, you didn't need to bother with a pillow, as I don't use one.

I sent in my CO registration this week. Here is a matter in which I am concerned at my own unconcern. Somehow I can't even pray with fervour that the Lord would let me finish Wheaton. I don't care what they do with me. Yesterday I prayed that God would take me to Peru or Brazil before I pass another October 8. I know inside that the flesh would like more training

—and perhaps I'm fitted to train more—everybody seems to be planning on it around here. But those generations passing away at this moment! They must hear of the Saviour! How can we wait? O Lord of Harvest, do send forth labourers! Here am I, Lord. Behold me, send me. How deaf must be the deafness of the ear which has never heard the story; how blind the eye that has not looked on Christ for light; how pressed the soul that has no hope of glory; how hideous the fate of man who knoweth only night! God arouses us to care, to feel as He Himself does for their welfare.

The journal continues:

October 9. "Every hour I need Thee."[13] My love is faint, my warmth practically nil. Thoughts of His coming flicker and make me tremble. Oh, that I were not so empty-handed. Joy and peace can only come in believing, and that is all I can say to Him tonight. Lord, I believe. I don't love, I don't feel, I don't understand, I can only *believe*. Bring Thou faith to fruition, Great Harvest Lord. Produce in me, I pray. This came today while meditating:

> *What is this, Lord Jesus, that Thou shouldst make an end*
> *Of all that I possess, and give Thyself to me?*
> *So that there is nothing now to call my own*
> *Save Thee; Thyself alone my Treasure.*
> *Taking all, Thou givest full measure of Thyself*
> *With all things else eternal—*
> *Things unlike the mouldy pelf by earth possessed.*
> *But as to Life and godliness, all things are mine,*
> *And in God's garments dressed I am;*
> *With Thee, an heir to riches in the spheres divine.*
> *Strange, I say, that suffering loss,*
> *I have so gained everything in getting*
> *Me a friend who bore a Cross.*

October 10. Have been vividly aware of seeking the praise of men today. Tonight the Lord Himself speaks from Matthew 6.

Lord, make me to forget myself. I would not be of those who already have their reward in receiving recognition from men. My God, Thou who dost see ἐν κρύπτῳ [in secret]! What dost Thou see in me? Purge! Tear off the shell and smash it to bits. Honestly, Father, I do not *now* want to be seen. Hide me in the brighter light of the Son within. And teach me to pray in simplicity as the Lord Jesus illustrated, concerned with seven things:

> *God's name*
> *God's kingdom*
> *God's will*
> *my bread*
> *my debts*
> *my debtors*
> *deliverance from evil*

Singleness, simplicity, is required of me. One treasure, a single eye, and a sole Master.

With a deeper love for Christ, Jim experienced what many others have found—his eyes were opened to beauty hitherto unseen, as another has written:

> *"Heaven above is softer blue,*
> *Earth around is sweeter green,*
> *Something lives in every hue*
> *Christless eyes have never seen.*
>
> *Birds with gladder songs o'erflow,*
> *Flowers with deeper beauty shine,*
> *Since I know as now I know*
> *I am His, and He is mine."*[14]

Jim wrote to me in October:

I wish I could describe the colour. You may remember the great oak, that sucks up sap from deep secret places and sends it to stiffen broad leaves unbelievably distant from the trunk. Chill nights have slowed its workings and the little sturdy green sentinels writhe in sackcloth now. Brilliant red sumac copses shout along the roads. The landscape has wholly gone surrealistic, unscathed greens boldly standing alongside fading orange, while yellow tries in vain to reconcile. And black starlings pepper bizarre, pungent sunsets which really need no condiment. I can't remember enjoying beauty in the fall as just now. Perhaps I am a little more aware than before.

Then in his next letter to his parents:

I was concerned after writing lest I should have been hasty in saying what I did as regards a soon removal to Peru. This morning the Lord came with thoughts of "hastening"—Proverbs 4:12, "When thou runnest, thou shalt not stumble," Isaiah 40:31, "They shall run, and not be weary," *et cetera*. Now, I know that this could never mean that I should rush out to the field. But it does mean that if I go in a hurry, there is nothing inherently wrong with hurrying if God is leading. The urgency impressed me mostly because of the language difficulties. If I ever intend to do any work among South American Indians, I might just as well determine to learn tribal languages as well as Spanish. One learns faster at 21 than he does at 25.

On the same day his journal contains this entry:

Father, if Thou wilt let me go to South America to labour with Thee and to die, I pray that Thou wilt let me go soon. Nevertheless, *not my will*.

By this time he had heard from his parents in answer to his letter about me. His father wrote:

Jim, I am jealous of any thing or person who could retard your progressive course to everlasting riches and a life completely devoted to that supreme and glorious Man at God's right hand.

Jim replied:

I wish I could describe the rest of soul I have just now. I believe in the God who pulls strings through circumstances. As regards Bets, I would have it no other way. God has made me as eager to go singly to the work as I ever was. It would be fine with me—and I say this as praising His over-abounding grace—if I never saw her again. Our fellowship has been wholesome and entirely beneficial. But as for talk of my getting married—I stand aghast at the suggestion! I have no clear leading as to what work I am to be doing, so that a wife simply cannot be decided upon. I fear for Dad in this regard. I know your heart, Padre— it beats often with my own, and God has made me willing for Christlike loneliness, thanks to your prayers. But cannot we leave all that with Him? We shall not be without signs when there are turns in the road.

And to me, his confidence in God was expressed in a letter dated October 24:

The confidence of Philippians 1:6 assuages all doubt for me. He cannot fail us. Oh, He may lead us oceans apart (and can we not trust Him for that, too?), but are we so childish (I do not say childlike) as to think that a God who could scheme a Jesus-plan would lead poor pilgrims into situations they could not bear? Dost thou believe that God doth answer prayer, my heart? Yea, I believe. Then will He not most assuredly answer that frequent cry of thine, "Lead me, Lord"? I am as confident of God's leading as I am of His salvation. May He not so often have to address us ὀλιγόπιστοι ["little-faiths"]!

The journal continues:

October 26. Prayed a strange prayer today. I covenanted with the Father that He would do either of two things: either glorify Himself to the utmost in me or slay me. By His grace I shall not have His second best. For He heard me, I believe, so that now I have nothing to look forward to but a life of sacrificial sonship (that's how my Saviour glorified Him) or heaven—soon. Perhaps tomorrow! What a prospect!

The month of October ended on a happier strain than it had begun, as a letter to me, dated the 31st, evidences:

It's a late Sunday afternoon, a grey, gloating October day of the sort that makes you downcast when you have not had any mail all week. It would make one that way if God had not previously foxed grey October and the mails and a whole lot more by providing what Nehemiah called "the joy of Jehovah",[15] which is also to be one's stronghold. I almost took offence at the post-mistress when she said all the mail was put out, and I had an empty box. However, this queer "joy" is a patent panacea for all such ills and I marvel at my light heart while looking at the date of your last handwriting.

He is giving me such good things I wonder that I could want more. Much impressed lately with the blessing of being called to battle on the Winner's side. Think of it, sister—you and I shall one day share with Him the promised triumph when He comes with blood-bathed garments and eye of flame, mocking at twentieth-century wiseacres. Exulting we shall follow and wonder then that we ever disbelieved. Does He seem slow? Let not the counsel and spirit of a clod whose life is vapour cause us to think anything but that a "little while"[16] is just that! Not only is He sure to come, but suddenly and soon!... As soon as we believe, He will do. "The hour is coming,"[17] He says, but there's the rub—mustard seed is rare stuff today.

Notes

1. Psalm 18.
2. Isaiah 59:9.
3. Malachi 3:16.
4. Isaiah 33:17.
5. From 'Rutherford's Hymn' by Anne R. Cousins, 1857.

6. Song 1:4.
7. From 'Rutherford's Hymn'.
8. Lamentations 3:2.
9. From the hymn 'I've Tried in Vain' by James Proctor, in *Victorious Life Hymns* (Philadelphia: The Sunday School Times Co.).
10. Ephesians 2:17.
11. Matthew 5:3, Goodspeed's translation.
12. Matthew 6:21.
13. From the hymn by Annie S. Hawks.
14. From the hymn by G. Wade Robinson.
15. Nehemiah 8:10, ASV.
16. John 16:16.
17. John 5:25.

— 7 —

Wine of Bewilderment

Now Christ is the visible expression of the invisible God.... He is both the First Principle and the Upholding Principle of the whole scheme of creation.[1]

ESPITE THE PRESSURE of studies, Jim found time at midday to spend in the Word. He wrote to his family on November 7:

Beloved Family: Sunday night again and high time I was getting something on paper to let you all know what great faithfulness the Father continues to manifest on my behalf. I can never remember being busier with details (all of them "things honest"[2]) yet with such a happy state of rest of soul. "They that wait upon the Lord shall renew their strength."[3] Of course I can't do all I would like by way of service for the glorious Servant who offers me the yoke-sharing next to Himself in this "field" He has purchased, but I do certainly rejoice at the abiding source of power found through the supply of the Spirit. Been much in the psalms lately at noontime—incidentally, I would exhort you each to begin taking a few moments out with your Lover at midday, according to the pattern of the woman of the Song, "Tell me, where thou makest thy flock to rest at noon; for why should I be as one veiled beside the flocks of my companions?"[4] Often at noon there is a tendency for the soul to be "veiled", clouded with world-lore, filmed over with temporali-

90

ties. Just a few moments spent before the Shepherd, listening to the silence of His love and telling Him the state of your soul even if it's not warm toward Him, just to keep short accounts by simple confession—this has been a great blessing to me.

As for coming home at Christmas, you will not understand why I feel a responsibility to be at the Student Mission Convention here at Illinois University. And I will not take time to say why, except that I am trusting God to make that a powerful force in His hands to the thrusting forth of labourers and also to speak to me regarding a definite field. I have not been able to shake a pervading concern for Moslem work, especially as it relates to unreached India. But He knows, and I wait.

Amused and a little mad at myself when you mention reading my description of Betty last spring, Mom. I hate to break the news to you now, but you have reared a good hypocrite in your youngest son. I was deliberately striving for effect in that letter, which I thought I had happily achieved. I was trying to throw all you hounds off the track completely. One of your late letters confirms that I succeeded in this and held up a fair front in August. When I wrote that letter no one but me had any inkling that I had feeling for Betty. She had none herself until I told her on May 31. Even Dave had to be tipped off and he was thunderstruck. Don't ask me why I held back from telling anyone my feelings. I was, frankly, scared, not knowing my own heart in the matter—and I have said some strong things about boy-girl relations, you know. In it all I have been transparent before the Lord. I did not court Betty's affections, though I may have done some "stage-setting" which impressed her. I dated her once in early spring; all other contact was commonplace and academic. This will probably inspire more questions. I will try to be more honest from here on out. As to her being critical and bossy, Mom, those are things she never dared be with me. That information comes from crafty drawing out of Dave things he never knew he revealed. Betty is the sledgehammer type of personality when she knows you, though she may appear quiet at first glance. She is blunt and dominating and this makes her tend to domineer, but I can't explain her. You must get to know her yourself. This may never be necessary, as my life and hers are "committed". I must feel more definite evidence from God and circumstances before I take any more steps that way. He has not led me to pray for this.

On November 16 Jim wrote:

Enjoyed your letter, Padre, but find you are very evasive as regards what I am really concerned with, i.e., going to the mission field next year. Next time you get inspiration please give a line or two on what you think of my possible leaving. And Mother, please let's not have any more of this talk about staying home, telling people of the "need". That would be *augmenting* the need. There are too many good preachers berating people night after night about a lost world who have never faced the challenge of sacrificial foreign service themselves. I feel as if I haven't got any excuse whatsoever to let a body such as you have given me get fat leaning on pulpits. There's work to be done, and skilled labourers are needed to complete the building of God. May He grant that I be one of them. What greater privilege than to be able to aid in presenting a glorious Church to such a worthy Redeemer?

From the journal:

November 18. "...all the days of his vain life he spendeth as a shadow."[5] I find now the literal truth of these words in my daily round. I watch sunrise silhouette the Tower from my window, and without any sense that day is gone, see grey November deepen into moon-mixture. How few, how short these hours my heart must beat, then on— into the real world where the unseen becomes important. O my soul—what shall it be for thee in that Day when thou standest before the God who breathed thee?

Jim had been made president of the Student Foreign Missions Fellowship (FMF) on campus, and this, with other extra-curricular activities, made for a heavy schedule, which he outlined in a letter to me:

November 20. "They made me a keeper of the vineyards, but mine own vineyard have I not kept."[6] So the Lover of the Song. How I experience this daily only one who knows responsibility can understand. You wonder what it's all about. Here are some typical examples: FMF team to Aurora College (three meetings, for planning and prayer); complete reorganizing of FMF literature, plans for advertising a new practical missions course under Prof. Winsor and Dr Martin; gospel team to Baptist Church in Chicago Sunday night; Student Council meeting Monday night, prayer group leaders and Relief Board meetings Tuesday; FMF Wednesday; Christian Council meeting Thursday, and trip to North Central College with Student Council; Friday—FMF executive prayer meeting, then the sending of 800 packages of books to alumni missionaries in a workshop that lasted till 11.30 pm, and they're not stamped yet! Well, I think you get the idea. A yoke is a good thing for a young man, according to Lamentations 3:27, good for his neck and will, but oppressive to a zealous spirit. Especially when I'm supposed to be an honour student, and there is not a single course of which I can say, "Well, I've got *that* one under control." And ringing in my ears is Coach Olson's last remark, "Why weren't you out to practice last night, Elliot?" This is, I know, a wonderful context in which to bear Spirit-fruit.

And to his parents he made this comment:

Not that I don't enjoy the work, or would complain under responsibility—but I fear my heart is wizened and chilled, while my head is widened and warmed! Likely the same struggles will be faced anywhere else, but I like to dream of a little less *activity* and a little more production beyond that sheepskin which will make of me a BA, whatever that means.

The same letter continues, speaking of the partisan spirit which was destroying unity among Christians:

I am more convinced than ever that God deals with individuals as they individually respond to his Word, *regardless* of their

Church association. So that I am beginning to think that the thing to be stressed is not the form of assembly worship, but eager searching and obedience to the Scriptures. Nothing else will make the man of God "throughly furnished",[7] fruitful in every good work.

Discouragement is a Satanic tool that seems to fit my disposition and the Enemy knows it. When I look at the work in the assembly, and realise that I've been there almost four years but have not seen a single soul led to Christ, my increasing tendency is to throw in the sponge and call it quits. Gospel meeting after gospel meeting, with no one strange coming out—and worse yet, none of the saints seem very deeply exercised about it. "How long, Lord, when wilt Thou come unto me?"[8] Why does He wait till the fourth watch to come to us instead of in the evening? Well, all my doubts and fears (hinges on which swing the gates of Hell) cannot prevail to take Him from His throne nor stop Him from the building of His Church.

The journal continues:

November 24. My spirit is all aruffle again at the vast, inexplicable complexities of humankind, and the careless, ineffective manner we fool "fundamentalists" use in answering the cry of hearts which cannot understand themselves. I don't know what the Ecclesiast meant when he said "God hath set the world in the heart of men,"[9] but it might be suggestive of my feelings now. The world, with its huge broil of minutiae, is within! Time with its tempest; space with its apparent infinitude, motion, change, that sense of "something far more deeply interfused"— with the psychological and physiological factors—all these, and more. Whatever can relate them and bring meaning to this all? Surely not our little church-goings and doctrine-learnings. It overwhelms me. I would despair indeed were it not for things like this: καὶ αὐτὸς ἐστιν προ πάντων καὶ τὰ παντα ἐν αὐτῷ συνέστηκεν ("He is both the First Principle and the Upholding Principle of the whole scheme of creation.")[10]

November 25. What I will be doing one year from today is a complete mystery. Perhaps a sick bed or a coffin—glory! Either of these would be fine, but the latter would be immortality, a swallowing up by Life. For this I am most anxious.

To me on November 27 Jim wrote of a talk he had with a fellow student on Thanksgiving afternoon:

He was ready to throw Christianity overboard and turn modernist, terrifically confused because of all he saw pawned off in the name of Christ. Well, I happened to run into this fellow last Tuesday, and, sensing a little of his trouble, made a date to talk with him yesterday. He thinks now that he and I are the only heretics around here, and is glad he has found such a liberal as I am who believes that a man does not have to come all at once into the family of God with a jolt and accompanying spinal exhilarations. Personally, I wasn't "saved" all at once, but took some years coming into my present settled convictions about the truth of God. So why should I demand that conversion be immediate in all others? Christ healed men differently. Some, *in absentia*—He spoke a word, and there was a lightning-fast reaction. Others He touched, spat upon, made clay, spoke to and questioned, then when they saw men "as trees walking"[11] He went through the whole process again. Let not him who accepts light in an instant despise him who gropes months in shadows. It took the Twelve three years to apprehend what was being shown them. The natural, so often illustrative of the spiritual, teaches that healing and growth, yea, even birth, are processes, and I think we altar-callers often perform abortions in our haste to see "results".

Well, let's see—that takes us up to 10 am Thanksgiving Day. A couple of hours in Hebrew, then a turkey dinner in the dining-hall. Noon devotions (if you haven't begun yet, I exhort you, get started), then some time in the patristics and over to Auntie's for a 4.30 turkey with Ron. Home again by 7.15 for a time of soul-tonic with Dave, Art Johnston, Bob Weeber, and Bob Sawyer. Ah, what times! I'll look back on those hours of mutual exhortation, heart-searching, and prayer as building blocks which have laid the foundation of my life. We miss this intimacy with our insistence on "let's have a crowd out"—while

the few gathering expressly "in His name"—find of a surety
that He is in the midst. . . .

God has blessed me with a queer twist that makes me laugh at
almost anything, though sometimes it gets way out of hand.
This may not be valid, but what do you think of translating
μακάριος as "happy"? If this will pass the lexicographers I
suggest it for I Timothy 1:11, "the gospel of the happy God".
Whenever I get downcast, the Lord feeds me pills of praise.

A letter to his parents written the following day, typical in
its occupation with Christ and eternity of many he wrote, is
worth quoting almost in full:

November gone, and still no real winter in these parts. Frosty in
the mornings but days are usually bright. Were it only for the
weather I would be encouraged beyond measure, but the work
schedule keeps me snatching at every moment for what it's
worth. I suppose time has always gone as fast as it does now and
it is silly to say "how time flies!" since it has always been the
nature of time to "fly" and we are carried along in its current at
the same rate from cradle to coffin, and should not act surprised
at its passing. Only one is increasingly conscious of the rate as he
finds more to be done and discovers the enormous obstacles,
within and without, which oppose their accomplishment. Life?
"It is even a vapour that appeareth for a little time."¹² And this
musing spurs me on: "For yet a little while and He that shall
come will come and will not tarry. Behold, I come quickly and
my reward is with me."¹³ What a challenge! What shall be my
reward in that day? How much will have to be consumed at the
glance of His "flaming eye"? How little remains to His everlasting praise? Looking at my days—how short they are, how
unproductive, how full of incidentals, how little real production
for the Harvest-Master.

Spent this afternoon with Ron at ———'s. They were most
hospitable and were eager to be remembered to you all, especially
you, Mother. E. says she has never met another like you or one
even comparable, and I think I should countersign that with a
hearty amen! They have a nice home and belongings and two

cute kiddies, but are so like the rest of us that it is again disheartening. We are so utterly ordinary, so commonplace, while we profess to know a Power the twentieth century does not reckon with. But we are "harmless", and therefore unharmed. We are spiritual pacifists, non-militants, conscientious objectors in this battle-to-the-death with principalities and powers in high places. Meekness must be had for contact with men, but brass, outspoken boldness is required to take part in the comradeship of the Cross. We are "sideliners"—coaching and criticizing the real wrestlers, while content to sit by and leave the enemies of God unchallenged. The world cannot hate us, we are too much like its own. Oh, that God would make us dangerous!

Thanksgiving spent at Auntie's with the annual turkey and trimmings and accompanying results. Not much done for God that day, I fear. But had one suggested that we throw out convention and fast or pray, all would wonder what he had been reading or where his aesthetic sense of sentiment was buried— so why suggest, one so seldom finds a kindred heart. . . .

Hard to imagine you so crippled, Mom. Auntie thinks you should come here and she could get you to rest a little. Utopian ideal, of course, but a noble suggestion. A deep sense of remorse prevails when I think of how much you have sacrificed on my account with such scanty results. God will have to reward you. I cannot. "Thy Father which seeth in secret shall reward thee openly." [14]

No opportunity to get into the big Chicago conference where the brethren rally year by year to encourage themselves in the grand old tradition. I fear I'm getting a bit cynical about these smug, powerless "PB's". [15] When it is good, it is very, very good, but when it is smug, it is horrid. I have met several earnest kids here from various backgrounds, completely muddled because of the confusion of "Fundamentalism" with what the New Testament represents as Christian. Talk of Evolution! One would hardly recognise the species today if it were not clinging to the old names. I sense fires burning, within which may make of me a fanatic reactionary, but as another has prayed, "Lord, deliver us from our sad, sweet, stinking selves." Oh why stand we debating whether or not children under the "age of accountability" (whatever that may mean) are going to heaven when we are dead sure that multitudes round us are pouring hourly into hell?

You ask whether Betty will go to Portland if I asked. I mentioned it, but she hasn't said a word. I'm quite sure she won't be going to Jersey and the only way I can think of getting a definite response is to just flat invite her. She certainly will not invite herself and I don't feel up to sending her home without your making the first move. Naturally I should like you to meet her, but you won't get to know her in a week or two. My mind is free from concern in the matter. I'm not ashamed of her nor of you all, nor of my present esteem of you both. Do as you feel the Lord leads.

If Mrs Rossler can secure at a rate any of that light airmail paper we got a year ago, I would appreciate some.

". . . in His temple doth everyone say 'Glory'." [16] The Lord is a hard taskmaster, telling me to rejoice and sing a praise-psalm when things oppress. Naturally, I rebel and quote Proverbs 25:20, "As he that taketh away a garment in cold weather . . . so is he that singeth songs to an heavy heart." "Sympathise," I cry, and He peels off my overcoat of self-pity by saying, "Praise, child, and be warmed within!" Ever notice that? Whenever I want comfort He tells me to "count it all joy" [17], and then, queerly, I heed, and it all becomes sweet.

> "If our love were but more simple,
>   We should take Him at His word,
>   And our lives would be all sunshine
>   In the sweetness of our Lord." [18]

Ah, how many Marahs have been sweetened by a simple, satisfying glance at the Tree and the love which underwent its worst conflict there. Yea, the Cross is the tree that sweetens the waters. "Love never faileth. . . . Many waters cannot quench love." [19]

Resting in *that* love, then, and praying that we may be found abiding therein at the last trumpet, I wait as a loving son and brother, Jim.

The journal continues on December 4:

What would it be with no Spirit to restrain? Thou hast done well, my God, in getting hold of me. I would set this world ablaze with passion didst Thou not possess me. And even now I tremble lest, succumbing to these things, I should openly sin and bring reproach to Thy great Name. Listen, soul: "In that day that I am afraid, I will confide in Thee. I will not fear; what can flesh do unto me?"[20] "Thou hast delivered my soul from death. Wilt Thou not keep my feet from falling?"[21]

December 5. Deep sense of uselessness this morning. Enjoyed prayer, not for the thrusting out of labourers so much as for their heart-preparation in learning to know Christ. What a ragged, shoddy thing Christianity has come to be, honouring men and means, places and crowds—O Lord, deliver me from the spirit of this faithless generation. How I should long to see the simplicity and powerful beauty of the New Testament fellowship reproduced, but no one seems to be similarly exercised here, so I must wait. O Christ, let me know *Thee*—let me catch glimpses of Thyself, seated and expectant in glory, let me rest there despite all wrong surging round me. Lead me in the right path, I pray.

His Word came clearly just after writing the above, "Take heed . . . be quiet . . . let not thy heart faint. . . . If ye will not believe, surely ye will not be established."[22]

On the same day, Jim wrote:

Dearest Family: Much cheered in receiving two letters this week from Dad and Bob, with your enclosed note, Mom. It's a real joy to know your prayer fellowship on my behalf. Be assured of my burden for you each. . . . And your exercise re: waiting upon the Lord for thrusting forth into His harvest, Bob—how anxious I am that we should be accounted worthy of such a calling. . . . Fret not to go ahead in surgery or fracture or tropical disease, Bob—as your life is in His hands so are the days of your life. Remember you are immortal until your work is done. But don't let the sands of time get into the eye of your vision to reach those who still sit in darkness. They simply *must hear*. Wives, houses, practices, education must learn to be disciplined by this rule: "Let the dead attend to the affairs of the already dead. Go thou and attend the affairs of the dying."[23]

Wondering if Mom is at seaside this week-end. Wish she could get somewhere where honest-to-goodness rest would be possible, about six months of it. Don't know what I would like to do more than come home and pitch in and help a little. Likely, though, what's needed there is not more help but a little more discipline to "come apart and rest awhile"[24] with the Seated Saviour just a little more every day. Such would lubricate the days much better than another voice-box and two more hands.

December 7 (from the journal). Lord makes Himself very near and tender tonight. Spirit of gratefulness and much peace combined with an unworthiness so utter I hardly dare speak of it. War with Japan began seven years ago today. Thankful for peace and confidence within.

December 8. "Thou hast made me to drink the wine of bewilderment."[25] Strangely excited with—just the forces of Life, I guess. Feel "poured out" over a great many interests with intense desire to do but so little power and time to accomplish. For example, wrestling: I would love to be on the mat right now, not to be seen so much as just to be struggling, putting out for all I'm worth. And here I kneel, at 2.45 pm, writing! Hebrew: I can think of nothing I'd like better than to be able to pick up a page of Hebrew Old Testament and read it at sight. Greek loses a lot of its challenge when one gets to know a little. Betty: had a letter from her just now. Long to be with her, or at least sit down and write to her. Thus the body, the mind, and the soul are all pretty much awake, and I don't feel at all like studying. Perhaps this is the "wine of bewilderment". O Father, let me not be dissipated on non-essentials. Bring the Word to me in power; sublimate these huge hungers to the obedience of Christ. Above all these things, I would have holiness. Teach me the path of faith.

A letter to me, dated December 9, says:

Snow greeted me as I stepped from the gym after wrestling practice tonight—fine and silty, falling ever-so-softly on a wizened, autumn-swept turf, and mantling cheerless sidewalks with myriad diamonds which jump and vanish as one walks along. I get hungry for the big, husky mountains at times like this when seasons change—out West where evergreens are free for the hacking, where footprints of other than these sleek squirrels pattern an unusual trail. I get a little nostalgic and read Robert Service:

"They have cradled you in custom, they have primed you with their
*   preaching,*
They have soaked you in convention, through and through;
They have put you in a showcase; you're a credit to their teaching—
But don't you hear the Wild?—it's calling you.

Let us probe the silent places, let us seek what luck betide us;
Let us journey to a lonely land I know.
There's a whisper on the night-wind, there's a star agleam to guide us,
And the Wild is calling, calling . . . let us go."[26]

The stuff really goes to my head and gets to be a real snare sometimes. He writes one piece called "The Men That Don't Fit In" that suits my spirit pretty much.

Your letter came yesterday but not until waiting had spawned fears and even doubts, I must confess! I think Solomon remarks somewhere that "hope deferred maketh the heart sick"[27] and perhaps this has been what's given such an unconventional spiritgraph this week. Jubilant and garrulous for a time, eager to wrestle or bat the breeze in the training room, then "vacant and pensive" (Wordsworth's "Daffodils", I think) with a gnawing yen to read Hebrew but little will to stick out the grind of consistent study for any length of time. Joy and confidence, then tight-lipped bitterness at nearly anything. Have felt an honest lonesomeness for Mom and Dad and an urge to be unclasped by all responsibility around here. And yet, with the covers tight around my neck last night in the dark, I felt as close to the Saviour as I have ever been, holding quiet communion. I think these are signs of the birth of that second kind of faith—expressed by Spurgeon in the now familiar phrase, "Little faith will bring the soul to heaven, but much faith will bring heaven to the soul."

On December 11 Jim wrote to his family:

Only a week more of school and a term paper due at the end of this week, so I suppose the prospect of rest over the holidays will grow sweeter as the next six days pass. As yet I don't know what I'll do for vacation. Dave has invited me home to Jersey and I would like to go except that it involves more expense than I care to lay out just now, and then too it's only for a week so it would be kind of a rush trip. We must be back to Urbana by Monday the twenty-seventh, for the Student Missionary Convention. Auntie has asked me to spend the vacation with them, and this seems most plausible, as I feel the need of rest more than anything else just now. It's all in the hands of the Mighty "Planner of Lives" so I am at rest.

We lost our first wrestling meet to Illinois Normal today. Quite a blow, since it's the first time they've beaten us in remembered history and we're supposed to have an experienced team. I took my match by a decision of 14 points to 3, but couldn't seem to pin the guy. Sure fun and keeps me fit.

A couple of your late letters mention the thought that I am not happy. I can't understand what nuances my letters contain, but I fear you have misinterpreted. It is true I feel as never before the pressure of studies and responsibility around here. The uncertainty of the next year adds its sobriety to my thinking, but for all these things, I would have no cause to call upon the Remover of Hindrances. Banish your fears; my soul is glad in God, though I tend to aggrandise the difficulties and fail often to give glory to the Great Solver thereof.

You are all worried that my faith in the simple New Testament principles of gathering for worship is being shaken. I think my chief interest lies in the New Testament, and I can offer no harsher criticism. Fret not yourselves as to my sincerity in sticking on at the assembly; it is because I am positive that

God's pattern is preached there, if not practised. Mind you, there is much better "preaching" in the independent groups here in Wheaton, and far better practice, but the preaching is often man's pattern. The great mistake is in preaching to our fellow-believers, "Come out from among them and be ye separate,"[28] with the suggestion that they should come out to us and be separate. It struck me forcibly that only Almighty God can make that exhortation—for only He is above and beyond all our petty walls of party separation. Our exhorting should conform to Hebrews 13:13, "Let us go forth unto Him." Preach this and we shall not divide but unite. Ours is not to say "come out where we are" but to take our position within the admitted bounds of human doing and say, "Let us go forth unto Him." As for Betty: if she were not capable of receiving as the Word of God New Testament truth as it is *on the page*, though such reception lead her to do the costly unconventional, she would have no attraction for me whatever. In fact, I am coming to think that it is this—her divergence from the run-of-the-mill stock—that appeals to me most.

On December 18, in another letter to the family, Jim wrote:

I was quite startled to read the new wedding [brother Bert's] date. It falls exactly at mid-semester time. Exams start January 21 and it is possible I could take mine early so as to get home by Tuesday or Wednesday. School does not begun until Thursday, February 3, and I could preregister so as not to miss anything. However, the old problem of expense seems to me most pertinent now. Especially as you say what you do about next semester's tuition. Let us pray much before coming to any exciting conclusions. I would sure like to be there, but an extra $100 right now would seem pretty costly. . . .

"And the work of righteousness shall be peace, and the effect of righteousness quietness and assurance forever."[29] "In quietness and in confidence shall be your strength."[30] I think the devil has made it his business to monopolise on three elements: noise, hurry, crowds. If he can keep us hearing radios, gossip, conversation, or even sermons, he is happy. But he will not allow quietness. For he believes Isaiah where we do not. Satan is quite aware of the power of silence. The voice of God, though persistent, is soft.... I am finding your counsel to get enough sleep most practical, Mother. Not only to be fit for the day and able to relax, but for spiritual awareness and reception one must simply be rested if he is to be blessed. Let us resist the devil in this by avoiding noise as much as we can, purposefully seeking to spend time alone, *facing ourselves* in the World.... Satan is aware of where we find our strength. May he not rob us!

The journal continues on December 22:

Feel deep urge to be moving above this slough of mediocrity which seems to characterise my days. Father, if these strong currents be flesh-driven, staunch and slay them. But if they can be sublimated, channelled, into courses which will do Thy service, then intensify them, mobilise them, give them direction. For I long (Thou knowest how earnestly) that the Bride of Thy dear Son be made perfect and entire in my day. Yea, Lord, if it cost me my bride in this life, let me have Thy grace and power to bring to the Lamb the reward of His sufferings. "If Thy dear Home be fuller, Lord, for that a little emptier my house on earth, what rich rewards that guerdon were!"[31]

He wrote to me on the same day:

I trust the Source of Sacred Gladness will find you ready soil to receive the abundance of His showers. Somewhere Amy Carmichael writes of little joys, like flowers springing by the path unnoticed except by those who are looking for them. So have I known it since last writing—little things, like a quietly sinking sun, a friendly dog, a ready smile. We sang a little song in kindergarten which I've never forgotten:

> *"The world is so full of a number of things,*
> *I'm sure we should all be as happy as kings."*[32]

Simple, but such a devastating rebuke to the complaining heart! I am impressed with the joy that is ours in Christ, so that heaven above and earth below become brighter and fairer, would we only exult in our possessions.

I have recalled several times this week last Christmas time. I thought of the sledding that night in Philadelphia—how we called each other "brother" and "sister" every time our paths crossed. And it doesn't take vacation to recall those late conversations in the kitchen and living-room at Birdsong. I mulled over those times all summer, and have had to turn on my mental heels many a time, quoting "vanity of vanities" [33] from the Preacher. Much as I like to reminisce, I find it saps one's powers of meditation and concentration. But memory keeps throwing little lapping waves on to the shore of immediate consciousness, and one must keep the Son before his eyes, remembering heart-fixation that makes men flint.

Finished my seminar term-paper for Dr Stone Friday afternoon, on the ecbatic use of *ἵνα* in the New Testament. Saturday went by as I painted signs for the conference display. Monday I wrote letters, did a little Greek for Patristics, went sledding and snow-balling with some of the Lombard kids. Yesterday I went to Chicago with Uncle Earl to get a new suit, as he and Auntie had decided I needed one for Christmas. Good thing they're here—I never realised I needed one! Last night a gang of us went to the Inter-Varsity Christian Fellowship office in Chicago to pack some things for the conference. Bed at 1.00 am, up at 9 this morning. Encouraged my pagan instincts (and my Auntie) by putting up their Christmas tree this morning. I must go back there now, as they're having a missionary from Trinidad for supper, and I want to quiz him about a thing or two.

And now men talk of Christ-mass—weird monstrosity and mixture of bright lights, reindeer, tissue paper and scraggly evergreens; jumbled mobs, bargain-baited, "striving after wind", [34] singing "Silent Night"—but what know they of Immanuel? How can they understand the God who once was wrapped in swaddling clothes? How long, Lord, ere they bow the knee?

This week comes your birthday. I think you're twenty-two,

but I don't feel that merits congratulations. Lots of folks make it past that. This can be said appropriately, however: of our God the psalmist said, "Thou crownest the year with Thy goodness (*this* year, particularly). Thy paths exude abundance."[35] For the next, I charge thee, Beloved, seek *His* counsel. The next will be a crisis year for us both and we must individually find His path. His Word is sure, "Thou shalt guide me with Thy counsel and afterward receive me to glory."[36] He is called the Wonderful Counsellor. I think the first modifies the second. And listen as He speaks: "I counsel thee to buy gold."[37] Consider not the cost; get His gold, and your riches will be eternal.

Notes

1. Colossians 1:15,17,JBP.
2. Phillipians 4:8, para.
3. Isaiah 40:31.
4. Song 1:7,ASV.
5. Ecclesiastes 6:12,ASV.
6. Song 1:6.
7. 2 Timothy 3:17.
8. Revelation 6:10, AV, and Psalm 101:2, ASV, (both para.).
9. Ecclesiastes 3:11.
10. Colossians 1:17, Greek text.
11. Mark 8:24.
12. James 4:14.
13. Hebrews 10:37 and Revelation 22:12.
14. Matthew 6:6.
15. 'Plymouth Brethren', the name given by denominationalists to certain groups of Christians who seek to imitate (as literally as possible) the New Testament pattern for the local church.
16. Psalm 29:9, ASV.
17. James 1:2.
18. From the hymn by F. W. Faber
19. 1 Corinthians 13:8,ASV and Song 8:7.
20. Psalm 56:3,4.
21. Psalm 56:13.

22. Isaiah 7:4,9, ASV.
23. Luke 9:60, para.
24. Mark 6:31, para.
25. Psalm 60:3, JND.
26. From 'The Call of the Wild' in *The Complete Poems of Robert Service* (New York: Dodd, Mead & Co., 1940). Used by permission of the publisher.
27. Proverbs 13:12.
28. 2 Corinthians 6:17.
29. Isaiah 32:17.
30. Isaiah 30:15.
31. From poem by Amy Carmichael.
32. 'Happy Thought' by Robert Louis Stevenson, from *A Child's Garden of Verses*.
33. Ecclesiastes 1:2.
34. Ecclesiastes 5:16, para.
35. Psalm 65:11, para.
36. Psalm 73:24.
37. Revelation 3:18, para.

— 8 —

Sheep—Destined for the Altar

But he made His own people to go forth like sheep, and guided them in the wilderness like a flock. And He led them on safely, so that they feared not.[1]

THE END OF THE YEAR 1948 found Jim attending the International Student Missionary Convention at the University of Illinois. A letter to his parents described his impressions:

Conference here is more than half over, and I have mingled feelings about it all. I had come half-way expectant for a time of deep heart-searching and -breaking, with a resultant turning of lives to the more real things—the unseen treasures. That has come to my own heart in a sense, for I have had keen certainty of the Lord's presence in prayer and meditation at noon times in a quiet little Episcopal church near the campus. But the spirit of desperation to do God's will has not gripped this group of 1,450 as a whole—yet. We lack the intensity of feeling deeply, that sense of inevitable *must* which Christ possessed, the zeal for God's house that consumed Him. As I look about here in this comfortable lounge in the Student Union Building, I see all sorts of people. Two Anglican padres from Toronto converse in one corner. A prim little Mennonite bishop walks by. A dark-visaged Latin reads the daily announcement sheet directly in front of me. A nervous-looking Britisher purrs rapid cockney phrases into the ears of a painted American co-ed at my left. Plain grey-haired missionary ladies look wistfully about. Some read Scriptures, others write or gabble happily on any number of subjects.

Think for a moment of the potential here: students from all over the country and other parts of the world, met here specifically to study missions. How long shall we sit analyzing, questioning, arguing, discussing, before God lays hold on us with power to thrust us out to the billion and a half who have not yet heard? But one can pray—and I ask this of you *all*. Lay hold with all your powers upon the Lord of the Harvest that He would make the effects of this convention resound in dark places for His Name's sake.

He wrote to me of the convention's significance for him personally:

The Lord has done what I wanted Him to do for me this week. I wanted primarily a peace about going into pioneer Indian work. As I analyze my feelings now, I am quite at ease about saying that tribal work in the South American jungle is the general direction of my missionary purpose. Also, I am confident that God wants me to begin jungle work single. Those are some good-sized issues to get settled finally in a week.

And on January 18 he continued:

My decision was based on seeing a man from central Brazilian jungles who has done a work comparable to the sort I feel exercised for. He told of the impossibility of marriage in his particular context. That was all—no voices, no Scripture, just the settled peace of decision which often comes to the exercised soul. I will *not* say God is leading me to a life of celibacy. *I only know what I need to know for now*, and that is that the Lord does not want me seeking a wife until I have His definite sign. And apparently there is no immediate reason to expect that sign.

Let me tell you a story. When I returned from Birdsong last January, I had fallen—or grown very much into attachment to the girl you know better than anyone else. Because of heart-searching I had had regarding God's use of those who have made themselves eunuchs for the kingdom's sake, I determined that none should know of my affinity for that girl, even though it was evident that we should be much together. I can remember confessing to the Lord what I called "my love for her", and striving daily to forget and swallow hard. In those days of decision to keep silence, it seemed as if I had sealed the course of my whole life, and I must confess, I felt as if I were somewhat of a martyr. There came to me then this song:[2]

> *Why should I droop in sorrow? Thou'rt ever by my side!*
> *Why, trembling, dread the morrow?*
> *What ill can e'er betide?*
> *If I my cross have taken, 'tis but to follow Thee;*
> *If scorned, despised, forsaken, naught severs me from*
> *Thee.*[3]

And in my hymn-book, there is a blue line drawn, with the date as I have indicated.

Dearest Betty, I charge you in the name of our Unfailing Friend, do away with all waverings, bewilderment, and wonder. You have bargained for a *cross*. Overcome anything in the confidence of your union with Him, so that contemplating trial, enduring persecution or loneliness, you may know the blessings of the "joy set before".[4] "We are the sheep of His pasture. Enter into His gates with thanksgiving, and into His courts with praise."[5] And what are sheep doing going into the gate? What is their purpose inside those courts? To bleat melodies and enjoy the company of the flock? No. Those sheep were destined for the *altar*. Their pasture feeding had been for one purpose, to test them and fatten them for bloody sacrifice. Give Him thanks, then, that you have been counted worthy of His altars. Enter into the work with praise.

This letter roused in me the old fear that I might be the means to turn Jim aside from God's purpose for him, and I wrote again, asking if he was sure that we did right to continue our correspondence. He was sure.

God has led us together in writing, and I have no sign that His will is anything else than that we continue. If such a course leads ultimately to a more bitter renunciation than withdrawal just now should mean, the more bitter way is to be God's way. Remember Marah. "And the Lord showed him a tree, which, when he had cast into the waters, the waters were made sweet."[6] The *cloud* led Israel to Marah.

Notes

1. Psalm 78:52,53.
2. January 8, 1948.
3. From the hymn 'Lord Jesus, Friend Unfailing' by Samuel C. G. Kuster.
4. Hebrews 12:2, para.
5. Psalm 100:3.
6. Exodus 15:25.

— 9 —

Goaded by God

My son, hear the instruction of thy father, and forsake not the law of thy mother: For they shall be an ornament of grace unto thy head, and chains about thy neck. [1]

IN JANUARY Jim's proposed trip West to attend his brother Bert's wedding began to materialise when his professors consented to his taking the final examinations early. Upon receipt of this news, Jim's parents sent him money for the train fare, begging him to come. He replied:

If I do come, may I make one stringent request? That there be *no* eating engagements planned prior to the wedding—either our going out or anyone's coming in. I should like if possible to get in a time of real quiet with you all and feel that since this may be the last family get-together before Glory, we should make it specially *family* with sufficient time for family prayer and Bible study. If it's to be a week of social hubbub, I refuse to come home. I can have that here on campus with bands and flowers. Promise?

He went home, and, as he predicted, it was the last family gathering for the Elliots. Jim spent much time with his father, and wrote to me:

Betty, I blush to think of things I have said, as if I knew something about what Scripture teaches. I know nothing. My father's religion is of a sort which I have seen nowhere else. His theology is wholly undeveloped, but so real and practical a thing that it shatters every "system" of doctrine I have seen. He cannot define theism, but he knows God. We've had some happy times together, and I cannot estimate what enrichment a few months' working with him might do for me, practically and spiritually.

The journal adds this:

January 29. When I think of how far he has gone into the secret riches of the Father's purposes in Christ, I am shamed to silence. O Lord, let me learn tenderness and silence in my spirit, fruits of Thy knowledge. Burn, burden, break me.

> *O God that goadest me*
> *With hunger pricks for Thee within,*
> *By stealing from my heart its dearest stays,*
> *And staying me with tendrils of Thy love—*
> *A token of friendship from a dear one in Thee,*
> *A word of Holy Writ, a song,*
> *A thousand things of spider-thong*
> *Which lift my heart from seen things, sturdy, strong,*
> *And rest me, relaxed, hung from an unseen stay above—*
> *Wise-goading God, teach me to rest in love.*

Undoubtedly it was his father's counsel which prompted this journal entry:

January 31. One does not surrender a life in an instant. That which is lifelong can only be surrendered in a lifetime. Nor is surrender to the will of God (*per se*) adequate to fullness of power in Christ. Maturity is the accomplishment of years, and I can only surrender to the will of God as I know what that will is. Hence, the fullness of the Spirit is not instantaneous but progressive, as I attain fullness of the Word, which reveals the Will.

If men were filled with the Spirit they would not write books on that subject, but on the Person whom the Spirit has come to reveal. Occupation with *Christ* is God's object.

After a week in Portland, he said good-bye to Bert and his bride, who were soon to leave the United States for Peru, and travelled east on the streamliner. He wrote his parents:

Never have felt such difficulty in leaving home as yesterday. Always before I've been possessed of some sort of youthful bravado which gloried in being unaffected. Yesterday's leaving, somehow, forced me to concerted action to keep a stiff upper lip as this steel serpent wound eagerly through Sullivan's Gulch. The "City of Portland" is running true to form, two and a half hours late. Snow was beautiful as it caught the first slants of dawn this morning, appearing a glistening sea of coiled and choppy billows. In some places the little slat snow-fences protruded just an inch or so above the swirl, causing long series of streamlined drifts trailing from the wind. Just now the sky is ice-blue, thawing into an occasional blur of cloud. The hills are ribbed with crusted sheep trails and broken with scrub brush. Most of those on board, however, are unappreciative. Cards, westerns, comic books, cigarettes, and worn timetables occupy the attention of most.

Still exceedingly grateful to God for the opportunity to come home this past week. Can't say why He should allow it as far as my ministry is concerned, for I felt far more ministered unto than I should have been had the Spirit of the Great Well-Pleasing Servant been more in possession.

Arriving back at Wheaton, Jim began his final semester in college. The journal for that first day reads:

I note that my jotting of a year ago seeks a time when I shall forget all my failure. Psalm 107 has wrought much peace of heart in this regard. Just today I was thinking of how God loves in spite of all my sin and has promised to bring us to the "desired haven".[2] He will perform until the day. What matters then the resident Adam? What care for my bloating pride? What concern for attacking lust whose inner fifth-column betrays me to that enemy so often? Perfect love casts out fear, and this blessed rest—in knowing He loves through all these things—makes them seem too worthless even to be thought upon. I know them. God knows them. I confess them. He forgives them. Oh, that I might praise Him worthily!

February 23. Some time since I made any note, I see. Too busy to take time out...and then, too, I haven't been getting fresh things every day. "Too busy"—cursed words, those. Father, forgive me for being so academic and material in my outlook, so much feeding of the mind and outer man, so little genuine concern for spiritual things.

Wrestling was responsible for part of the 'busy-ness', and Jim tried to encourage his mother with his letter of February 26:

This is the Wheaton Invitational Wrestling Tourney, and I'm sitting in my room after having tucked away a steak after semi-finals this afternoon. Finals begin in an hour. I'm wrestling opponents ten pounds over my weight at 175, but have been fortunate in getting some easy material thus far. Pinned one man this morning and won on points this afternoon. Will hit the Chicago University 175-er tonight. We've got the meet in the bag with so many men running to the last bouts, but there'll be some rowdy times in the gym tonight. Take heart, Mom—only one more meet, and maybe I won't wrestle that one, unless I get hot suddenly and the coach decides to send me to the Cleveland Invitational in March, but there's little danger.

Two weeks later he wrote to his parents:

We came in second at Cleveland. I have not yet determined how much the Lord uses athletics to honour His name in the world, but I have wrestled my last collegiate match in faith that it was His will, and asked Him to establish the work of my hands.

And in the journal, this:

We won second place at the tournament in Cleveland, but what is that? Nothing abides. Behold, the Son of God comes! One flash of His burning eye will melt all our polished marble and burnished gold to nothing. One word from His righteous lips will speak destruction to the vast rebellion we call the human race. One peal of His vengeful laughter will rock the libraries of our wise and bring them crashing to a rubble-heap. The wise shall be taken in their own craftiness; mountains shall be brought low. What shall abide that Day? Lo, "He that doeth the will of God abideth forever."[3] Church of God, awake to your Bridegroom! Think not, America, to say in your heart, "We have upheld the common man; we have the godly for our heritage; we have respect to the religions." I say to you, God is able to raise up righteousness from your pavement stones. You have nothing but awful show before Him who comes. "O that Thou wouldst bow the heavens and come down."[4] Laodicea, when will you learn that fullness without Him is vacuum? Oh, the awful emptiness of a full life when Christ stands yet without.

Jim was responsible for getting speakers for the weekly meetings of the Foreign Missions Fellowship. He was not satisfied, however, with the emphasis that some of them had been placing on 'leadership' and training for the mission field. He wrote to me:

Everybody who comes to FMF these days tells us that we must be more educated than the past generation of missionaries. There is not a word in the New Testament about this "training for leadership". There all the training is for being a servant of everyone you meet. Training is to learn to follow, not to lead. But we must have "Christians who are leaders, you know". Jesus said, "He that is first shall be last."[5] "It is enough for the disciple that he be as his master."[6] That is the sort of training that we need, to be as He is, sharing His rejection even by well-meaning Fundamentalists.

116

His brother's leaving for Peru as a missionary caused Jim to rethink the cost of that choice, and he wrote to his mother, near the date of Bert's sailing:

Burdened to pray for you as Bert and Colleen leave, Mom. I can never share in the terrific struggles which you must know in this testing of your mother love. I only know that no testing can overtake you but what God will faithfully provide a way of escape so that you can endure it and glorify Him. Remember— and I don't want to sound pedantic or impudent as if I knew all the costs—remember that we have bargained with Him who bore a cross, and in His ministry to those disciples His emphasis was upon sacrifice, not of worldly goods so much as of *family ties.* Let nothing turn us from the truth that God has determined that we become strong under fire, after the pattern of the Son. Nothing else will do. Our silken selves must know denial. Hear Amy Carmichael:

> *"O Prince of Glory, who dost bring*
> *Thy sons to glory through the Cross,*
> *Let us not shrink from suffering,*
> *Reproach or loss."*

Notes

1. Proverbs 1:8,9.
2. Psalm 107:30.
3. 1 John 2:17.
4. Psalm 144:5.
5. Mark 10:31, para.
6. Matthew 10:25.

— 10 —

The Renaissance

Let no one boast of men. Everything belongs to you! ... For you belong to Christ, and Christ belongs to God![1]

SINCE HIGH SCHOOL days Jim had judged his own conduct, and probably the conduct of others, by what he later called his 'code of don'ts'. Late in his senior year in college he began to see that this was contrary to the teaching of the apostle Paul. Furthermore, it was cutting him off from a certain percentage of the student body whom he wanted to know.

Paul says,

One man believes that he may eat anything; another man, without this strong conviction, is a vegetarian. The meat-eater would not despise the vegetarian, nor should the vegetarian condemn the meat-eater—they should reflect that God has accepted them both. After all, who are you to criticise the servant of somebody else, especially when that Somebody Else is God? ... We shall all be judged one day, not by each other's standards or even our own, but by the standard of Christ.[2]

With a new understanding of these principles, Jim discarded some of the old inhibitions which before he had regarded as prerequisite to holiness. The Scriptural teaching was not always properly applied, however, as he later recognised, but he entered into many activities with a new liberty. Among these were the rivalries between the classes of '49 and '50. On March 19 he wrote:

Wednesday, besides being the 49-er's Centennial Day, was also our annual Reverse Day, when the girls date the fellows and open the doors and generally behave like gentlemen. They were far more interesting than the men, with their long hoop-skirts, bustles, piles of lace, and hair done up. One of them asked me to the student-faculty basketball game. I went over to uncle's and got his spats, top hat, stiff collar with wings, black bow tie, and then picked up an old Prince Albert coat with tails, and a cane (fancy dandy's, with carved dog's head and built-in gun chamber), and duded it in rare style. Set off shouting "Hail 49!" with great gusto. I have never in my wildest dreams hoped to see Wheaton, from prexy to janitor, in such high spirits. The faculty put on a skit between halves of the game that laid us all out. Strangely, I have never sensed a more unified school in four years. I received a tie, along with about twenty other faithfuls, for sticking out a three weeks' beard-growing.

On March 26 Jim wrote:

Dear Mom, Dad, and family: Good to get two letters this week: yours Monday, Mom, and then the combined of yours and Dad's this morning. Thanks for the two dollars, as well, and the stamps. Haven't the faintest idea when I will have opportunity to get the stamps in order of classified, but I'll keep hoarding them anyhow.

Sylvia MacAllister just interrupted this letter by walking by our window on her way over to Jackson's place. Couldn't resist shouting to her for old times' sake. Auntie invited her for the week-end, but since they're invited out for the evening, I volunteered to take Sylvia to the Chapel Choir concert tonight. All the boys in the house have dates and we are coming here for cookies and ice-cream afterwards. Four of us worked up a little harmonica quartette for entertainment.

I bought a harmonica last week in Maxwell Street—saw a German double-reed job brand new at $1.50. That's less than half what I priced the same thing for in Cleveland, so I bought it right off.

Saw the buds begin to sprout for the first time today. It's grey and dripping out, but we've had two warm spring days this week and things are on the burst. Just ten more weeks of classes. Junior-Senior activities are showing dangerous rival sproutings as well. Both classes are determined that the other shall be chagrined. The Forty-Niners showed such spirit as Juniors last year and did such a bang-up job with this Centennial Day affair that the Class of '50 is rankling with jealousy. My room-mate is a junior. They had a big party last night, and I noticed he came in with a sheet of most derogatory and barbarous songs about the senior class. The house lights grow dim—a hush comes over the audience—and the curtain rises on Act I——

In a letter of a week or so later:

Wrestling banquet is tomorrow night. It will likely be a high time. I'm to quote "The Shooting of Dan McGrew" and "The Cremation of Sam McGee", besides singing some of the old songs with my southern date, "Tex" Carlson. She owns a ukelele, so we'll harmonise and dummy around till the boys feel entertained. They sure do put one to work if he shows the least tendency to combine audience ability and foolishness. The thing that bothers me most is that I enjoy it.

Paul exhorts: 'Take care lest this liberty of yours somehow become a stumbling-block to the weak.'[3] Jim's liberty to participate in class activity to the extent of growing a beard was an offence to at least one fellow student. A girl came to him one morning to say that she considered his beard a sign of vanity. 'It went down the drain the next morning,' he wrote to his parents.

The journal continues:

April 14. Fellowship with the gang is enticing fun, but I feel carried away tonight with soul-excitement. Nothing bad—just nothing good. Taken up with comp studies, Robert Service, the old songs that keep ringing in my ears. Strange place, this soul of mine. I think it is more *place* than *person*. It rings with whatever enters, be it high thoughts of the seated Christ or idle rhymes from any poet. The soul does not seem to mind what it is occupied with, but only cares that it be kept occupied. It is passive as to choice. I choose, my soul responds, with ringing laughter, emotion, or pure worship. It is a tool, not a craftsman, and must be controlled. It is as amoral as a bed, but beds can become places of illegitimate activity. Son of God, Purger of the inner parts, Discerner of my sittings down, my risings, wilt Thou hallow this soul of mine? The choice is mine, you say? Ah yes, the choice is mine.

From a letter of April 16:

Went to Lake Michigan sand dunes with a gang of seniors. Had a good time. Wish I didn't have to go to class at all, but could just fellowship with these Wheatonites. So few of them understand life lived to the hilt for and with the Lord Jesus. I wish now that I had understood how to deal with them. Seems like I've only caught on myself this spring.

He wrote on May 10:

This week-end a gang of seniors is going to Rockford and camp out on one of the girls' farms. We'll be leaving Sunday night, skipping classes on Monday, so it looks like we're in for a high time. Pray that I'll be a help, they've asked me to take devotions. Next week-end after is the "Sneak", leaving sometime Friday and returning Monday. They've asked me to take Communion Service there. I've never done anything like that, so pray for me.

I thought of you all yesterday with Bert and Colleen leaving. Bet you felt it hard, Mom and Dad, and the Lord knows why. It's hard to know how to pray in such instances, except that each find strength in the Lord's goodness, as Amy Carmichael puts it,

> *"For my beloved I will not fear,*
> *Love knows to do for him, for her,*

> *As hitherto. Whom my heart cherishes*
> *Are dear to Thy heart too!"*

Seems that the Lord Himself must do. I cannot, cannot even pray aright for you. But if He has called them, what right have we to even whisper to our sleep-, ease-loving souls, "Why this waste?"[4] And yet we must learn to pray in words for them. God grant us grace that we may learn travailing intercession first for their soul's edification and strength and then for those to whom they are to minister. Paul wrote to the Philippians that although they were not in bonds nor in open battle with the enemy, *their faith was*, and he exhorts that they should enter into the conflict of the gospel, since it was given them not only to believe, but also to suffer for Christ's sake. So let us learn to strive together with them.

The moon is almost full tonight. It could be seen nearly all day up in the "brooding blue".... Just think—about one month from today I'll be seeing you. Hope you will feel well enough to enjoy your stay here, Mom.

The end of May was the time for the 'Senior Sneak', when the class of '49 successfully evaded the class of '50 to go up to Wisconsin for a week-end retreat. A year earlier Jim would probably not have allowed himself to indulge in this sort of fun, but, as he wrote to me:

A disruption of my previously pious "code of don'ts" that used to motivate much of my action has occurred in the last three months. The Lord has freed me from many things—good, "consecrated" attitudes, priggish little laws whereby I used to govern my conduct. I experience new fellowship, new freedom, new enjoyment. But my pendulum swung too far. My liberty became licence in some things, and a stumbling-block to some people.

He wrote to his parents while on the 'Sneak' on May 22:

Sitting by Lake Michigan with a gang of '49-ers on this terrific Sunday afternoon. Best loaf I've ever experienced. All inhibitions released by this northern Wisconsin air and outdoors, things really have cut loose. You'll be hearing reports and seeing pictures later. The Juniors didn't get a clue as to our luggage or destination, so this was a Sneak with a vengeance.

Thought about you much last week but failed to get a letter off to you. Wondering how the farewell was, and the trip to LA. Ed McCully, our senior class prexy, won the national oratory contest in Frisco last week. He's from the assembly in Milwaukee and a good buddy of mine. He flew back here yesterday and we promptly chucked him in the lake for his success.

Trust Bert and Colleen will have the confidence and peace of sensing the Lord's nearness on the trip. Been exercised afresh about the unreached "of every tribe"[5] today. Wish there was more wide-awake interest in the regions where pioneer efforts are needed. But one must be sure of a call to such a work and I'm not sure yet just where the Lord is preparing me for. . . .

I passed comprehensive examinations without undue strain on my part, though I don't know how I rated as yet. Still have two term papers to do before next week, so will be a busy little beaver till then. . . . Seems like there have been entirely too many worthwhile activities for me to do some very insistent writing which I have been neglecting. Pray that I might not become so involved that I fail to apply myself to the Scriptures and apply all the Scriptures to myself.

To me, on May 26, Jim wrote:

The Sneak is over, with much indecision on my part as to what profit it brought. I had one terrific lot of fun, got to know some kids on a spiritual plane whom I had always hankered to know. Sorry I was so foolish as to believe I could have a good time without the regular emphasis on the Word in private. *Nothing* substitutes for that.

You would have enjoyed the Communion Service we had during that week-end. We had a huge glass flagon and an oversized loaf of bread. After a few opening remarks we began to pray and sing familiar hymns as different ones led. McCully broke the bread and gave thanks for the cup. It took a long time for the single cup and plate to get around to 180 people, so we sang as it was passed, "Spirit of God descend upon my heart", "When I survey the wondrous Cross", "Amazing Grace", "O Love that will not let me go", "Crown Him with many crowns", etc. Hardly a soul that wasn't moved to worship. Oh, why cannot the Spirit lead us more often thus? How long shall we trust in man's programming to accomplish the work of His Spirit in men's souls?

One of the lessons Jim felt that his 'renaissance' experience had taught him was expressed in a later letter to me:

One of my renaissance experiences was to get among kids who were on a different spiritual level than my own, and enjoy fellowship with them. I found a very subtle snare in so doing. I sought their fellowship in order that I might minister to them, "be a help", you know, to these "weaker" ones. What a rebuke came when I sensed my real motive—that *I* might minister. Love hacks right at this, for she refused to parade herself. I learned to recognise no "spiritual planes", but simply to *love*, purely, in every group. Trying to "be a help" even has a smell of good works in it, for it is not pure. Our motive is only *to be*—do nothing, know nothing, act nothing—just to be a sinful bit of flesh, born of a Father's love. Then you see, Beloved, there can be no defeat.

> *"If you can meet with triumph and disaster*
> *And treat those two impostors just the same....* [6]

So whether knowledge tends to swell me up, or the despair of the flesh would make me shrivel up, the love of Christ "holds me together". [7] Any little occasion that has meaning, if only I can love while it lasts. Keble reminds us of Christ, who with a great task before Him.

> *"Yet in meek duty to abide*
> *For many a year at Mary's side,*
> *Nor heed, though restless spirits ask,*

'What? Hath the Christ forgot His task?'"

Only a few weeks remained before graduation, and Jim was seeking the will of the Lord for the summer. His brother Bob had written him of plans for building a house for himself and his wife, and Jim looked forward to helping on that project.

I feel sure that three months' building would prepare me more for the mission field than another three months in the books. Most pressing is a sense of responsibility to the home which has made me all I am, and paid all the bills without a question. God knows best. He will not reveal His will by fires nor earthquakes but by that quiet dwelling in His presence which sons soon learn to interpret in their lives. Strange that we should be so slow to "tame". Brute flesh is rebellion incarnate within, and it takes some seasons of hammering and healing both, to bring it into subjection.

Let us earnestly have these decisions before God. I think we can all sense that this is a crisis year both for family and country. Let us not be found with the frenzied of earth, cast about with no foundation upon which to base their lives. We can boast with David in his prosperity, "I shall never be moved."[8] "My heart confided in the Lord and I was helped, therefore my heart exulteth."[9]

Notes

1. 1 Corinthians 3:21,23, JBP.
2. Romans 14:2–4, 10, JBP.
3. 1 Corinthians 8:9, RSV.
4. Matthew 26:8, para.
5. Revelation 5:9, para.
6. From 'If', by Rudyard Kipling in *Rewards and Fairies* (Garden City: Doubleday & Co., 1910).
7. 2 Corinthians 5:14, para.
8. Psalm 30:6.
9. Psalm 28:7, JND.

PART THREE

Portland—Oklahoma—
Wisconsin—Indiana—
Illinois—Portland,

1949—1952

— 11 —

The Test of Free Time

When the time came for God to reveal His Son within me so that I might proclaim Him...I did not, as might have been expected, talk the matter over with any human being...I went away to Arabia...It was not till three years later that I went up to Jerusalem.[1]

AFTER GRADUATING with highest honours from Wheaton, Jim drove West with his parents, expecting to spend at least the next three months there. It had not been easy to leave the 'old gang' at college, especially since Jim was not yet sure of God's intentions for him in the coming year. When asked the usual question posed to seniors, 'What will you be doing?' he had no answer. But he knew where to find it. In his journal on July 8, 1949, he wrote:

Home at last. Mingled feelings of "not belonging" and of thanksgiving for all God's grace these past four years. God, preserve me from living a life which conforms to the general pattern. Oh to live above the world, "in public duty and in private thinking", as J. G. Holland puts it. How many Christians will find with the character in Service's poem,

"Came out with a fortune last fall, —
Yet somehow life's not what I thought it,
And somehow the gold isn't all"?[2]

To whom shall I go for counsel for a way of life? To whom for example? To Thee, Lord? Yea, I come to Thee.

The Lord's counsel this time was that Jim spend a year in Portland, helping where he could in the assembly, but most of all preparing his soul through concentrated study of the Bible. He started out by helping to paint the assembly hall, but used even these hours for spiritual profit, as will be seen by a letter written to Bill Cathers on July 12:

While high up on the hall tower with a paint brush on a swinging scaffold with Dad the other day, we got talking about methods of preparing young fellows for the Lord's work. We agreed that the artificial atmosphere of Bible school was unsatisfactory, then started discussing Paul's way of training those about him to teach others. By the time we reached for the ropes to lower the pulleys to an unpainted place, he was saying, "Well, Jim, you pray about it, and if it is the Lord's mind I'll go with you and Billy into Montana next summer." What say you, brother? Of course it will mean no wedding plans for you, until some time after graduation, since I feel it is God's order to relieve young married folks from the burden of active battle until they are settled. Check Deuteronomy 24:5 on this. Pray about it, and I will, too. We would support ourselves, hold tent meetings and open-air meetings, or wherever there is an ear for the Word, and if we find interest and can help souls we would stay as long as is necessary to get them established and formed into assemblies. We ought to know how to do this in our own language before we try it in another, don't you think?

Your word about serving the Lord as Paul and Barnabas did together was not a new idea to me. It has often been my secret wish, and I should not be surprised if it is one of those things that is in the mind of our Great Shepherd-God to stir us on by one another's faith. But we can wait His time in this, too.

I have experienced some little stirring in my soul since last I wrote. The study of Acts has been engaging much of my time, and I sense hunger to know His way, that is, His method of doing His work. Oh, how we need the Holy Spirit to give us a godly distaste for Laodicea! And not to go sour, but to maintain the gladness of heart that is to characterise that people whose God is the Lord.

> *"Aye, amid all men bear himself thereafter,*
> *Smit with a solemn and a sweet surprise,*
> *Dumb to their scorn, and turning on their laughter*
> *Only the dominance of earnest eyes."*[3]

I charge you, by the concern we bear for one another's souls, and by the love of God, that you warn and exhort me with patience if you see in me those turnings back of heart which I do not perceive in the blindness of my flesh. Rest in the knowledge of His doing all for you, Billy. —Earnestly, Jim.

On July 19 he wrote to me:

These days seem strange ones of waiting, sorta marking time till all the red-tape gets time to pass, but I am sure I have not missed the Lord's mind. We have not yet begun building [a house for his brother] because of a little snarl with the city over property lines, getting a loan, and agreeing with each other on blueprint details. Meanwhile Dad and I are working around here, painting the house, fixing the car, cleaning up the meeting-hall, details that seem so unimportant, but somehow needful.

How easy it is to lag spiritually at such times! Though there is challenge among the saints to stir them up and Sundays are crowded with jail and street meetings, there is a very decided tendency to let the days slip through your fingers. The Lord challenged me from the eighty-fourth Psalm last Saturday night. A different translation of verse 5 is "Blessed are they whose strength is in Thee, in whose heart are the *highways*". For me it meant, is your heart really in this business of getting out into those byways or are you willing to settle down and lag while others wait help? Just now I don't happen to *be* in the highways —my experience is more like the sparrows' of verse 3, resting beneath the altar. But that need be no cause for my heart to lose its eagerness for the highways. Then, too, verse 7 is both a warning and a promise "strength to strength"—but each one shall appear before God. How then, my soul?

I have had to reconcile myself to staying in the US until I've proved myself in the work here. The brethren would have it no other way, so unless I go out with Dad to British Guiana [this had seemed a possibility for a short time] I will have to wait until the way is clear for the Regions Beyond. Still, it is not wasted time, as I'm sure you, if anyone, will understand, Bets.... Confident of the Lord's glad promise, "He will give *grace* and *glory*; no good thing will He withhold from them that walk uprightly."[4]

The journal continues on July 23:

Painted part of the hall today. Restless to do other things more directly related to the Lord's work. Longing for a companion who will be a David to me, and me his Jonathan. Lack spiritual stamina to keep fresh in all this eating and doing. Oh, there is time to read and seek God, but my desire slackens. Lord, uphold Thy lily-saint. Stay me, Jehovah, for Thine is a strong right arm, and mine so weak! Saturday night again, and weary from work, but seeking something from the Lord now. How shall I build with these weak and slack hands, Lord?

Tuesday, July 26. Confession of pride—suggested by David Brainerd's Diary yesterday—must become an hourly thing with me. How vile and base my thoughts have been lately. Not just unkind or unsympathetic, but rotten, lewd thinking that cannot be overcome simply by *willing* to be rid of them. How dare I minister to God's saints in such a condition? Lord, rebuke my flesh and deliver my heart from evil.

August 4. I must confess much leanness of soul today, oh Patient Shepherd. How often I have been angered at delay, short-spirited, anxious to criticise. I noticed tonight, too, that one does not live to himself in this regard, but that a little leavening of dissatisfied temper will spread through a group and change outlooks. Then too, Meek Saviour, I must bring a boisterous tongue, roguish lips to Thee for cleansing. Oh to be holy! Just to sense for a moment that I have somehow, however feebly, simulated some measure of Thy character, Lord Jesus. A word from Horatius Bonar spoke to me tonight: "Holiness is not austerity or gloom; these are as alien to it as levity and flippancy; it is the offspring of conscious, present PEACE."

August 21. I sense tonight that my desires to be great are likely to frustrate God's intents for good to be done through me. O Lord, let me pray again with earnest, honest heart: I will not to be *great*—only, God, grant to me Thy *goodness.*

In September, at the repeated invitation of Jim's mother, I visited Portland on my way home from Alberta, Canada, where I had spent the summer in rural missionary work. Jim met me at the station, and drove me out to Mt Tabor, where his home stood facing snow-capped Mt Hood. The house had been greatly enlarged since the Elliots had first moved into it in 1922, and now it sprawled comfortably over a steep hillside, surrounded by fruit trees and flowers of many varieties. The glassed-porch was filled with flowers and plants, set in pots of every description.

Inside, I met for the first time Jim's mother. Soft grey hair and a wide, loving smile contributed to the general impression of motherliness. Mr Elliot, stocky and of strong build, with grey hair betraying its former redness, greeted me next. Then 'Auntie Frostie', a little old lady for whom Mrs Elliot had cared for over twenty years, prim and tiny, with a slight British accent. Jim's sixteen-year-old sister Jane and older brother Bob, a chiropractor, were also there.

One day Jim took me to the beautiful Oregon coast, where we swam at the foot of a great headland of rock, and, later, sat by a driftwood fire, watching the sun die in the Pacific. On other days we hiked on Mt Hood, canoed in the Columbia River, drove to Multnomah Falls.

'Strange, but oh such happy days,' Jim wrote later. 'Were those not of Thee, my God? And wilt Thou deny fruition to such love as we have known? As Thou wilt. But how impossible it seems—to wait—yet, with God nothing shall be impossible.'

After we said good-bye at the Greyhound Bus station, Jim
wrote in his journal:

September 13. She has been gone one hour. What thunders of
feeling I have known in that short time. I could not read the
neon lights as I turned away from the bus, and couldn't face the
people as they passed me. Leaving her is terrible. Teasdale's
poem comes back:

> *"I asked the heaven of stars*
> *What I could give my love—*
> *It answered me with silence,*
>   *Silence above.*

> *"I asked the darkened sea*
> *Down where the fishes go—*
> *It answered me with silence,*
>   *Silence below.*

> *"Oh, I could give her weeping,*
> *Or I could give her a song.*
> *But how can I give silence*
>   *My whole life long?"*[5]

Each time I see her, I have no answer. Only that I must wait.
How long? For what? I know not. O God of my bitter moments,
Father of Christ who wept, grant me guidance directly from
Thee. May I ask it in Spirit-spawned faith? Please let us not part
again in silence. How bitter is love unexpressed!

These words came as I wept between sunset and moonrise on
the side hill beneath the firs:

> *"Wheels carried her into silence,*
> *Out of my reach.*
> *I feared, lest darkness closing round us*
> *Might gain our souls,*
> *And we lose sight*
> *Of real things.*

But nay, the Sun that ruled our days
Has lit the moon to rule our night.

October 7. Realised today that I am on a very stiff trial—it is the test of free time. The Lord took away all outward activity. No work, no money to spend, nothing to do. I fear lest I should waste such days. Spent this one in writing, reading, and a little prayer.

October 16. Very happy in the Lord tonight. Sense that I am being tested in the matter of learning to "abound".[6] Everything seems directed to my good. I am free now of all work obligations except what minor affairs living at home entails. My health is perfect. The state of the assembly is happy and there is evidence of prosperity in the fellowship, though the miraculous is little known among us. Still there are many burdens to be lifted if I choose the path of sacrifice here at home. Lord Jesus, Lord of the apostle who knew how to abound and how to be abased, grant to me faithfulness this week. Let me not retrograde.

October 18. Last night those great, sweeping desires for the glory of God seized on me, seasons when the thoughts pour ahead of the words in prayer and my attitude is as one heaving great gasps of want. Desire there is aplenty. Words are few at such times and faith, I must admit, is not really great.

October 24. I see the value of Christian biography tonight, as I have been reading Brainerd's Diary much today. It stirs me up much to pray and wonder at my nonchalance while I have not power from God. I have considered Hebrews 13:7 just now, regarding the remembrance of certain ones who spake the word of God, "consider the outcome of their life, and imitate their faith."[7] I recall now the challenge of Goforth's *Life* and *By My Spirit*, read in the summer of 1947, the encouragement of Hudson Taylor's *Spiritual Secret*, and *The Growth of a Soul*. There are incidents which instruct me now from the reading of J. G. Paton's biography, read last winter. And now this fresh Spirit-quickened history of Brainerd. O Lord, let me be granted grace to "imitate their faith".

October 27. "Enjoyed much sweetness" (as he puts it) in the reading of the last months of Brainerd's life. How consonant are his thoughts to my own regarding the "true and false religion of this late day". Saw, in reading him, the value of these notations, and was much encouraged to think of a life of godliness in the light of an early death.

October 28. One of the great blessings of heaven is the appreciation of heaven on earth. He is no fool who gives what he cannot keep to gain what he cannot lose.

October 29. On reading a letter to Bert from Wilfred Tidmarsh I responded to a simple urge to offer myself for the work there in Ecuador. This morning it struck me as quite a presumptuous action and I covenanted with the Lord quietly that I would not post the letter unless I had some definite word from Himself. It seems the situation he is in demands that he abandon the Indian work among the Quichuas, because of his wife's health.

Later: after reading in Ephesians 4, 5, and 6, the words "redeeming the time"[8] struck me. The marginal reading encouraged me even more, "buying up the opportunity". And when I turned to the Greek, ἐξαγοραζόμενοι τον καιρόν, I had certainty that I should mail the letter.

On October 31 Jim wrote to me:

Today I went out to the Christian School to place my application as a substitute teacher. Tonight I went to the local detention home for boys to tell a Poe mystery story at their Hallowe'en Party. Tomorrow eve I am to help in a newly beginning craft class for unsaved kids in one of the suburban assemblies. Wednesday afternoon, children's meetings at the hall; Friday morning, chapel service for the Goodwill Industries employees. Days I spend in the books. Tell your father I was deeply impressed with Brainerd's Diary which I finished last week. Other reading material is a book on Ephesians by Van Ryn; Orr's *View of God and the World; The Pilgrim Church* by Broadbent; *The Holy War* by Bunyan. I try to get in what I call "reprobate reading", a little every day, just to keep from dropping into the stereotyped and conventional. This is either *Thus Spake Zarathustra* by Nietzsche, something from Service or Poe, the *Rubáiyát* of Omar Khayyám, John Masefield. It takes strict and careful discipline to keep my heart in Bible study in the forenoon, and in prayer. The rest of the day is desecrated with these others, secular and sacred.

From the journal:

November 6. Sweet, sweet grace of God! It was a happy day, spent with saints and sinners. Street meetings tonight brought me into contact with a successful man who has an empty heart. How shall I praise God sufficiently for the inexplicable miracle of divine grace in my soul? And how explain it to others? I have committed this man's soul to God, and His Word, expecting to write one day in these pages of his turning to the Lord and finding great peace. You see these words, Lord, and are my Judge as to whether they are in faith.

Had thoughts of eternity lately. Eternity shall be at once a great eye-opener and a great mouth-shutter. It shall be the Rectifier of all injustice and how vast is injustice!), the Confirmer of martyrs' blood, the Explainer of years of labour swallowed up in meaningless ruin on earth. Lord, deliver me from sweet doctrinal nothings.

November 8. I had just discovered Paul's use of the word καρπὸς ["fruit"] in Galatians, Ephesians, and Philippians when Mom called me to vacuum the living-room. Finishing that I noticed the table decoration was meagre, so went out and cut a couple of holly sprigs. That reminded me of the shoots growing under the chestnut tree (from seeds dropped by birds in the tree) that had to be moved if they were to grow. Decided to put a hedge of them around Jane's wing of the house, so removed the azalea that was there to the rockery and put in a dozen holly roots out there. Heigh ho! So goes the Greek for this morning!

November 9. It's almost midnight. Don't feel like bed. Spent the evening in the *Reader's Digest* and Wordsworth and Coleridge. Not profitable for sanctifying, but good broadening. Stepped out just now to mail a letter. The moon seems ulcerous, oozing yellow through torn gauze of cloud. Slow-drying pavements, the gutters sopping rotten leaves, motionless cold whose intensity lies in its quiet qualities rather than its chill.

November 10. The gaining of Christ is both an inward reckoning of loss and an outward suffering of it. I have known myself to lose something for Him, yet cherish it in my thoughts. Paul says, "I not only reckon them scraps fit for the heap but I have actually undergone loss of them."[9]

November 11. I am spending this drizzly afternoon reading *The Pilgrim Church*, by Broadbent. Who can describe the waves of pity, excitement, self-searching, and holy desire that have gone through me as I lift my eyes from the page to stare upon the soaked side yard? I find myself constantly trying to bring these ancient arguments up to date, to apply anabaptism, separation from nominal reform, fasting, Quaker freedom, etc., to my own day. "But Thou, O Lord, how long?"[10]

I see clearly now that anything, whatever it is, if it be not on the principle of grace, it is not of God. Here shall be my plea in weakness; here shall be my boldness in prayer; here shall be my deliverance in temptation; at last, here shall be my translation. Not of grace? Then not of God. And here, O Lord Most High, shall be your glory and the honour of your Son. And the awakening for which I have asked—it shall come in your time, on this principle, by grace, through faith. Perfect my faith, then, Lord, that I may learn to trust only in divine grace, that Thy work of holiness might soon begin in Portland.

November 19. Stupefying weakness and dullness in the things of the Lord. Seemed to lack communion on the Holy Spirit for spiritual energy. Show me my failings and goings-backward, Lord, for who can understand his own faults? Depressed and sensible of uselessness tonight. Satisfied that Fritz (see entry for November 6) is in the Lord, a brother. Thanks be to God for His deliverance!

November 24. Lord, give me firmness without hardness, steadfastness without dogmatism, love without weakness.

November 25. I see that a year ago today I was questioning what I would be engaged in today. Of six possibilities then supposed, I am engaged in none. The first two are still the most real exercises of my heart. Still, even in meditating on these (Peru or India), fears seize me and my inadequacy and unpreparedness, my real lack of intensity regarding them, come to me so forcibly that I can hardly believe I am being led in either direction. Yet, I say, "Lead on, O King Eternal, I follow, *not* with fears." [11]

Enjoyed the truth of singing "psalms and hymns and spiritual songs" [12] this morning. Found my prayer list so unstimulating to real prayer that I laid it aside and took the Inter-Varsity Hymnal and sang aloud with much heart-warming such songs as seemed to fit my need. This is as decidedly a means of grace as anything given by God to His people, but how little we use it!

November 29. I think there is nothing so startling in all the graces of God as His quietness. When men have raged untruths in His NAME, when they have used the assumed authority of the Son of God to put to death His real children, when they have with calloused art twisted the Scriptures into fables and lies, when they have explained the order of His creation in unfounded theories while boasting the support of rational science, when they have virtually talked Him right out of His universe, when they, using powers He grants them, claim universal autonomy and independence, He, this great Silent God, says nothing. His tolerance and love for His creature is such that, having spoken in Christ, in conscience, in code of law, He waits for men to leave off their bawling and turn for a moment to listen to His still, small voice of Spirit. Now, after so long a time of restrained voice, bearing in Almighty meekness the blasphemies of His self-destroying creatures, now—how shall break upon the ears, consciousnesses, hearts, and minds of reprobate man the Voice of one so long silent? It shall thunder with the force of offended righteousness, strike with lightning bolts upon the seared consciences; roar as the long-crouched lion upon dallying prey; leap upon, batter, destroy, and utterly consume the vain reasonings of proud human kind; ring as the battle-shout of a strong, triumphant, victory-tasting warrior; strike terror and gravity to souls more forcefully than tortured screams in the dead of night. O God, what shall be the first tones of that voice again on earth? And what their effect? Wonder and fear, denizens of dust, for the Lord Himself shall descend from heaven with a battle-cry, with the voice of the archangel and the trumpet blast of God Himself, made more terrible, if that could be, by the long-suffering of His silence.

December 1. Much disturbed at noon today by a report that "people are talking" about my not being employed. I trust I have had more exercise than they all in this matter. Some think I ought to go to work for a year. God knows I am willing. Felt this charge came as a cutting criticism and sensed a strong desire to retaliate by justifying myself before them, telling them of my application for three jobs lately; of my prospect of going to British Guiana; of my Bible studies; of reading and work—small indeed—of keeping up the place here. But the word of the Lord Jesus came to me. "Ye are they which justify yourselves before men."[13] Not wanting to be found such, I knelt to pray and read the noon psalm for today. It was number 17. Verse 2 smote me: "Let my sentence come forth from Thy presence.... Thou hast tried me...my steps have held fast to Thy paths.... Deliver my soul from men who are Thy hand (v. 14, margin), from men of this world whose portion is in this life...they are satisfied with children, but I shall be satisfied when I awake with Thy form." So, Lord, I am in Thy hand, and say now in faith that Thou hast led, searched, exercised, and tried me. If there lacks now that which I should be doing and am not, hide it not from Thy servant who would follow Thee.

December 5. "Give attendance to reading."[14] Finished a short biography of Allan Smith, missionary to the Paraguayan and Amazonian river systems. Stirred for Tidmarsh's work among the Ecuadorian Quichuas again. Prayed to be sent out soon with definite steps of guidance for my path. Took some confidence from Psalm 18:36, "Thou has enlarged my steps under me and my feet have not slipped."

On December 17 Jim wrote me a letter which showed that his field of vision was at last being focused:

I have had detailed correspondence with two missionaries to whom I wrote; one, Wilfred Tidmarsh of Ecuador (whose wife was injured in a Missionary Aviation Fellowship plane crash when Nate Saint was pilot), who is having to leave an established forest work among Quichua Indians; the other Rowland Hill of

Bangalore, India. Both describe fields of tremendous interest to me and both are quite anxious regarding my leading from the Lord. From one standpoint the works are almost opposite, as the Ecuadorian work is among primitive unlettered tribespeople, while the Indian project is among high school and college-age upper-crust Hindus who are studying in English. Brother Hill wants to start a Bible school for some of them, and is looking for someone who would qualify as a teacher of Greek, etc., as well as work in the wide-open schools. How is one to decide when the heart is equally torn for both works, and one's capabilities fit either sphere?

This was a new test of faith, in view of the decision to go to South American Indians, which Jim had made a year earlier at the Student Missionary Convention. But he believed that the way would be obvious when the time came, provided he continued fulfilling the duties which stared him in the face. As George Macdonald wrote, 'Obedience is the opener of eyes.'

For December 19 the journal contains this note:

I must act in a holy manner, not for reward or appearance, but because of God's nature. The Law continually reminds me that commandments are to be kept, not for their own sake, but for God's sake. I will be righteous, then, because God's nature is such. His character determines my conduct. "This do... for I am Jehovah." [15]

Jim wrote to me on December 27:

I forgot to mention your birthday in my last. I can't remember if we ever discussed giving gifts or not, but somehow it seems such a cheap sort of thing to do—entirely too conformist a practice to have much place in our relationship! The practice at Christmas has gotten to be such a commercialised hoax that I will be sincerely glad when all good Christians abandon it. The excitement of the week-end left us all weary-eyed and untalkative at supper tonight. Seems to me we would have a better attitude toward the whole thing if someone would write a realistic poem on the "Night After Christmas", to counterbalance the magical effects of the imaginative "Night Before".

The journal entry for the same night reads:

"The thirst that from the soul doth rise doth ask a drink divine."[16] Felt deserted this morning and utterly unable to pray because of the crowded passages within. Too much excitement at the reunion last night. I was reminded of the "rubble"[17] instruction of last fall. Desire for the earthly was increased and enlarged, still I recognised that were it sated I would not be at rest. Left my Greek to turn to Ecclesiastes, which I read partway through. The kindred pessimism helps me some, but I cannot tell why. Passages that seemed to say what I feel stood out:

"All things are full of weariness, man cannot utter it: the eye is not satisfied with seeing, nor the ear filled with hearing."

"I said of laughter, it is mad; and of mirth, what doeth it?"

"So I hated life, because the work that is wrought under the sun was grievous to me; for all is vanity and a striving after wind."

"I have seen the travail which God hath given to the sons of men to be exercised therewith."

"Better is a handful with quietness than two handfuls with labour and striving after wind."

Let me read this page when I get to hungering after civilisation's excitements and excesses in some lonely place. Take counsel, then, my soul; the whole of life is vanity and you would be no happier in brighter atmospheres. Woe and loneliness may be miserable, but hollow happiness and many in a crowd are much more so. You may say justly of it all, sighingly, "When will it end?" Shelley's "Ozymandias" fits fairly:

> "I met a traveller from an antique land
> Who said: Two vast and trunkless legs of stone
> Stand in the desert. Near them, on the sand,
> Half-sunk, a shattered visage lies, whose frown,

> *And wrinkled lip, and sneer of cold command,*
> *Tell that its sculptor well those passions read,*
> *Which yet survive, stamped on these lifeless things.*
> *The hand that mocked them, and the heart that fed:*
> *And on the pedestal these words appear:*
> *'My name is Ozymandias, King of Kings:*
> *Look on my works, ye Mighty, and despair!'*
> *Nothing beside remains. Round the decay*
> *Of that colossal wreck, boundless and bare,*
> *The lone and level sands stretch far away."*

"One moment in annihilation's waste" (Omar Khayyám).

"O Lord, be not silent unto me, lest I become like those that go down into the pit."[18]

Evening—Much comforted later, though conscious of sin. Read Hebrews through aloud in English.

December 31. This is New Year's Eve. Light-hearted and empty all day. Moved to sober prayer again. O Lord, you see the places secret in me, you know all my wanderings and reserves. If you see anything in me that is holding back the clear revelation of your will about Ecuador, uncover it to me, I pray.

To me, he wrote:

Had a letter from India today which ended, "I would rejoice to think the New Year would find you here." Still I am waiting. I was challenged by that word of Abraham in reading Hebrews tonight. "He went forth, not knowing whither he went."[19]

"I know that the way of man is not in himself—it is not in man that walketh to direct his steps."[20]

With a prayer for 1950 for you that is both directed by the will of Christ and executed by His power,—Jim.

Notes

1. Galatians 1:15—18, JBP.
2. From 'The Spell of the Yukon' in *The Complete Poems of Robert Service* (New York: Dodd, Mead & Co. 1940), p. 3. Used by permission of the publisher.
3. From 'St Paul' by F. W. H. Myers, in *Collected Poems* (London: Macmillan & Co., 1921), p. 138.
4. Psalm 84:11.
5. 'Night Song at Amalfi' by Sara Teasdale, from *The Collected Poems of Sara Teasdale* (New York: The Macmillan Co., 1937), p. 97. Used by permission.
6. Philippians 4:12.
7. RSV.
8. Ephesians 5:16.
9. Philippians 3:8, para.
10. Psalm 6:3.
11. From the hymn 'Lead On, O King Eternal' by Ernest W. Shurtleff.
12. Colossians 3:16.
13. Luke 16:15.
14. 1 Timothy 4:13.
15. Allusion to the commandments in Leviticus, e.g. Leviticus 19:30.
16. From 'To Celia' by Ben Jonson.
17. Nehemiah 4:10, para.
18. Psalm 28:1, para.
19. Hebrews 11:8, ASV.
20. Jeremiah 10:23.

— 12 —

The Test of Service

Concentrate until my arrival on your reading and on your preaching and teaching. Never forget that you received the gift of proclaiming God's word. . . .[1]

On January 3, 1950, Jim wrote to me:

THIS BEGINS a new file on the second half of the twentieth century according to the conventional reckoning. But what am *I* doing here? What is the significance of my being one of the elect upon whom the end of the ages is come? It gives me a sense of what I heard C. Stacey Woods call "destiny" to think I live in a day so near the Great Precipitation. The elders got to discussing prophecy in our prayer meeting last night and suddenly brother Gill looked me straight in the eye and said, "We are within forty years of the millennial reign of Jesus Christ, and that's a conservative estimate!" At supper tonight, Dad said, "Children born today will see the wind-up of the age." Do consider this, Bets, slowly, and for several minutes at a time. What is my relation, practically, to the end of the age? Oh, it is gripping to think that our eyes are to be so blessed as to see Him, "so coming in like manner"[2] as He went away. What means the enormity of faith in a returning Christ in such an hour? How poorly will appear anything but a consuming operative faith in the person of Christ when He comes. How lost, alas, a life lived in any other light!

144

Yes, I read with avid eagerness *Life's* editorial [on America's failure to produce great art because of the lack of a sense of sin] last week. Even went so far as to pay twenty cents for the fool magazine! It denotes the swing of the pendulum from fearful realism to a little softer, if less surely defined, way of thinking. Pessimism, the anodyne of all pantheism, is a bitter pill and does not well suit man, the laughing mammal.... The armchair American, untrained in brutality, will find palpable the honeyed lie of the False Prophet. Neo-Orthodoxy will be the rage; church union the patriotism, God the common topic of conversation, but not Paul's Orthodoxy, nor Christ's Church, nor my God. "The people imagine a vain thing!"[3]

A later letter comments on my reply to this paragraph:

I share your sentiments about the *Life* magazine editorial. I hope I hadn't a sneer in my tone. Despisers are not in the way of righteousness. Nietzsche would have his disciples learn great contempt; Christ would teach His great compassion, *tender* feeling, not *bitter* feeling. As Bunyan says, "Bowels becometh pilgrims." Maxwell quotes a quoter of Carlyle this month similarly: "Contempt is a dangerous element to sport in; a deadly one if we habitually live in it." I think we both need this. Criticism of things in general is so distant from Christlikeness, and I am sure the healthy attitude toward Mr Luce's recent word on belief is to rejoice.

The letter of January 3 continues:

The volcanic upthrusts we imagined as frozen explosions on Mt Hood are pure white, dazzling against late Wednesday's blue sky. A carload of us went up again yesterday and skied all day. I feel like the first day following wrestling work-out in the fall. I am no skier at all, usually ending up in a soft but chilly bank of snow. It's far more thrilling a sport than skating, on any surface, though I am no better on skis than on skates.

Snow came on here last Sunday night. We have about two inches now, but rain and warmth are predicted for tomorrow.

The full moon on the snow and the freighted evergreens, the scarlet spots in the holly, and the silence—dozens of passages from Service come to mind. Somehow it amuses me every time you quote him. I never knew anyone else who took him seriously, I guess. All literature profs I ever talked to sorta look wise and remark, "Well, his writing is not in the best taste." I have not had much peace to read during the holiday, but things have blown quiet now and I must get at my books again.

I got my acceptance letter from Camp Wycliffe[4] for this summer. Feel as though the Lord would have me take the time there, whether I go to India or South America. The British Guiana project is dragging, so I will likely spend my spring here. Pray for more openings for the Word, will you? Oh that God would cause His Word to "run and be glorified".[5] The Christian High School board verified a standing offer for me to take two weeks' meetings in their high school. I wish you'd enlist some prayer help on this score. The series is to begin January 15, half-hour morning sessions. I have never done any such thing, and feel quite insufficient for a crowd of active minds such as they will have. Pray that the Holy Spirit will do His work of lauding, lifting, and enlivening Christ before them.

The diary continues on January 4:

I have been musing lately on the extremely dangerous cumulative effects of earthly things. One may have good reason, for example, to want a wife, and he may have one legitimately. But with a wife comes Peter The Pumpkin Eater's proverbial dilemma— he must find a place to keep her. And most wives will not stay on such terms as Peter proposed. So a wife demands a house; a house in turn requires curtains, rugs, washing machines, *et cetera*. A house with these things must soon become a home, and children are the intended outcome. The needs multiply as they are met—a car demands a garage; a garage, land; land, a garden; a garden, tools; and tools need sharpening. Woe, woe, woe to the man who would live a disentangled life in my century. II Timothy 2:4 is impossible in the United States, if one insists on a wife. I learn from this that the wisest life . simplest one, lived in the fulfilment of only the basic requi. ments of life—shelter, food, covering, and a bed. And even these can become productive of other needs if one does not heed. Be on guard, my soul, of complicating your environment so that you have neither time nor room for growth!

I must not think it strange if God takes in youth those whom I would have kept on earth till they were older. God is peopling Eternity, and I must not restrict Him to old men and women.

January 10. The announcement of Einstein's new theory of gravitation—which I fail to understand in any degree—caused no small stir in the news this week. All I see is the "integration process" at work again, the "One World" idea of Wilkie's. World Government, World Council of Churches, unification of ideals, and now, the explanation of all phenomena on the basis of a single formula—these are the signs of the End. Social, religious, political, and technical unification, men will find. But where will they find a Moral Integrator, a common denominator for Good and Evil? There is no unification of these, nor understanding of them apart from the consideration of the Christian God.

January 11. Most encouraging letter from Fritz today. Thank God for the faith to believe for him, that first night in November. He grows daily, it seems. How faithful my God!

January 15. Deserted all morning. Much time on my knees, but no fervency or any desire for prayer. No heed or hearkening in the study of the Word, either. What good are Greek, commentaries, insight, gift, and all the rest, if there is no heart for Christ? Oh, what slackness I feel in me now. Wasted half a day. Was to have spoken in chapel again at the Christian High School, but because of snow, school was closed. Good thing—I had nothing to say to the kids anyhow.

January 18. Spoke on fellowship with God at the nurses' and med-students' meeting. Felt that I wandered and joked over-much. I must learn to be more sober, Lord, in such serious matters. How carelessly I handle the Holy Word, how danger-ously off-handed. Help, Lord; let my ministry be Spirit-empowered, not put over by my personality. Feel I failed the

Lord in too much digging for sermon thoughts, and not enough time letting the Scripture speak to me.

Despite the near-despair which some of these journal entries reveal, Jim was being strengthened, in the long hours spent at the old roll-top desk in his bedroom, for later conflicts. On January 19, out of his own discouragement, he was able to write a letter which was of great encouragement to me. I was facing a decision which I feared considerably. His reply to my letter:

> I pray for you, that all your misgivings will be melted to thanksgivings. Remember that the shadow a thing casts often far exceeds the size of the thing itself (especially if the light be low on the horizon), and though some future fear may strut brave darkness as you approach, the thing itself will be but a speck when seen from beyond. Oh that He would restore us often with that "aspect from beyond", to see a thing as He sees it, to remember that He dealeth with us as with sons. Amy Carmichael's words come to me:
>
> > *"He hath never failed thee yet.*
> > *Never will His love forget.*
> > *O fret not thyself nor let*
> > *Thy heart be troubled,*
> > *Neither let it be afraid."*[6]

The journal presents evidence that God was offering him opportunity to give out some of what was being taken in.

January 20, 21. Four meetings with an Inter-Varsity Christian Fellowship gang at Jennings Lodge. Spoke on New Testament semantics and on what a Christian is called: Believer, Disciple, Brother, Saint, Christian—and the relations they entail. Felt the sustaining power of the Spirit, but oh, how I need Him!

January 23. Disheartened tonight because of my lack of discipline. How dare I be so careless and preach as I do? "To him that knoweth to do good (as I have been taught and taught others to be hard on ourselves) and doeth it not, to him it is sin."[7] Sinned by being intemperate in working all day on my stamps—while keeping up a rationalization that I would quit at any moment. Oh, what hypocrisy, what a heart of sin—and how it deceives! Father, forgive it, and let not those who put their trust in Thee—for tomorrow's high school chapel—be ashamed *on my account*. Deliver me from this strong conscience of sins. Let it not have dominion. Give the spirit of forgiveness, I pray.

Not only was his own soul's state the subject of much lamentation, but the state of his own generation as well.

January 24. Ah, tolerant generation, who pay the prophets and fondle them who are sent unto you—Woe. How much better had it been for you and for them if only they had found death at your hands! Cursed be your Judas-embrace. Damned be your friendliness. It speaks not well for you; it lays a shattering condemnation on your prophets.

Ah, generation that hears, but feels not, listens, but aches not, harks, but knows not pain nor the pleasurable healing-balm thereof. Tell me, does all fire extinguish save in Hell? Damned be this tepidity. Have we no fire to hate? Does no flame seize our prophets? Show me one burning heart. Let me see a single worldling afire with true passion, one Heavenling consumed with his God's eternal burnings. In them I would find excuse for you, my cheating, shamming, joyless generation. Well has your own poet said, you live and die "ox-like, limp, and leaden-eyed".[8]

February 4. Difficulty in getting anything at all from the Word. No fervency in prayer. Disturbance in the house, cold weather, and occasional headaches have made spiritual things less precious this whole week. I find I must drive myself to study, following the "ought" of conscience to gain anything at all from the Scripture, lacking any desire at times. It is important to learn respect and obedience to the "inner must" if godliness is to be a state of soul with me. I may no longer depend on pleasant impulses to bring me before the Lord. I must rather respond to principles I know to be right, whether I feel them to be enjoyable or not.

I do not understand why I have never seen in America what missionaries write of—that sense of swords being drawn, the smell of war with demon powers. Corresponding is the unity among Christians on the mission field, forced by the onslaught of a very real foe. Satan is not real—though we talk of belief in a "personal devil". As a result, our warfare takes on this sham-fight with shadows, a cold war of weary words. There is no shouting; rather, yawning. Laughter long ago stifled sobs in our assemblings together. Woe, woe, woe unto us. We have not submitted to sacrifice. We have not guessed the power of the calling to which God has called—its power to ruin and to revive, its strength to slay. Service's "Law of the Yukon" has some words peculiarly applicable to the life to which I think God calls:

"Send not your foolish and feeble; send me your strong and your sane—
Strong for the red rage of battle; sane, for I harry them sore;
Send me men girt for the combat, men who are grit to the core;
Swift as the panther in triumph, fierce as the bear in defeat,
Sired of a bulldog parent, steeled in the furnace heat.

And I wait for the men who will win me—and I will not be won in a day.
And I will not be won by weaklings, subtle, suave and mild,
But by men with the hearts of vikings, and the simple faith of a child;
Desperate, strong and resistless, unthrottled by fear or defeat,
Them will I gild with my treasure, them will I glut with my meat."[9]

February 20. Finished the chapel services at the Christian High School. Forbid, Lord, that any of those to whom I minister should be so foolish as to take my word as though it were Thine; or so daring as to set aside Thy Word as though it were mine.

Whether Jim knew of any results from that series of talks I do not know. But after his death I received a letter which demonstrates that prayer was answered. Evelyn Corkum, a student in the high school at that time, wrote:

> I was a sophomore, a little more conservative than the average. In all these years there are certain specific things Jim said which have stood out and become very basic factors in moulding my character and way of life.
>
> His entire series was based on Timothy. He explained that he chose that book because it was written to a young man. . . . It was through this series that I finally began to have a rather regular daily time with the Lord. Jim did not suggest that we start the morning out with five minutes of Bible skimming and hasty prayer. He challenged us to get up forty-five minutes early, ahead of the rest of the family, get to a place where we could be alone with the Lord, without interruptions if possible. At that time, the suggested forty-five minutes seemed to me a huge sacrifice, but it was like him not to try to *edge in* counsel in the hope of gaining the students' favour.
>
> One day he spoke frankly of boy-girl relations. . . . "Don't put yourself in a position to see how good your resistance is. When you feel temptation coming, *get out of there!*" . . . It was new to me to see a good-looking fellow so sold out for the Lord. His personality was magnetic and his spirituality did not in the least make him "creepish" or "fuddy-duddy".
>
> He dared us to give up ourselves to Christ. . . . I am sure I am not exaggerating when I say that Jim had the greatest influence on my life of any single individual outside of my parents. I do not regret having taken his advice seriously. I believe that because of it my life has been full and that I have known and am experiencing the Lord's leading.

Jim's journal continues:

February 11. I see tonight that in spiritual work, if nowhere else, the character of the worker decides the quality of the work. Shelley and Byron may be moral free-lancers and still write good poetry. Wagner may be lecherous as a man, and still produce fine music, but it cannot be so in any work for God. Paul could refer to his own character and manner of living for proof of what he was saying to the Thessalonians. Nine times over in the first epistle he says "You know", referring to the Thessalonians' first-hand observation of Paul's private as well as public life. Paul went to Salonica and lived a life that more than illustrated what he preached; it went beyond illustration to convincing proof. No wonder so much work in the Kingdom today is shoddy—look at the moral character of the worker.

February 13. Spoke tonight at the quarterly meeting of the Christian School Association. Touched on demon powers in the classroom ("We wrestle not against flesh and blood"[10]) and of the *institutionalization* of the child—the ability to develop good deportment without godly devotion; scholarship without spirituality; sincere, pure minds, without spiritual, powerful motives. Felt clumsy in expressing myself and not too sure all I said was of use. Oh for the lips of Samuel, from which the Lord let not a single word fall to the ground!

February 18. Teaching seventh and eighth grades all this week in the Christian School. The board want me to decide soon about what I'll be doing next fall, as they want me to teach for a year. O God, so many turns, so many ways, so many pits! Help me to do Thy will without consideration of any man. I can make no decision unless I hear Thee speak, Lord.

The same day Jim wrote a letter to his high school friend, Dick Fisher, who he felt was missing God's way for his life:

Have you sent in your Wheaton application yet? You are losing valuable time in your GI-bill money for school. I exhort you, Richard, to drop these lumbering trivialities pronto, pay your debts, and hit the road to college. If you can't get into Wheaton try something else. Further, I sense that you are in real need of some stalwart Christian companionship in both sexes, and feel that the conditional environment of a Christian college campus would supply your present lack. You can't fool yourself into thinking you can get along without more contact with the people of God than you have been having. I say this not without forethought, for I have felt often when with you that you and I should have been more together, or at least that you learn godliness along with some friend, as did Christian in *Pilgrim's Progress*. I know that it is not my place to tell you what you should do, but I feel this strongly for you, brother. It is dangerous to have companions among the devil's flock, and know little of travelling behind the Great Shepherd of the sheep of His fold. It is probable that you have before you a multitude of hopes and plans for work around Astoria, but I feel that you should take all that to the Lord and tell Him that you want more than a good business. In fact, this is so pressing and so important to your welfare that I even dare to say that the telephone company doesn't need you any more. It is evident after several years with them that you have gotten very little for all your pains. Certainly the work has been of little profit to you spiritually, your bank account is no larger, and I daresay that you are no happier personally than you were when you started with them. In short, you are getting nowhere.

It seems like this is sorta stern stuff to be coming from me, but I got keyed up about it today and thought I had better exhort you, because I can see the Great Day approaching fast, and perhaps it hadn't occurred to you that you have got to render up an account right away. I'd like to see you to talk it over, for I am afraid that I won't be around here this summer, and may miss a chance to spend much time with you. If it sounds like I'm sticking my nose into your business, remember that I say this with a regard to the eternal profit of your soul, and that the Lord has stirred me up to write of this.

Christ needs some young fellows to sell out to Him and recklessly toss their lives into His work. It seems to me like you ought to be one of them, Fisher. — Earnestly in the Lord Jesus, Jim.

A letter written on February 22 to his father, who was preaching in eastern Washington, reveals the seriousness of Jim's intent to see the New Testament church pattern set to work in modern practice. The letter shows, too, that his time was not entirely spent in the academic (teaching and studying) and the spiritual:

Beloved Dad: Your insistence upon short notes leaves me without excuse not to write, so here is one for you. Long pause here. I wrote the first sentence too hastily, I guess. Just as I clicked off the last who should come bursting in the door but that mad Dutchman Werner Durtschi, who had brought his mother and two sisters over for a lesson in knitting Argyle socks from Mom. So went the evening. It's late now, and I had to run in second gear all day today because of a late night last evening.

Much longer pause here. Thursday filled with work and study. No time for letter writing.... Got my first pay cheque from the Christian school today. They're paying ten dollars a day minus tax. Sizeable, and giving an increased responsibility in stewardship to me. Things are going a little more smoothly as I get to understand the kids more. Discipline remains a problem. Do you think that the fall set the human heart against all learning? Why must all be pushed and driven to that which can only do them good, even in the field of secular knowledge? I see that the heart rebels at all light, not only at the knowledge of God.

The meeting of two weeks ago at the Stark Street assembly was enjoyable, though not as well attended nor as warm as the previous one, I thought. The setting up of men on the platform discourages contributions from the floor. I have been under some exercise as to running our gospel meeting as the saints used to, not announcing a leader nor appointing a song leader, but waiting on the Lord for individual exercise in these matters. We saw the method work well at Forest Grove one night some years ago.

The chickens are producing five or six eggs a day. We noticed that the leaving off of the light at night does not affect their production, so we have abandoned the practice of keeping the light on. We got an oversized egg today that measured 2¾ inches long.

The Buick slipped out of reverse and low again, but Bob had it back with a few minutes' work. Same trouble we had in Bozeman, you'll remember. The Plymouth is grinding gears badly, so we use it very little, not knowing what might happen next.

Bryson cut down the two remaining trees on his lot, and I hauled them down to the chestnut this morning. Have not had time to buck them to lengths yet, but we need little wood just now. The bulbs are springing all over the place, but won't be blooming for another two or three weeks, I guess.

I must get some papers corrected and do some other correspondence, so will call this the end. I made this translation of 1 John 2:7,8 this morning. What do you think of it?—"Beloved, I am not writing a new commandment to you, but an old commandment which you have held from the start; the word which you have heard is the old commandment. Still, I am writing it as a new commandment because the darkness is passing along, and the true light is shining on." This last means, I think, that the command to love one another takes on fresh meaning as I step into new light, and the darkness dissipates. With the growth in my knowledge of the implications of the love that I am taught, I am determined to apply that love in an increasing number of situations.—Earnestly, your son Jim.

February 25. Spoke last evening to the junior class at Multnomah School of the Bible, on 2 Timothy 2:4 [says the journal]: the war with spirit-forces, disentanglement, and something of the call to service. What a mockery! I felt as though little or nothing was accomplished.... The Lord has been distant most of this week, and I have found myself too weary and sinful to draw near to Him. Desire seemed to fail and my soul lies faint, lapping at its own stale dregs.

February 26. I was asked to give up the breaking of bread meeting for a "service" next Sunday morning. What folly! Ah, for the spirit of Rutherford,

> "E'en Anwoth were not heaven,
> E'en preaching were not Christ."

How can one explain without bringing offence? I offended in refusing, but oh, the Lord was real tonight out underneath the moon. A February night it is, pregnant with spring.

*"Too many devious paths lead down the land
And I shall need in that strange, vast unknown,
Thy hand upon my hand."* [11]

March 6. Dave was here last week-end, and wants some answer regarding Inter-Varsity and Foreign Missions Fellowship work. I see several restrictions, the primary one being the compromises I would be called upon to live under in recommending mission boards, while knowing that the way of God is so far from organised methods that none with whom I would deal would be able to see the consistency of my own attitudes and the things I would have to recommend. Further, the leaping from place to place, here a night, there a day, has been shown to be ineffective, in the summer of 1948, lacking the substantial quality of settled local building.

My exercise seems to be undergoing crucial fires just now. I sensed afresh last eve the truth of Paul's word, "How shall they preach except they be sent?" [12] O God, here I am. Send me, oh send me afield.

But further preparation was still needed. Instead of being sent "afield" Jim was sent to a small town in southern Oregon to preach in a series of meetings. At the beginning of the two and a half weeks there, he wrote:

The fulfilment of Psalm 65:5 is hoped, "By terrible things in righteousness wilt Thou answer us, O God of our salvation; who art the confidence of all the ends of the earth, and of them that are afar off upon the sea." I hardly dare believe for this, since my own soul is in such a state that I cannot find faith to lay hold on God prevailingly.

March 26. Spoke this morning on the Triumphal Entry.... Some freedom but much unnecessary shouting.

March 27. Spoke on Mark 14. Felt deserted, though much prayer had ascended for the meeting. Only two sinners out. Much humbled in heart afterward.

March 28. Spent this afternoon visiting with Phares about the country. Some stir, a certain "sound of going" [13] there seems to be up the valley, but no conviction generally among the people.

O God, soften sinners and save them to Thine eternal glory!

March 31. Spoke on Gethsemane.... Went into the meeting with a shaking at the horror of sin. Conviction sensed, but the souls of men were not shaken with the trembling as we had hoped. Came home questioning the Father's goodness and was rebuked with these answers:

(1) God is not frustrating our prayers. He has heard, and in wisdom withheld an unusual work. The wisdom of God seemed a good thing to ponder, though I could not understand it. God withholds blessing only in wisdom, never in spite or aloofness.

(2) James' word about asking came.

  (a) I had not been asking definitely enough—"Ye have not because ye ask not."[14]

  (b) I had not been asking purely enough. "Ye ask and receive not because ye ask amiss, that ye may consume it upon your lusts."[15] I still had my own concerns, my own name connected with the work, and had God granted it hitherto I would have consumed the answer in pride and selfishness.

A letter to his father dated April 13 indicates that the meetings were not without effect.

Beloved Padre: Just a brief note-report on the Lord's work down at Williams. I just now got in after an eight-hour bus ride since midnight. Am unpacked now.

The Lord gave me much freedom in the meetings and was Himself obviously working over the whole valley area. The town's chief drunkard and his wife came to the Lord one afternoon and both gave public confession of faith last night. One or two of the young folks came into assurance of salvation and are making a good beginning at the study of the Scriptures. Phares and I met with twenty-five young people, high school age and over, last night after the meeting before I went to the bus and had a serious time dealing with them about private study of the Scriptures, personal holiness, and down-to-business living for Christ. I think God wrought wonders—nothing emotional (except in me personally, where I felt much conviction for my inward corruption), but a sane and scriptural building process, done, I trust, in the Spirit.

Never has the meaning of the death and consequent exaltation of the Saviour been so clear to me, and I praise God for plainness of speech in ministering some of the doctrines of grace.

The journal continues:

April 16. Inter-Varsity conference over the week-end. Exercised re: I-V staff work. No leading concerning the foreign field. Back to the Greek this morning, after three weeks away from it for all practical study.

April 17. Turned down offer by the school board to complete the school year as seventh-eighth grade teacher. Found some difficulty in discerning the Lord's will, but believe He has guided. It is easy to be swayed by minor (or even major) points when one comes to make decisions if one cannot hark back to *principles* of guidance. I have learned three principles recently which make a fair beginning at a code:

(1) Remember always that God has taught you the importance of a building ministry. Staying for some time in one group, stressing certain things consistently, is the best way to accomplish lasting work for God.

(2) Do not put yourself in a position relative to any man or group which permits them to direct policies which you know must be decided upon through your own individual exercise before God. Never let any organization dictate the will of God. A move which so ensnares cannot be of God for me.

(3) Whenever the choice is between the doing of spiritual work, of whatever sort, and a secular job, again of whatever sort, the choice of me must be the former regardless of financial conditions.

April 19. Seeking a promise of God's acceptance of my trust in Him for guidance in the next month and a half. I got this encouragement from Isaiah 42:16, "I will bring the blind by a way that they know not, in paths that they know not will I lead them."[16] I fulfil the qualifications for once, Lord; most surely I am blind.

April 20. I asked earnestly for some token of guidance to be shown concerning my going to the Summer Institute of Linguistics.[17] Got none. It is clear to me tonight that I can do quite well without that guidance for now. God is going to give me a specific leading—not when I ask for it, but when I need it, and not until then.

May 18. Took up and finished a hasty browsing of the *Life* of William Farel, a Reformer of note. It was three hours before I returned to the Scriptures and prayer. I trust I learned a lesson, for it took special concentration and considerable difficulty to begin to feel the power of the Word. Anything, good as it may be, put before my study of the true and living Word becomes a snare, and I must assiduously avoid such, if the Word is to be my fresh meat every morning.

Last night I took a walk around the hill. Found myself again dedicating my clay, asking for God's presence to be sensed more continually. Analyzed afresh and repudiated my base desire to *do* something for God in the sight of men, rather than to *be* something, regardless of whether results were to be seen. The clouds scudding over the west hills seemed to speak to me: "What is your life? It is even a vapour."[18] I saw myself as a wisp of vapour being drawn upward from the vast ocean by the sun's great power and sent landward by the winds. The shedding of blessing upon earth must be as the rain, drawn up first by God, borne along by His Spirit, poured out by His own means and in His place, and running down to the sea again. "As water poured out."[19] So my weakness shall be God's opportunity to refresh earth. I would that it should be as He has shown.

And to me, Jim wrote:

Though these days may be quiet, as far as doing is concerned, they are jammed full of excitement in the inner man. I exult to know the God who maintains the path of the just as a shining light, brighter by the moment toward the Perfect Day.

Notes

1. 1 Timothy 4:13, 14, JBP.
2. Acts 1:11, para.
3. Psalm 2:1.
4. A study-camp in Norman, Oklahoma, conducted by the Summer Institute of Linguistics, Inc., in affiliation with the University of Oklahoma.
5. 2 Thessalonians 3:1, ASV.
6. This was a quotation from memory and is not in the exact words of the author.
7. James 4:17.
8. From the poem 'The Leaden-Eyed' by Vachel Lindsay.
9. From 'The Law of the Yukon' in *The Complete Poems of Robert Service* (New York: Dodd, Mead & Co., 1940), p. 12. Used by permission of the publisher.
10. Ephesians 6:12.
11. Source unknown.
12. Romans 10:15.
13. 1 Chronicles 14:15.
14. James 4:2.
15. James 4:3.
16. ASV.
17. The University of Oklahoma.
18. James 4:14.
19. Psalm 22:14, para.

— 13 —

Impelled by These Voices

Unto the upright there ariseth light in the darkness. [1]

J IM ELLIOT'S April prayer for guidance concerning attendance at the Summer Institute of Linguistics was answered in the affirmative, and June 2, 1950, found him in Wheaton again, *en route* to Oklahoma. This futher step taught him something else about guidance, which he recorded in his diary:

> Impressed with Ephesians 5, "understanding what the will of the Lord is", and Romans 12, "proving what is the will of God". Every moment I may be conscious and rejoice in the knowledge of God's will. Obedience to every command puts me on the track and keeps me there. Decisions of course must be made, but as in railroad, so in life—a block signal, a crisis, is lighted only where there is special need. I may not always be in sight of a "go" light, but sticking to the tracks will take me where the next one is. Understanding the will of the Lord is believing Him, that he will—in all situations where I have obeyed—make that way His own way, effectual for eternity.

At the University of Oklahoma, Jim, along with several hundred other prospective or returned missionaries, spent ten weeks learning how to study unwritten languages—how to write them down and analyze them. Phonetics, the study of sounds, he found not difficult, with his native ability to mimic others' accents and dialects. His analytical mind tackled with zest the problems of morphology (the study of the structure of words) and syntax (the structure of sentences). The course also gave opportunity for each student to practise in a simulated field situation. Informants from various language groups were brought in to the University, and the students worked with them individually, collecting and organizing language data just as they would do in an area where the langauage is not yet in writing. For this study Jim was allowed to use as his informant a former missionary to the Quichuas of the Ecuadorian jungle. This afforded an excellent opportunity for a start on the particular language which Jim was beginning to feel would be his task in the future. The missionary from Ecuado was the first to tell Jim of the Aucas. Jim's heart was immediately set on fire. A tribe untouched by civilization? A people who had repulsed every attempt of the white man to contact them? The pioneer spirit in him was kindled at the very thought. Some may say his was a romantic temperament. Very likely it was. But Ragland, the pioneer of South India (1815—1858), said:

> St Paul considered it as wages to work at Corinth without wages, and had a feeling (which in anyone else we should call romantic) about preaching Christ where he had not been named before.... Indeed, I am not clear that the feeling commonly called "romantic" is not, as much as any other natural feeling, sanctifiable and applicable to Christ's purposes.

Jim thought of the correspondence he had had with Dr Tidmarsh. He thought of the Quichua country, where large areas were as yet not reached with the gospel. And now the Aucas. This, to a man accustomed to expect God to 'pull strings through circumstances' as he said, did not appear to be mere coincidence.

Was it Ecuador, then, rather than India, to which he was to go? His leading in this case was as remarkable as it was clear. On July 4 Jim decided to set aside ten days for prayer for God's definite answer.

'Make my path sure, Lord,' he wrote in his journal. 'Establish my goings. Send me when and where You will, and manifest to all that You are my Guide.'

Four days later he added:

These are days of vision for me, days wherein are revealed to me those great "oughts" which must be if Christ is to have glory. Partly they are revealed in what I see around me by way of departure from the Word of God in practice. Partly they are known in the reading of the Scripture as I see the ideal and its beauty in days past. Oh, what manner of men we ought to be in light of what is now on us! Lord, Thou hast spoken once and again in my soul. What ought to be can be. And I believe. Vindicate Thy Name, Thy Word, Thy pattern by accomplishing these many "oughts" I see but afar off.

July 14. I asked for some word from God ten days ago, which would encourage me in going to Ecuador. It came this morning in an unexpected place. I was reading casually in Exodus 23 when verse 20 came out vividly. "Behold I send an angel before thee to keep thee by the way and to bring thee into the place which I have prepared. Take heed before him." Coming as it did, with such preceding feelings and such simple believing for some promise, I take this as leading from God that I should write Tidmarsh telling him that I will go to Ecuador in the will of God.

It was not in answer to his own prayers alone that Jim was thus led. Only a few days later he received a letter from Eleanor Vandevort, a college friend who was by then a missionary in Africa. She told of a peculiar compulsion to pray for Jim at the very time he had set aside for prayer. He wrote to her:

Dear Eleanor: I suppose it is very early morning in the Sudan, and that you rise to face the day with Christ, or that you still sleep with His Spirit brooding over you. In either case, two four-line prayers from Amy Carmichael are being prayed for you now. If the former,

> "My Lord, My Love, my heart's Eternal Light,
> Shine on thy lover through the hours of night,
> Shine on my thoughts, my very dreams be found
> About Thy business, on some holy ground."

And if the latter, then:

> "Walking the dawn-wind, Jesus, Heavenly Lover,
> In the still beauty of the waking morn,
> Unveil Thyself to me, and with the vision
> Shall come the strength for trials yet unborn."

. . . Your letter is dated July 12 and you say I had been much on your heart thereabouts. It was of God you were burdened, Van. For I had been having ten days of special prayer about going to Ecuador, between July 4 and 15. A recently abandoned station among the Quichuas had been offered to whomever will take it. Some here knew of the work and encouraged us to regard it as a door to be knocked on. If God opens the door, who can shut? And if He says, "Go", who will dare stay? So pray that my faith be strengthened against opposing powers.

Then, on July 25, he wrote to his parents of further confirmation of the decision:

The confidence given of the Lord that this is His will for me grows daily, and is confirmed on every side. Not by spectacular means always, but by very little things, something dropped casually in class regarding the Quichua language; a $20 bill in an envelope in the mail-box with an unsigned note, "Philippians 4: 19. God bless you. This is for Ecuador." A letter from Dr Tidmarsh yesterday. He was encouraged but not elated, grateful to God, but will not yet assume that God wants us right in Shandia, knowing our interest in the Quichuas generally.

If it is God's will, I am ready to go immediately, and would wait only the decision of the elders in Portland. Bob's wonderings about the draft board do not even cause me the slightest worry. After all, he who sets the open door before me promised "no man can shut".[2] It may seem naïve to take such a view, but after all, there is nothing I can do to "draft dodge', or pull strings. The Lord's promise to preserve the simple applies in my case, I think. He is God who regards kings and rulers as very small factors in the affairs that concern His work. And I think we can afford to share that attitude with Him. This is not to say they will not try to shut the door. It is simply to say that God will keep it open, regardless of who tries to shut it, and how hard they try.

How I praise God for you all. What a heritage falls to them whose surroundings from childhood have been illumined by the Book of God, whose winds have been freighted with the prayer and concern of others for their souls. Think for an instant of the little children digging yams today at the crack of a whip in Quichua-land, many of whom don't know their own fathers. Romanism dominates their souls and intoxicates their bodies. Oh that God would plant His Spirit in some of those families, as He has so graciously in ours, that they might know the blessing and recompense of living for God as we know it today. The missionaries say the spirit of the people is utterly broken, having been so long enslaved in such frightful excesses. They have no desire to alleviate their own needs, but drink themselves into their graves.

> *"Not that they starve, but starve so dreamlessly;*
> *Not that they sow but that they seldom reap;*
> *Not that they serve, but have no gods to serve;*
> *Not that they die, but that they die like sheep."*[3]

Men who live and never understand what they were created for may be said indeed to be "dead" as the Scriptures say. "Where there is no vision, the people perish."[4]

Jim's parents, along with others who knew him well, could not help questioning whether perhaps his ministry should be among young people in the United States. His gift for Bible teaching and preaching was an unusual one, as had been evidenced in college student work, radio preaching, and evangelistic meetings. They wrote to him, telling him their feeling, and mentioning as well their own sense of loss at seeing him leave home permanently.

He replied on August 8:

I do not wonder that you were saddened at the word of my going to South America. This is nothing else than what the Lord Jesus warned us of when he told the disciples that they must become so infatuated with the Kingdom and following Him that all other allegiances must become as though they were not. And He never excluded the family tie. In fact, those loves which we regard as closest, He told us must become as hate in comparison with our desires to uphold His cause. Grieve not, then, if your sons seem to desert you, but rejoice, rather, seeing the will of God done gladly. Remember how the psalmist described children? He said that they were as a heritage from the Lord, and that every man should be happy who had his quiver full of them. And what is a quiver full of but arrows? And what are arrows for but to shoot? So, with the strong arms of prayer, draw the bowstring back and let the arrows fly—all of them, straight at the Enemy's hosts.

> "*Give of thy sons to bear the message glorious,*
> *Give of thy wealth to speed them on their way,*
> *Pour out thy soul for them in prayer victorious,*
> *And all thou spendest Jesus will repay.*"[5]

Does it sound harsh so to speak? Surely those who know the great passionate heart of Jehovah must deny their own loves to share in the expression of His. Consider the call from the Throne above, "Go ye,"[6] and from round about, "Come over and help us,"[7] and even the call from the damned souls below, "Send

Lazarus to my brothers, that they come not to this place."[8]
Impelled, then, by these voices, I dare not stay home while
Quichuas perish. So what if the well-fed Church in the homeland
needs stirring? They have the Scriptures, Moses, and the
Prophets, and a whole lot more. Their condemnation is written
on their bankbooks and in the dust on their Bible covers.
American believers have sold their lives to the service of
Mammom, and God has His rightful way of dealing with those
who succumb to the spirit of Laodicea.

The breadth of Jim's vision is suggested in this entry from
the journal:

August 9. God just now gave me faith to ask for another young
man to go, perhaps not this fall, but soon, to join the ranks in
the lowlands of eastern Ecuador. There we must learn: (1)
Spanish and Quichua, (2) each other, (3) the jungle and independence, and (4) God and God's way of approach to the
highland Quichua. From thence, by His great hand, we must
move to the Ecuadorian highlands with several young Indians
each, and begin work among the 800,000 highlanders. If God
tarries, the natives must be taught to spread southward with the
message of the reigning Christ, establishing New Testament
groups as they go. Thence the Word must go south into Peru
and Bolivia. The Quichuas must be reached for God! Enough for
policy. Now for prayer and practice.

Notes

1. Psalm 112:4.
2. Revelation 3:8.
3. From the poem 'The Leaden-Eyed' by Vachel Lindsay, in *Collected Poems* (New York: The Macmillan Co., 1925). Used by permission of the publisher.
4. Proverbs 29:18.
5. From the hymn 'O Zion, Haste' by Mary A. Thompson.
6. Matthew 28:19.
7. Acts 16:9.
8. Luke 16:27,28, para.

— 14 —

The Pattern Tested

I only say this, let the builder be careful how he builds! The Foundation is already laid, and no one can lay another, for it is Jesus Christ Himself.[1]

WHEN THE linguistic course was over, it seemed that the 'pillar of cloud'[2] was not lifting, and Jim decided to stay on in Norman, Oklahoma, for a month or two with Bill Cathers, helping in the small assembly in Oklahoma City, and in the Bible study group on the university campus. During this period he applied for a passport. Dr Tidmarsh had written from Ecuador to say he planned to take a furlough in the fall, and urged Jim and Bill to come as soon as possible.

Jim wrote to me on August 31:

We are trusting God to provide a place to live and eat here. We ran an ad as "handymen", in the *Norman Daily*, and we usually make enough money painting, repairing, or fixing up to keep us ahead financially. There is abundant opportunity to minister in the area: high school kids in Norman, needy country folk all around, welcome in the assembly, and when school starts, work on the university campus.

If it is God's mind we will leave for Ecuador as soon as we have passports and have seen home once more. There are some supplies to be collected, but nothing like most married couples require. Special stuff you could be praying about includes a radio set, some dental supplies, and medical tools (which Dr Tidmarsh will show us how to use), and, lest I forget, passage money. We are working on a deal which would take us there on a banana boat as crew members.

The journal continues:

September 7. These are waiting-days for Bill and me. We had hoped by now to have secured passports and begun work on collecting supplies, but God has had other things in mind. We have worked when the opportunity came, waiting for word *re*: commendation from the assembly at home. Tomorrow J. M. returns and we must leave his apartment. But where should we go? Norman is a good place to work, but finding a place to live and cook is not easy.

Psalm 31:15 was a blessing: "My times are in Thy hands." And Psalm 139:16: "In Thy book they were all written, even the days that were ordained for me."[3] Ordained days, then, whether spent in waiting, working, or whatever. We have asked for guidance, been obedient where we understood what was to be done, and now wait word for the next step.

September 29. Word came from Ed McCully today *re*: his exercise before the Lord to quit school and begin looking for open doors for a sold-out life. How I praise God to hear! Even wept as I read of the Lord's dealings, for my desire for him, and the spiritual exercise of his gift has been much enlarged. Now I wonder if he may not be the man God would sent with us to Ecuador? I have prayed for one more for the work, and perhaps God will answer thus. Grateful if so, Lord, very grateful.

October 18. I leave, God willing, tomorrow for Wheaton, though I cannot now see why. Things are so needy here. The meetings in Oklahoma City require much, much more prayer than we are giving them; visitation must be done. There are several recent contacts on the university campus that should be followed up with personal contacts. There are calls for painting jobs yet undone. Yet I feel constrained to go to Milwaukee to seek Ed McCully, much the same as Barnabas went to Tarsus to seek Saul long ago.

Lord, I have trusted in Thee with all my heart, and now I confess that I have no understanding upon which I can lean. Grant that my way may be prepared before me, at Homecoming in Wheaton, in Milwaukee, and in Huntington, Indiana. Do the first work of knitting Ed and me, opening the believers' hearts to the truth of the Sanctuary. Waste not my hours of travel, Lord. Flood my pathway with light and give me grace to walk therein pleasing to Thee.

On the way up to Wisconsin Jim ran the car he was driving into the high shoulder of the road, turning it completely over. A friend of Jim's had bought the car only a few days before, and had not a penny of insurance on it. Jim wrote:

I felt sick, but it was plainly an accident, and I know that God had lessons in it. Good to know Psalm 121 in these days—"Thy keeper . . . neither slumbers nor sleeps."

The McCullys had almost hired a painter, so I took the job and have it well under way now. Ed is working as a night clerk in a downtown hotel and I go down every other night to study the Word with him, sleeping while he does the bookwork, and getting in about three and a half solid hours of Bible study. The interchange of thought is stimulating.

There is little indication of where I should go from here. The Lord has supplied every need abundantly, and I rejoice in knowing His presence in all my "goings out and comings in".[4]

In a letter of a few weeks later:

I certainly enjoy being with Ed, and could hope the Lord would send us afield together, but I do not think the decision should be made while I'm here. We influence each other too easily and our natural compatibility would override the Lord's leading if we're not careful.

A letter from Tidmarsh tell us he is going to England on

furlough this month, and since we feel it imperative to be introduced to Shandia under his counsel, we will probably wait until then and return with him next year.

At this point Jim received word from Bill Cathers that he planned to be married. Since Jim had expected to go to Ecuador with Bill, according to the New Testament pattern of working 'two and two',[5] this news was a jolt. He told his parents of it in a letter, adding this comment:

Talk of marriage, rings, flowers, affairs, and (ugh!) housekeeping leaves me cold. I dread occasionally that my realism may keep me from really falling for anyone hard enough to feel like getting married. Rats. I am a bohemian loafer without enough sense of responsibility to keep my shoes shined.

His mother's reply was a defence of the institution, plus the gentle suggestion that Jim's attitude was perhaps one of sour grapes. Jim countered:

If I am envious of dear Billy in his marriage, Mom, it is certainly the newest kind of envy I have ever heard of. When it comes to marriage (since your last letter contained so much on the subject) I am still faced with serious problems. It does not necessarily mean that a bachelor must be egotistical, unbalanced, talkative, and overbearing because he has not got a wife. He may be all of these things, as some I know are, but there are married people in the same category. Besides this, Paul, Timothy (we are led to believe), and others of the New Testament figures, to say nothing of other godly men in history and our Lord Jesus Himself, were not married men. If marriage is the only cure-all for unbalanced young men, these must have been unbalanced, and from their work, one could not fairly say it. So, whether to get married is still a problem, aggravated by the peculiar demands put on one who would follow the Pauline pattern in a tropical-forest situation. Bill is being led to marriage, and I exult that it is so, rejoicing with those who rejoice. To envy him would be to covet his leading (and gift!), and covetousness in Scripture is denounced as idolatry.

By the 'peculiar demands of a tropical-forest situation' he explained himself thus:

It is difficult enough to get among people, learn their language and customs, get acclimated, and make all those emotional adjustments without adding the tremendous task of aligning to married experience. For the woman it is even more difficult and there have been cases where family responsibility so absorbed the wife that she never has become a missionary, simply lacking time to make the social adjustment because of the multiplicity of domestic details. W. E. Vine, whom I have been reading, shares this view, and believes that a man should go with another man until effective contact is made in the society. If, then, it becomes clear that one's testimony and effectiveness would be increased, one should marry.

From Milwaukee Jim went to a small town in Indiana in November where a group of young married couples was interested in studying the Bible. It was an opportunity for him to teach some of the truths which he had recently been examining anew.

Of the first Bible study he wrote:

I felt liberty to lay the cards on the table and flatfootedly blurted out something about the New Testament church pattern. Most of them were stunned, but came back eagerly for more. Have been visiting some of their homes since, and find a real stirring among half a dozen families, a hunger for the Word. Many are bound by traditional organization patterns and, although they feel something is wrong, are fearful of breaking the accepted modes of worship. Of course, I am already branded as a propagator of some new sect, but to this I exultantly reply in the words of the apostle on a similar charge, "But this I confess to thee, that after the way which they call a 'sect', so serve I the God of our fathers."[6]

I charge you to pray for the saints here. God must do the work of centring their lives in Christ. None know the Scriptures well because of the devilish schemes of the clergy to keep them from thinking for themselves. Do pray for wisdom and grace for me that my witness might be effective for the glory of the Man at God's right hand.

Jim's convictions on the importance of conforming to the New Testament pattern in the structure of the local Church underwent severe fire in this effort.

He wrote home on December 6:

All are willing to admit that the assembly pattern of the New Testament is ideal, but none are willing to commit themselves, particularly the men.... Let those who claim New Testament conformity beware: we commit ourselves to a way of life which must be conditioned by the New Testament, and disciplined by *all* the principles therein. So pray for these men—they do not lack desire, but practical devotion, a setting to the task.

After a month's studies with the little group, Jim wrote to his parents:

Generally I feel quite useless. They are helped by my being here, but total ignorance of the Truth is the general status of church-goers hereabouts. I know that my time is limited, and unless someone else moves here to help them, there is little chance of their going on. Oh that God would shake up some of those married couples around Portland with their prim unconcern for souls and saints, dabbling with building lots, houses, jobs, babies, silverware—while souls starve for what they know! God shall not hold us guiltless, either. "He shall suffer loss."[7] What is needed here is a family to move in, take work, open the home, and teach Truth without reference to the schismatic heresy of "Plymouth Brethren". The urge comes on me at times to write in scathing terms articles for these piddling little magazines of "comfort and kind words for God's little flock". Baloney! When are we going to rise like men and face the world squarely? This drivelling nonsense which condones inactivity because of the apostasy of the day needs a little fire to show up the downright ungodliness it hides. We cuddle around the Lord's table as though it were the last coal of God's altar, and warm our hands, thinking that will appease the wrath of the indignant Christ when He charges us with the unmet, unchallenged, untaught generation of heathen now doing their Christmas shopping. It makes me boil when I think of the power we profess and the utter impotency of our action. Believers who know one-tenth as much as we do are doing one hundred times more for God, with His blessing and our criticism. Oh if I could write it, preach it, say it, paint it, anything at all, if only God's power would become known among us! ICHABOD.

I had forwarded to Jim a letter from a friend in a foreign country, which told something of conditions among Christians there. His answer reveals the importance he placed on the corporate conduct of the Church:

J's letter was interesting. Her attitude toward the Church of God is like the multitude of Fundamentalists—"anything will do". The pivot point hangs on whether or not God has revealed a universal pattern for the Church in the New Testament. If He has not, then anything will do so long as it works. But I am convinced that nothing so dear to the heart of Christ as is His Bride should be left without explicit instructions as to her corporate conduct. I am further convinced that the twentieth century has in no way simulated this pattern in its method of "churching" a community, so that almost nothng is really "working" to the glory and pleasure of God. Further, it matters not at all to me what men have done with the Church over there or in America, it is incumbent upon me, if God has a pattern for the Church, to find and establish that pattern, at all costs.

The clergy of Fundamentalism is a direct descendant of papism, and in spite of what J. says, has no basic principle in Scripture—where the priesthood of all believers is taught.

Further, J. says "the worship service is most satisfying to me as an individual!" What in all eternity has that got to do with it? Have her personal likes and dislikes any right to dictate method in the holy church of God? It is this attitude that has brought hopeless confusion into our present order, for "holy rolling", and snake-handling are most satisfying to some folks as individuals. "Let God be true and every man a liar." Is it His way? Then let my personal likes be filed in the waste-can. Let me follow by afforded grace. It is neither J's job nor mine to commend or condemn any system of gathering. It is the responsibility of both of us to search the Scriptural principles, find the all-important "Thus saith the Lord".

In spite of this strong conviction, there were times when Jim was tempted to wonder if there was any use in expecting to see those principles actually at work. He wrote in his journal:

I have had such conflict of mind lately with unsettlement because of sin, and discouragement in this situation that the very idea of there being "pattern principles" upon which to build for God seemed absurd. Who cares these days if things are done according to Pauline method? Get on with the gospel; we haven't time to bicker over how the work is to be established. It seems I hear this on all hands.

First came the encouragement of 1 Chronicles 28:9, "My son, know thou the God of thy father, and serve him with a perfect heart and with a willing mind; for Jehovah searcheth all hearts and understandeth all the imaginations of the thoughts. If thou seek Him He will be found of thee; but if thou forsake Him He will cast thee off forever. Take heed now; for the Lord hath chosen thee to build a house for the sanctuary; be strong and do it."[8]

Merciful God, but speak this to *me*, actually; make this apply with all its power, promise of good and warning of evil.

God never built anything among men without first delivering to them a pattern; e.g., Moses, Noah, David, Paul.

Jim's next experiment in following the Pattern was to be in Chester, a small town in southern Illinois. Ed came down from Milwaukee and they arrived on December 13. Jim's journal entry that night was:

Feel that God is surely leading Ed and me there. Asking for (1) the establishment of an assembly, (2) radio, medical, and educational experience. Absurd to ask now for these things, as far as any outward possibility is concerned, but I think God is to be glorified in our asking the impossible of Him.

December 16. Back at work in the post office in Huntington. Slow going with souls here, but there are encouraging signs. Men unsound in doctrine complicate the issues. Ah, for a place where Scriptures have not been twisted! Lord, send me to Ecuador!

The decision to go to Chester, like every other decision, was tested almost immediately; this time by invitations to return to Portland to help in the Bible studies and evangelistic work there. He replied:

I firmly believe that God wants me to pioneer in Chester. I still maintain that there is too much collectivism of spiritual truth in Portland. There are sufficient numbers of believers to turn the whole city to God if they would once turn to Christ and confess their shameful neglect of His work. It is now time for a demonstration of God's power—and that is expensive in terms of sacrificial living, travailing prayer, and renouncing of private enjoyments. . . .

Pray for openings for us in Chester—in the gospel, in work, and ministry to "churched" believers. We do not want to build on another's foundation so are praying that souls will be saved there through our witness and that we can do a genuine New Testament work in seeing them drawn together.

As for 'renouncing private enjoyments' Jim practised his exhortation when Christmas time came and with it wistful hints from the family that a visit from him would be much appreciated, after his seven months' absence.

> Surely it would have been nice to be home, and I know it gives you joy to have me there; still, we must steel ourselves to sacrifice *joyfully*, exulting in the knowledge of the proven will of God, that sweet food the Lord Jesus tasted in speaking with the Samaritan. "It is my meat to do the will of Him that sent me."[9] Let us not say in our hearts that this is a heartless attitude; it may be realistic, and therefore harsh on our feelings, but it is always the *very best thing* that can possibly be, the doing of the will of God. There is no need to apologise for one's action, nor defend it if he is sure of God's will. And this is my confidence, that the Lord wanted me here for now.

Notes

1. 1 Corinthians 3:10,11, JBP.
2. Exodus 13:21, RSV.
3. Psalm 139:16, ASV.
4. Psalm 121:8, para.
5. Mark 6:7.
6. Acts 24:14.
7. 1 Corinthians 3:15.
8. ASV.
9. John 4:34, para.

— 15 —

Hemmed in to Nothing

I will say unto God my rock, 'Why hast Thou forgotten me?'... As with a sword in my bones, mine enemies reproach me: while they say daily unto me, 'Where is thy God?'[1]

JIM RESUMED HIS JOURNAL notes on January 6, 1951;

Chester, Illinois: Ed McCully and I returned here on Thursday, and were prospered on our way by the Sovereign; protected, provided for, and encouraged. We are seeking His face now with the prayer of Psalm 90:16,17, "Let Thy work appear unto Thy servants...establish the work of our hands." We want first of all to see His approach to this area, discover His method, and then see it established in our hands. Sense a high privilege as a Truth-bearer here, and want much grace to present the Word in power.

January 9. Last night Ed and I went to St Louis with Powley for a profitable visit with the aged Dr Morey and the young men of the St Louis assembly. Lord, the potential for work is tremendous, work among them, Spirit of God; deliver their souls from the conventional tediums, terms, and traditions. Raise up some men of God from the group.

January 10. For youth there is special wretchedness; for then the powers within conflict most bluntly with the powers without. Restraint is most galling, release most desired. To compensate for these, youth has special powers. "I have written unto you, young men, because ye are strong, and the word of God abideth in you; and ye have overcome the Wicked One."[2] Unusual strength is a premium for youth; acuteness and retentive powers are more real in youth; victory sweetest in youth. Lord, let me live to the hilt, exerting all its force, loosing all its fire. In Solomonic wisdom, I would *rejoice* in youth, yet *remember* my Creator.

January 15. There is that restlessness, that itching, urging discontent in me this morning. The milk of the Word curdles before me or seems to sour within. Hatefulness and rebellion against all restraint is not far from the surface; and it is good that I am not alone here. "Lead me not into temptation, but deliver me from evil."

January 16. Feel that I must write something tonight in praise of the God of delights. The day passed slowly with little affairs; two conferences for Hytool sales, contract signing for a radio programme, some poor script-writing, all with a sense of waiting on God for His time, His H-Hour. All day the sun dropped hints of spring, and at dusk, returning from the shop, I exulted in the distinct wall of purple—the Ozark foothills—close-guarded by the unblinking Venus. The night spread black and blossomed brilliantly with stars. I walked out to the hill just now. It is exalting, delicious. To stand embraced by the shadows of a friendly tree with the wind tugging at your coat-tails and the heavens hailing your heart—to gaze and glory and to give oneself again to God, what more could a man ask? Oh, the fullness, pleasure, sheer excitement of knowing God on earth. I care not if I ever raise my voice again for Him, if only I may love Him, please Him. Mayhap in mercy He shall give me a host of children that I may lead through the vast star fields, to explore His delicacies, whose finger-ends set them to burning. But if not, if only I may see Him, touch His garments, and smile into my Lover's eyes—ah, then, not stars, nor children shall matter—only Himself.

On January 17 Jim wrote to his parents:

Dearest Mom and Dad and all. Good to hear from you again and know that the grace of God abounds still among my dearest ones on earth. It is sweet, unspeakably sweet, to know the Father of Mercies, and to know He never forsakes, ever fortifies those whose confidence is in Him. Ed and I have been feeling more and more recently the need of Him. Here alone the fight is not so easy as when many surround to encourage. But He has been our encouragement, and it is in the Name of the Lord that we set up our banners here.

Friday morning we begin our radio programme. We signed the contract yesterday. Ed will be taking the fifteen minutes' programme on Friday and I will be preaching on the half-hour programme Sunday afternoon, each announcing for the other. Some earnest young men from St Louis will make up a male chorus. Never have I sensed such a great responsibility to do and say the right thing for God. We have entitled the programme 'the March of Truth', taking our theme from the Battle Hymn of the Republic, "His truth is marching on". Pray daily for this, as we are children here, needing more each day to know His grace to demonstrate that promise of Jesus' own lips. "He that believeth on me, the works that I do shall he do also, and greater works than these shall he do, because I go unto my Father. And whatsoever ye shall ask in my name, that will I do, that the Father may be glorified in the Son."[3] What a promise!

From the journal:

January 18. Seems like long waiting to get the work started in Chester. No sales or income thus far, just draining resources, and those will not last more than another week. I have had hopes of laying by some money for the field, but selling is not going to be able to do that, at our present rate.[4] Desired to share in the work of financing the radio here and other evangelical efforts otherwise, but God has hemmed me in to nothing, that I may have nothing, do nothing, want nothing, save Himself. Lord, Thou seest the impossibility of my hopes, and I expect deliverance from Thee in some days.

January 29. Sunday morning we had the service at the state prison, speaking to about 350 convicts up for everything from petty larceny to wholesale murder. A real thrill to declare the Word of forgiveness from Mark 2. "Who can forgive sins but God only?" That *means* something to outcasts of society who have to face both an unforgiving conscience and a bitter hard culture.

After dinner listened to Billy Graham, then went down "under the hill" (as they say of the river-front) to a small mission where a dirty-fisted little plumber proved the godliness of Saint Paul by saying something like this: "Ah tell yuh, they was thirty-five souls saved by the apostle between his dungeon and the chopping-block. They whacked off his head with a broadaxe and it bounced three times and rolled away. But everywhere it hit there busted out three fountains of water, and they tell me they are springing up with pure water to this very day!"

We figured we had plenty of "religion" for that day, so went off to "Zarit's" for coffee and contacting the high school kids.

We're having meetings every Thursday night in a town about twenty miles away. Also have an opportunity to conduct an assembly in the high school there. We are on the bill as a "programme for moral, religious, and uplifting purposes". By God's grace, we'll preach the Resurrection.

A later letter tells of the programme.

February 23. Today Ed and I had the assembly at the Sparta High School. It was a flop and we have been brooding all day. I can't figure it out. We prayed and trusted, but the message and music seemed to have little effect on the kids. It was a real privilege and I will be sorry if we find that we muffed it by some thoughtless neglect or lack of faith or some other thing. Tonight we went over to one of the town's dowagers and got her to grant us the use of a run-down store to begin Sunday School work in. It will give us something definite to stick to. It is not up in the part of town where most people live and shop, but down along the river, in the old dock town. We are thankful for this opening. Frankly, things have been very difficult to go on with here. There has been no real interest on the part of unsaved radio-listeners, a thing we had hoped for, and our efforts to get public places were blocked in a couple of ways, and so we feel frustrated. It is an easy thing to wonder, as we have done dozens of times, just why God sent us here. Six weeks so far, and no natives converted except that salesman who was from out of town. We feel God must be testing us, for He has certainly given us no evidence, beyond His provision of our needs, of any special sort that this move was His will. But what can one do? Doubt, after praying, waiting, and weighing as well as one can and still leaning on the Spirit to move? No. We cannot doubt, but search our hearts and pray more and believe more.... It would be easy to slip into the business world and just be a good guy with a lot of religion, rather than a producing son of God in enemy territory. Time's up. Look aloft and pray for me.

On February 24 Jim made this journal entry:

Ed and I have been in Chester six weeks. There has been no real work started here, and we have only this confidence: God sent us. It is Jehovah who has said, "I will work, and who can hinder it?"[5]

To me he wrote:

There is a certain despairing loneliness snooping about these days and I can almost hear the streets and buildings bristling with the note that haunted David, "Where is thy God?"[6] I don't mean to sound dismal, but there is bleakness about a place like this where no liberating truth is being sounded out. The synagogues[7] are full, but still hollow with unreality. Oh, if earth in its brighter shades be so drear, what must its denser ones be? Thank God for that sense of looking "for a city which hath foundations",[8] which prevails when one sees the basis of these. The business world is a crude one, almost animal in certain aspects, and powerfully affecting to a new-comer, as I regard myself. The very principle of making money by selling things at a profit is distasteful at times, but it seems to be my job for now. Made a couple of sales on Wednesday amounting to nearly $700 in turnover of funds, exhilarating but empty.

We went visiting in the slums last Monday night. Not easy, but comforting to be among those "blessed poor"[9]—with Jesus in a sense we are not when among the self-sufficient. We must go again soon. It makes one scornful of vanity and not much in love with life, especially this life of banks, bills, rates, and percentages.

When Jim and Ed returned from their selling jobs at night, it was to a cramped little apartment, where they took turns cooking their dinners: steaks once a week or so, accompanied by elaborate salads. After dinner, as they cleared up the dishes, the two men would often memorise poetry together. Ed had not been aware of this world of delight until their Chester days, when he 'discovered' Shelley's Ozymandias, first of all, and then Omar Khayyám, Coleridge, Poe, and others. They even copied poems and stuck them up on the wall with adhesive tape, to aid in memorisation.

Their mood was not always serious. One day as they stood waiting for a bus in Chester, Ed went into a nearby store, leaving Jim standing beside a little old lady on the street corner. Presently Ed barged out of the store, coat collar clutched up over his chin, hat pulled down over his eyes. He shoved up to Jim, snarled out of the side of his mouth, 'Meet ya tonight at the Blue Parrot at nine,' and vanished around the corner. The lady, darting a terrified glance at the criminal beside her, edged away.

The incident was only one of many which Ed and Jim staged, without rehearsal or discussion of any kind beforehand. They worked together; they were a true team.

The journal continues:

March 5. Started River Rat Sunday School yesterday. Seventeen out. Encouraged. I am learning the vanity of words. If God does not speak through me, as it is plain He does not through most preachers today, I had better leave off trying to preach. Have been praying the prayer of Psalm 51:15, "O Lord open Thou my lips", and trusting that promise made first to Jeremiah, "Behold I will make my words in thy mouth fire, and this people wood." [10] Mere declaration, no matter how eloquent or impelling, will never kindle the fire God's Word, spoken by God's man, will kindle. Lord, give me Thy Word for this people.

March 22. Felt assured again that the Lord is sending me to Ecuador, having no more place in the States since so many possess so much truth here. Checked on a passport again last week.

The following is from a letter to his parents, dated March 31:

Easter found all the folks of Chester out to church. We had a record crowd at "Club 66" as well, totalling 43 "river rats". They are utterly devoid of any knowledge of God and I suppose that work among them is the nearest thing I've ever done to moving into a pagan culture with the gospel. They had yesterday off from school, so we took two loads into the "Thunderbird" [11] and carted them off to the big ball park for a game. They insisted we repeat the process today, so we're stiff from throwing and running two days in succession. We'll see how effective our methods are tomorrow morning at 10 o'clock. We are praying that God will enter this gang and give us some lives for the glory of the Lord Jesus. They don't bother much about making moral distinctions, though we've noticed a decrease in swearing since we've been playing with them.

Sales dribble in, and I don't work too hard at it. Peole have read that note about our evangelistic efforts in *Letters* magazine, and are sending funds liberally. This we are not too happy about. In the first place we didn't volunteer the information to the magazine and didn't look for publicity. Then too we feel that the work is so very small and we so ineffective in it, that it does not deserve much financial support.

These months of working with Ed led Jim to hope that he was the answer to prayer for a single partner with whom to begin jungle work in Ecuador. This hope, too, was frustrated, as he wrote on April 28 to his parents:

> Ed's diamond arrived this morning. By the time you get this he
> will be officially engaged, for Marilou is coming on Monday for
> a week's visit. I cannot condition myself to think of marriage
> now, in spite of all the bells and rings, not to mention the
> abundance of marriageable women on the horizon. Things are
> too unsettled with me, and I do not feel it fair, either to the girl
> or to the work of the Lord, to tie myself up now with all that the
> relationship involves. I admit, it is not easy to see the wedding
> bells break up the old gang, and sit by immobile, but, though a
> wife would be lawful (even desirable at times) for me, it is not
> now expedient.
>
> We are in the middle of our two rallies in the Chester High
> gymnasium. We had about eighty out last night, not a third of
> what it should have been in view of the heavy advertising we've
> been doing. However, we feel that we are delivering our souls of
> the blood of the community. They know we are here, and that
> we are having meetings regarding the reality of the Lord Jesus.
> If they do not want to hear, then their blood is on their own
> heads.

Jim's preaching in meetings of this kind was usually
simple, very direct, and serious. He was offended by men
who began their sermons with a joke. As he gained in
experience, he learned to eliminate a great deal of shouting
which had characterised his earlier efforts. When he used
notes, they were written on small slips of paper which fitted
inside the pages of his Bible. He stood behind or beside the
pulpit, body thrust forward, his gaze 'reaching out' to his
audience. Whatever he said was linked closely with the actual
words of Scripture, which he read or quoted from memory
throughout the talk. He did not make a practice of asking
members of the congregation to make any overt response to
the message, feeling that if the Holy Spirit was at work in the
mind and heart of the listener during the meeting, He would
continue that work later.

On April 16 Jim wrote to me:

Your last letter was, like Paul's to the Corinthians, at once rebuking and comforting, and I am grateful for it. The *trial* of faith, a court-room drama constantly in session for believers, is more precious than gold, Peter says. It has been that here. Faith has been under fire, and I think because its Source is Christ, it has been strengthened and proved precious. Now problems have arisen and combined with some unsettled old ones sufficiently to dishearten me, but God is faithful and the prayers of His Son effectual when He prays that my faith fail not.

During their last month of working together in Chester, Jim and Ed held meetings in a tent in town. Crowds were small, but there were several who indicated a desire to follow Christ.

Jim wrote:

Why, oh why, are the forces of God so few and feeble while the Enemy counts multitudes on his side? Lord, how long will you hide yourself, concealing your power and letting men think low thoughts of you? Begin to move, Lord, for the sake of the *Name*! Move me, as well, and let me know the fullness of the Spirit.

June 14. Finished tent meetings in Chester, preaching from Acts 1:11, "This Jesus shall so come." [12] Impossible to register the good God has done in Chester. I can see several reasons for coming now that I did not see in January. Surely the Lord has led. Still nothing "big" or extraordinary in the work of the gospel, and this I judge to be only because I lacked intensity and perseverance in prayer. Lift me to heights of desire, Lord, and teach me to pray.

Looking over the last two years since graduation gives me a funny sense of uselessness. The way for me has certainly not been conventional or predictable in any way. But I have sought the will of God, and in this I rest. It is no use arguing what might have been if so and so had happened. We are only asked to do what we are told—small, strange, or simple as that may be—our orders are to obey, and in this my conscience is clear. I have walked in integrity, not purposing according to the flesh, that my path should be yea, yea, and nay, nay. But having purposed in Christ to do what is pleasing to Him, I find His approval (yea) and seal (amen) in the very smallest and unlikely things. Especially is this true of these months here in Chester. Who shall doubt, or say that our labour is in vain? "Thanks be to God, who *always leads us in triumph*."

Notes

1. Psalm 42:9, 10.
2. 1 John 2:14.
3. John 14:12, 13.
4. There is a marginal note here in a different-coloured ink: 'Little did I know! Saved nearly $500 by June!'
5. Isaiah 43:13, ASV.
6. Psalm 42:3.
7. Jim's poetic use of the New Testament term, applied here to churches.
8. Hebrews 11:10.
9. Matthew 5:3, para.
10. Jeremiah 5:14.
11. Jim and Ed's pet name for their rattletrap.
12. ASV.

— 16 —

Exactly Timed for Good

*Moreover we know that to those who love God...everything that
happens fits into a pattern for good.*[1]

JIM TOOK PART in the weddings of his two friends, Ed
McCully and Bill Cathers, and then headed West once
more, arriving in Portland in July with a dollar and
twenty cents in his pocket. He set to work immediately at
odd jobs, and in August took a brief vacation with the family
at Ocean Park, Washington. I was vacationing in New
Hampshire when he wrote to me:

> The Tidmarsh family were here for ten days. Their visit served
> to fix my purpose regarding Ecuador. Things are working out,
> but slowly. My passport number is in progress for visa in
> Ecuador. The draft board has given an OK to leave the States. A
> cautious estimate for a sailing date is December 1, probably
> from Los Angeles. First, I'm coming East.
>
> Bill and I are scheduled for meetings in the New York-New
> Jersey area from September 21 to October 12!—some ministry,
> some missionary, but mostly to get acquainted with the
> believers. I have a few days open in a rugged schedule and would
> certainly like to see you if the Lord would have it. Will you be at
> Birdsong [my family home in Moorestown, New Jersey]?
>
> Ed and Marilou will be in the medical school of the Bible

Institute of Los Angeles this year, and we pray will follow us to Ecuador next year. Pray, will you, that God will strengthen Ed's conviction? I am asking still for a single fellow to accompany me to the school in Shandia, and a young brother from Seattle seems interested. You may remember Pete Fleming, the rather intellectual young blade from the University of Washington. We have had some keen times lately and he is definitely waiting the Lord's command.

On the same day Jim wrote to Pete:

Dear brother Pete: Thanks for your letter of last Thursday. Glad you enjoyed Tidmarsh. We missed you on Mt Adams—sorry I didn't get word to you about it sooner. It was a much more rugged climb than Hood. Choppier snow face, steeper, two miles longer, but some warmer, and done on a much clearer day. There is a false summit which we nicknamed "Frustration Point". You think the hike is all over at 7.00 am and then you round this ridge and see the real summit 1,500 feet above you and a mile beyond. However, it was great; indeed, the life we were made for—though we were all sick until we had a snooze on top.

Our family decided to take this week off, so we are at the beach just now. Won't be home until late Saturday, so I cannot make Seattle this week-end. Besides, I was drafted for two meetings and a special dinner date this Sunday. I intend to be at the Conference Labour Day week-end, and am in hopes the Lord will make your way clear to come. We have much still to discuss—which does not come easily or well out of a typewriter or the barrel of a pen.

I have no word for you *re*: Ecuador. I would certainly be glad if God persuaded you to go with me. But *He* must persuade you. How shall they preach except they be *sent*? If the Harvest-Chief does not move you, I hope you remain at home. There are too many walls to leap over not to be fully persuaded of God's will. All I can do is pray for a cleared path for you. The command is plain: you go into the whole world and announce the good news. It cannot be dispensationalised, typicalised, rationalised. It stands a clear command, possible of realisation because of the Commander's following promise. To me, Ecuador is simply an avenue of obedience to the simple word of Christ. There is room for me there, and I am free to go. This of course is true of a great many other places, but having said there is a need, and sensed my freedom, through several years of waiting in prayer for leading on this very point of "where?", I now feel peace in saying, "I go, sir, by grace."[2] My experience is by no means restrictive to your persuasion. You may require more or less of subjective evidence to find certainty. I have not the foggiest idea how or where God will lead you. Of this I am sure. He will lead you and not let you miss your signs. Rest in this—it is His business to lead, command, impel, send, call, or whatever you want to call it. It is your business to obey, follow, move, respond, or what have you. This will sound meaningless to you, unconvincing and "old stuff", and that is what it should sound, for it is only a man's counsel. The sound of "gentle stillness" after all the thunder and wind have passed will be the ultimate Word from God. Tarry long for it.

We are leaving for the East September 7, if the Lord directs as we now plan. Will be returning late in October, hoping for passage in late November from Los Angeles.

Seems craziness to speak of leaving alone that soon...and it must be either craziness or faith. But, remember the words of Amy Carmichael? "The vows of God are on me. I may not stay to play with shadows or pluck earthly flowers, till I my work have done and rendered up account."—Looking forward to Labour Day weekend, Jim.

En route to the east coast Jim wrote me a note from Chicago:

I am grateful to the Lord Jesus for allowing another meeting with you. There is much to speak of. Dave mentioned the South Pacific possibility, and I am praying.—Gladly, Jim.

At my home on September 20 he wrote in his journal:

Arrived at Birdsong. Nearer to her now than ever, yet more confident that God is leading me away from her, to Ecuador with Pete, and she to the South Seas! This is a strange pattern.

Between the date of this entry and Jim's next visit to Birdsong several events indicated that the door to the South Seas was closed to me. Had our experience of God's leading throughout the course of our relationship been other than what it had been, it would have appeared simple: become engaged, and go to Ecuador together. For a long time there had been no question in either of our minds as to whom we should marry should marriage be the will of God. Had He indicated that this was His will? For each of us, the answer was still No. Jim felt, however, that this was no reason to dismiss from our minds the possibility of God's leading me to South America. He asked me to consider this seriously before the Lord, fully realising that such a course would lead to criticism and misunderstanding. We knew our Guide, and had experienced His clear direction at every point thus far. We knew, too, that He leads 'in a way that they know not'.[3] Indeed, what need had we for a guide, were the path a familiar one?

So we set ourselves to pray, well knowing the difficulty of discerning God's will where our own wishes were so strong. Often the prayer written by Amy Carmichael of India was ours:

> *"And shall I pray Thee change Thy will, my Father,*
> *Until it be according unto mine?*
> *But no, Lord, no; that never shall be, rather*
> *I pray Thee, blend my human will with Thine.*
>
> *I pray Thee hush the hurrying, eager longing,*
> *I pray Thee, soothe the pangs of keen desire,*
> *See in my quiet places wishes thronging—*
> *Forbid them, Lord, purge, though it be with fire.*

And work in me to will and do Thy pleasure,
Let all within me, peaceful, reconciled,
Tarry content my Wellbeloved's leisure
At last, at last, even as a weanéd child."

Jim went back to New York City for more meetings, and a few days later wrote me this letter:

The will of God is sweet tonight, altogether "good and acceptable and perfect".[4] The considerate love of the Lord Jesus for us seems such a kind thing now. I know it has always been so, but somehow I didn't see how *wise* it was when it didn't seem kind. "With mercy and with judgment my web of time He wove, and aye, the dews of sorrow were lustred with His love...."[5] You know the rest. Remind me of this when I cannot regard His love as considerate some time.

Stayed overnight with a brother in Queens who raises chrysanthemums. He was telling me that they don't bloom until every other flower is gone or going with the frost. I suspected that the frost might be what brought them to bloom, but he said, "No, it's the longer nights". I really had never realised the point of Rutherford's

"But flow'rs need night's cool darkness,
The moonlight and the dew...."[6]

not just for rest, but for blossoming. Need I allegorise?
... Waiting on Him for whom it is no vain thing to wait,
Jim.

The answer given during the next four weeks of prayer, "cool darkness," and waiting, was that I should go to Ecuador. This decision led Jim to hope that God meant marriage for us eventually, but, believing that he should ask for no commitments whatsoever until he had lived in the jungle and evaluated first-hand the requirements of that life, he steadfastly kept his course, telling me nothing of his hope. His commitment was to God alone, for he believed, with Paul, that 'He is able to keep that which I have committed unto Him'.[7] No attempt was made to explain our position to others. To us, the reason was eminently adequate—this was God's way.

Driving West with Pete Fleming, who had flown to New York to share Jim's meetings, Jim wrote to me:

> If I went to the mission field singly of my own will, I should certainly halt. But God has directed, Betty. He knows I would rather go with you, were not His mandate the better good.

And, like everything else in his life, Jim accepted this gladly.

> I thank my God. Life has been made so rich, so full for me. Sea-like, but having no ebb. Nature, Body, Soul, Friendship, Family—all full for me, and then, what many have not—the *capacity to enjoy*. "And He said, 'Lacked ye anything?' And they said, 'Nothing.'"[8]

The past is gone, and I am glad, both for its going and for the way it went. God has led in, through, and out, by the best route possible, we may believe. I am particularly conscious of the Christian's right to expect events to be *exactly timed for good*. "As for God, His way is perfect."[9]

Notes

1. Romans 8:28, JBP.
2. Matthew 21:30, para.
3. Isaiah 42:16, RSV.
4. Romans 12:2.
5. From 'Rutherford's Hymn'.
6. From 'Rutherford's Hymn'.
7. 2 Timothy 1:12.
8. Luke 22:35.
9. Psalm 18:30.

— 17 —

The Hand Is on the Plough

*Anyone who puts his hand to the plough and then looks behind him is
useless for the Kingdom of God.*[1]

AFTER ARRIVING in Portland, Jim was busy buying
supplies for Ecuador, speaking in the north-western
area, and packing. But he kept up his private times
of prayer and study, recording in the journal things he felt no
liberty to speak of to others. On November 23 he wrote:

Just read again the story of Abraham. Convenient food just
now—with this pressing sense of need, the want of warmth and
woman, tenderness, relief, and children. The God who "prepared
laughter"[2] for Sarah in her old age, whose promises made
Abraham himself fall to the ground and laugh because they
seemed so goodly and impossible—fitting thoughts for my
present attitude because I feel now as though it may mean five
years of single life, these next five resilient years, years when I
will most want her, most need her, and best be able to satisfy
her. These years, I see in the plan now, must be spent alone.
Then, maybe after I'm thirty, getting paunchy, wrinkling and
balding even—then the marriage bed! Mother said the other
day "Who wants to wait until they're thirty to start raising a
family?" Certainly not I. All I knew to say was, "You raise a
family when God wants you to." And I believe. I feel sure that
God is doing the best for us, and that in the face of what seems

194

most unlikey. Perhaps I'm wrong in thinking I have years to wait—but a man can't feel "lustihood of his young powers"[3] swell and surge inside him and not be affected by restraining them. It may be that He hasn't planned to make us wait years, but it certainly looks like it from here. Of course I hope I'm wrong. But if I'm not, then El Shaddai, the God who saw and heard Hagar, considered Sarah's laugh, and disregarded Abraham's 100th year—this God is the One I believe to be guiding and governing me in these affairs. And in this, in prospect, I with Abraham can laugh.

November 28. The dozens of little arguments that flood me when I think of waiting to take Betty amount to considerable force if I let them work on me. But my refuge is not in answering them one by one and arguing them down—my refuge is in Jehovah, Whom I have asked to preserve me. For now, and always, "Jehovah is the portion of my inheritance and my cup; Thou maintainest my lot"[4] (Comforting in the extreme, that word "maintainest"—stronger than the prayer word "preserve".

Relegating all problems directly to the Lord, trusting implicitly in His guidance for past and future experience produces the remark: "I will bless Jehovah, who hath given me counsel."[5] My going to Ecuador is God's counsel, as is my leaving Betty, and my refusal to be counselled by all who insist I should stay and stir up the believers in the US. And how do I know it is His counsel? "Yea, my heart instructeth me in the night seasons."[6] Oh, how good—for I have know that "my heart" is instructing me for God. "My heart said *for Thee*, 'Seek ye my face.'"[7] No visions or voices, but the counsel of a heart which desires God.

And so I sense that I may share the Christ's words, "I have set Jehovah always before me; becuase he is at my right hand, I shall not be moved."[8] Not moved? With all the awful pressure of inward desire to move me to lust? Not moved. With all demonic hatred to move me to fear and doubt? Not moved. Wherefore? He is before me and at my right hand. THEREFORE MY HEART IS GLAD!

November 29. I am reading *The Return of the Native*. Poor Hardy. If only he could have once seen the hand of God. The

s of Egdon Heath form patterns which resist any idea
rking of the Will. If he could once have experienced a
ed incident that wrought the greatest possible good,
he would not have written as he did. Each event is so
meshed with unreasoning ill, and the reader gets to expect the
blackest. Really he does in the negative what poor novelists do
in the positive—accentuates improbabilities—only he does it
to the detriment of his heroes; they, to the betterment of theirs.
Neither is true to life. Granted, fate and tragedy, aimlessness
and just-missing-by-a-hair are part of human experience, but
they are not all, and I'm not sure that they are even a major part,
even in the lives of men who know no Designer or design. For
me, I have seen a keener force yet, the force of Ultimate Good
working through apparent ill. Not that there is rosiness ever;
there is genuine ill, struggle, dark-handed, unreasoning fate,
mistakes, if-onlys, and all the Hardyisms you can muster. But
in them I am beginning to discover a Plan greater than any
could imagine. Witness three years of relationship with Betty!

December 1. In reading the Scriptures I find a great moral
power. Therein I am made aware of two great forces for good in
human experience: the *fear* of God and the *grace* of God. Without
the fear of God I would not stop at doing evil; the fear of God
restrains. Without the grace of God I would have no desire to
approach positive goodness. The one is a deterrent from evil; the
other is an encouragement to good. "Wherewithal shall a young
man cleanse his way?"—not so much make up for what is past,
but perfect what is future—"by taking heed thereto (from now
on) according to Thy word."[9] "These things I am writing to you
that you may not sin."[10] The Scriptures were written to this
very intent: to be a means of grace in struggling against sin.
Would that Christians read their Scriptures. We should have a
holier band for it.

December 5. Terribly depressed after preaching tonight. Felt
as though I had no preparation, no liberty, no power. Once I felt
compelled to stop during the sermon and tell the people I didn't
have a message from God, but then thought better of it, or
rather thrust it from thought altogether. I never want to preach
that way again. Lord God Almighty, let me speak Thy word as

going forth out of Thy mouth. How sadly and how slowly I am learning that loud preaching and long preaching are not substitutes for inspired preaching. Oh, it's awful. To see a room full of people, waiting to hear a word from God, and to have no word. And then to try to make up for it by jumbling unripe, untested ideas with old, dry words, and to know that your heart isn't in it. El Shaddai! Deliver! Worst of all, the people can't even seem to tell the difference when I feel the Spirit and when I can't. Either I'm a frightful bluff, or the people are utterly undiscerning . . . maybe all of both.

December 6. Passion, bordering on frenzy, grips me at times; — not always, thank Heaven, but often enough to make my denial of her for the work's sake a very real, poignant thing. In this, just now, I feel more than ever the Lord Jesus' requirement, "Except a man forsake. . . ." [11] Well, thank God for the privilege of giving up ought for His sake.

December 24. Just finished *For Whom the Bell Tolls*. A most intriguing work which raises some problems for a Christian. Realistic, psychologically penetrating, compactly detailed, it represents a literary landmark for me for its style alone. Would that I could be as aroused about experiencing *God* in life as these modern writer are aroused at just experiencing life. They make no comment, draw no conclusions, point no moral; simply state things as they are. Perhaps it is for this very lucidity that they hold such grip on me. Must we always comment on life? Can it not simply be lived in the reality of Christ's terms of contact with the Father, with joy and peace, fear and love full to the fingertips in their turn, without incessant drawing of lessons and making of rules? I do not know. Only I know that my own life is full. It is time to die, for I have had all that a young man can have, at least all this young man can have. If there were no further issue from my training, it would be well. The training has been good, and to the glory of God. I am ready to meet Jesus. Failure means nothing now, only that it taught me life. Success is meaningless, only that it gave me further experience in using the great gift of God, *Life*. And Life, I love thee. Not because thou art long. or because thou hast done great things for me, but simply because I have thee from God.

A letter to me, of December 28:

I'm glad your last letter was a long one. It was mailed the fourteenth, and was good to have something more to think on while waiting your next. I've been expecting one every day this week, but know you must have had a busy holiday. I couldn't go to sleep last night for some reason so I took to piecing together our meetings and conversation in order for September and October. I am thankful, deeply thankful for such happy memories. Well may we bless God for them, Betty. He was kind, *very* kind!

Monday. Perhaps your letter will come today. I woke this morning with my left eye badly swollen and sore. Certainly gives me a curious squint with one eye closed. You'd have trouble loving me if you went by looks today. I'm certainly glad that we have not based our relationship on good looks. "Favour is deceitful and beauty is vain."[12] Oh, Betty, we owe praise to God for teaching us the worth of inner adornment. There are so many painted and well-dressed butterflies around here. They distract the eye but do not touch the spirit, and it is good to know the God who looks within to the "hidden man of the heart" and to enjoy that part of a person with Him. True, there are some here with this meek and quiet spirit, but I have found in none of them the response and stimulation which I find in you—the understanding you have of me and the spoken witness of it. Others listen and assent; you seem to *hear*, "savvy", and contribute some return. It is as you said, "The marriage of true minds". You said that was from Shakespeare, I think.

January 1, 1952. This has been a good day, full of visiting and chatting, resting and remembering. No small sign was given me confirming my going to Ecuador via the *Santa Juana*. I have been asking God to seal my leaving, not knowing what to expect. Yesterday several cheques came in the mail, and I intended to cash them and send a cheque to Kelly, the travel agent, for my passage. But the bank was closed when I finally found a parking place and finished other pressing things yesterday afternoon. Today when I picked up some purchases from Tommy Dryden he gave me a cheque for fifty dollars. I made no special note of it until I got home and put it with the cheques I got in yesterday's mail. Then I discovered that they totalled $315, my exact fare to Guayaquil! All in twenty-four hours, from five separate sources. This is the first of these miracles I am encouraged to expect. Hallelujah! Praise to the King of Heavenly coffers. Cheques confirmed my leading to Milwaukee last fall, to Sparta this spring, home this summer, and home now, since all came from individuals whose contacts depended upon my being in those places. Wise God, my God. This is to encourage me for 1952.

Letters written during Jim's last two weeks in Portland were filled with the details of packing, farewell meetings, and other things. The following are samples:

Equipment is piling up all over my room, and I hope to get to packing today. Correspondence is stacked up here on my desk and invitations to speak piling up....

I'm in the midst of a series of injections. Typhus reacted strangely this week, centring in my eyes and making them itch and colour red. More shots Monday....

Spent some of the week organising about 1,500 slides given me by a brother here. Besides Bible-story pictures, there are also nature pictures, through butterflies and giraffes to snowflakes. A godsend for the Indians.

Mail came in the middle of my packing books. Tomorrow, that barrel. It's been staring me in the face for two weeks and I haven't had the heart to begin filling it. Now it's a must. The *Santa Juana* will be in Portland on the 18th, and we must have it on the docks when we leave here the 10th. Pete is putting his stuff aboard in Seattle and Mom and Dad will drive us south.

January 10. Last day in Portland. The past week has been very busy, full of visits and interruptions while packing. But God has been good and exceeding loving-kind toward me. The saints have given unhesitatingly at every turn and every need has been met, even beyond the need. It is as in the wilderness, "for the stuff they had was sufficient for all the work to make it, and too much."[13] Peter will arrive today and we will drive to Williams tomorrow. That will be the first step away. It is hard to say goodbye, but, as Pete wrote yesterday, "the hand is on the plough".[14] I have had difficulty keeping spiritual pace these last days, rushing through prayer and scanning the Word only. This is no way to have confidence in the soul. Still, God is gracious.

> "We change, He changes not;
> Our Christ can never die.
> His love, not ours, the resting place,
> His truth, not mine, the tie."[15]

January 15: Oakland, California. Your letter came a week ago today and I opened it with the end of the paint brush with which I was lettering my name and destination on my packing barrels. Later that evening, after a meeting and supper at Herb Butt's, I had a chance to read it over. Wednesday, more packing. Thursday, all the stuff had to be taken to the dock and billed for lading. I ended up with two steel barrels (the best way to pack anything), two foot lockers, two wooden crates, and a wardrobe trunk—seven pieces, 1,400 pounds. Pete had only 900 pounds, but I had most of the heavy stuff: slides, recorder, tubs, guns, pots, kettles, and dishes.

We're in the middle of visits and engagements again in Oakland, and I find no time at all for closet prayer. We haven't a room of our own and I miss the sense of "bowing my knees"[16] as Paul says. Privacy before the God who sees in secret is an integral part of true prayer, and one hates to be obvious in asking for privacy. God knows and hears, however. What will Shandia be with the curious eyes of Quichua boys!

January 25: Sunland, California. The tumult of these last days is ruinous to correspondence with you, but things are settled sufficiently today to write. We have our passports visaed, all but one crate on the docks, and are waiting for our tickets from Grace Lines.

Leaving the States is not too exciting yet. I feel very little emotion, and will probably undergo the whole gamut of good-byes without a tremor. Not that I don't feel sorry to leave the folks, but only that this part of the will of God is of little more significance than any given part of it up until now....As for you, it may be that it will be worse when I am gone, but I can think of nothing to help. Only to say that the will of God is "good, acceptable, and perfect".[17] May it be for you acceptable.

January 26; Tujunga, California. Must write some acknowledgements and finish packing a box this morning. The afternoon we spend with Ed and Marilou. Tonight a big rally and they're expecting me to do something great in sermonising. "Let not them that trust in Thee be ashamed because of me."[18]

January 28, Monday. Perhaps you've noticed that our ideas merged about this matter of Ecuador only being one of many steps of obedience to the Will, and leaving the dock only one more, hardly any more thrilling than the initial realising, months ago, that the Will would have it so.

The *Juana* isn't in yet, and I doubt if we sail before Thursday.

January 30. What is one supposed to do with three extra days? Spent the morning reading family mail, getting in a little reading from Leviticus, writing a couple of business letters. When I came here last fall I brought a twisted little tree from the Grand Canyon, and today I got a chance to mount it so it will be usable for a centre-piece. Something like a ming tree, but without the rounded limbs and heavy leaves. There is a small, moss-like leaf on parts of it, dried green now, but which used to smell strongly of sage. The trees at the Canyon are fascinating in their ruggedness and this one seemed to be a perfect miniature of many I saw there. Aunt Mabel likes this kind of stuff.

When I expressed to him something of the sense of loss which I felt at missing out on these important events, Jim wrote:

Your "sense of loss" at our not being able to share things these past few months is not new to me. I *know* it, and often tell Him about it. And such thoughts as

"*If Thy dear home be fuller, Lord....*"

are a consolation. And then the realistic facing of non-accomplishment comes to me and crushes to silence all telling. For if, really, we have denied ourselves to and from each other for His sake, then should we not expect to see about us the profit of such denial? And this I look vainly for. It comes to this: I am a single man for the Kingdom's sake, its more rapid advance, its more potent realisation in my own life. But where is that advance and that realisation? I am willing that "my own life. But where is that advance and that realization? I am willing that "my house on earth be emptier", but not unless "His house be fuller". And I think it right that we hold God to His own bargain. I err, of course, in making the *visible* results of our separation the final test, and, I trust, rejoice in seeing beyond results which are obvious. But I reason thus that I should be more importunate in prayer, more "dogged" in devotion, and should not get, as you say, to a "weary acceptance of things as they are...."

Besides this there is the somewhat philosophical realisation that actually, I have *lost* nothing. We may imagine what it would be like to share a given event and feel *loss* at having to experience it alone. But let us not forget— that loss is *imagined*, not real. I imagine peaks—enjoyment when I think of doing things together, but let not the hoping for it dull the doing of it alone. What is, is actual—what might be *simply is not*, and I must not therefore query God as though He robbed me—of things that are not. Further, the things that *are* belong to us, and they are good, God-given, and enriched. Let not our longing slay the appetite of our living!

Notes

1. Luke 9:62, JBP.
2. Genesis 21:6, ASV margin.
3. From 'The Hound of Heaven' by Francis Thompson.
4. Psalm 16:5, ASV.
5. Psalm 16:7, ASV.
6. Psalm 16:7, ASV.
7. Psalm 27:8, JND.
8. Psalm 16:8, ASV.

9. Psalm 119:9.
10. 1 John 2:1, para.
11. Luke 14:33, para.
12. Proverbs 31:30.
13. Exodus 36:7, ASV.
14. Luke 9:62, para.
15. From a hymn by H. Bonar.
16. Ephesians 3:14, para.
17. Romans 12:2.
18. Psalm 69:6, para.

PART FOUR

Ecuador

1952—1956

– 18 –

Under Way

'I promise you,' returned Jesus, 'nobody leaves home or brothers or sisters or mother or father or children or property for My sake or the Gospel's without getting back a hundred times over, now in this present life, homes and brothers and sisters, mothers and children and land—though not without persecution—and in the next world eternal life.' [1]

WHITE STARS BREAKING through a high mist. Half moon. The deep burn of phosphorus running in the wake. Long, easy rolling and the push of steady wind. The *Santa Juana* is under way.

Thus began Jim's journal for February 4, 1952.

We've just come from a walk on the upper deck after a meal served in the officers' dining-room. Black cod, mashed potatoes au gratin, fresh vegetable salad, good black coffee. The stateroom is quiet now as Pete begins a little typing. All the thrill of boyhood dreams came on me just now, outside watching the sky die in the sea on every side. I wanted to sail when I was in grammar school, and well remember memorising the names of the sails from Merriam-Webster's ponderous dictionary in the library. Now I am actually at sea—as a passenger, of course, but at sea nevertheless—and bound for Ecuador. Strange—or is it?—that childish hopes should be answered in the will of

206

God for this *now*.

We left our moorings at the Outer Harbour Dock, San Pedro, California, at 2.06 pm today. Mom and Dad stood together watching at the pier side. As we slipped away Psalm 60:12 came to mind, and I called back, "Through our God we shall do valiantly." They wept some. I do not understand how God has made me. I didn't even feel like weeping, and don't, even now. Joy, sheer joy, and thanksgiving fill and encompass me.

In his first letter to his parents written en route, Jim said:

I surely praised God for the valiant way you both took my going. It is true that I know very little about how you feel at seeing me leave. All I understand is that it must be very keen, deep, and closely linked with all that this life involves for you. I pray for you whenever you come to mind, asking the "help that is from God" [2] for you both. You are as well a constant source of praise for all that you have given of yourselves for my sake. The will of God is always a bigger thing than we bargain for, but we must believe that whatever it involves, it is good, acceptable, and perfect.

Weep not for me. We abound in everything here. This tramp steamer is the best set-up I've ever been in. We eat like horses—egg plant, zucchini, potatoes au gratin, fresh buttermilk, fresh-baked rye bread are some of the staples. For meats we have had ox heart, lamb curry, beef roast, stewed tripe, and, tonight, sirloin steak. It would be all right if I could ever get enough exercise to get hungry. We have complete liberty over the whole ship, and believe me, we take it. Poop to prow, that's us. Our fellow-passengers number seven: two married couples who sit all day and read novels and soak up sunshine, and three women. Of these latter, two are middle-aged married women who wear jeans and short suits, and the third is a semi-peroxided case who is always wishing we'd get shipwrecked. I'd judge she's about 37, but tries desperately not to let that be known. In all, what I would term a "hot sketch".

The crew is much better company, many of them being young men our age. We have met and spoken with several.

Everybody knows we are missionaries, and it makes it easy to talk of the things of God, though we haven't been satisfied with our contacts yet.

The sheer joy of being in the will of God and the knowledge of His direction heretofore is my general experience now. God has been in our going to now, and if life were to end at this point, I feel I could say with Simeon, "Now let Thy servant depart in peace."[3] Not that I feel in any way that my work has been done, but only that I am satisfied that God has been confirming His word to me. The evidence is before me of the veracity of the Lord, and with Jacob I can say, "It is enough."[4]

The clear weather and oncoming humidity tell us we are approaching the tropics. Further evidence is the wildlife that surrounds us out here. Today I saw a bird standing on what looked like a piece of wood, but after the man on the bridge pointed it out and gave me his glasses I discovered that it was a great sea-turtle. While I was looking at that a flurry of water startled me right near the ship. It looked much like the pattern made by a star-bomb on the fourth of July, sending spurts every which way from the centre. Just a school of flying fish, I am told. Yesterday we sighted some large lance-nosed marlin leaping toward port, and a whale spuming not far off. Who said the sea was monotonous?

The journal gives further cause for thanksgiving:

Our stateroom was to have had three in it, but we bless God that He has ordered it so that we are alone. It would be a little awkward with another. "Your Father knoweth."[5] Ah, we've proved that lately! When the Chrysler was being repaired, we needed a car for running around Los Angeles, and God gave us one. He knew we needed a near-by bed the night the ship failed to leave. Helen and John provided that. He knew we needed the extra time for equipment, and the *Juana's* delay from January 20 until February 4 gave us that time. We needed, too, the breaking of bread at Glendale yesterday morning; the presence of Jesus the Lord was real. Thanks, then, to you, Good Lord. I'm glad the Lord knows the way of the righteous. He knows the way that I take.

"Oh well it is forever, Oh well for evermore,
My nest built in no forest of all this death-doomed shore.
Then let the vain world vanish, as from the ship the strand,
For Glory, Glory dwelleth in Immanuel's Land."[6]

He wrote to me on February 9:

> We are in the Gulf of Tehauntepec tonight, fairly close to shore, passing the city of Salina Cruz. The wind is wild. I've never felt such blowing. Just returned from the flying bridge where I was able to do something I've wanted to do for a long time—literally lean on the wind. One can stand effortlessly at a fair degree of slant, feeling the air misshape the face or hearing it really whistle if you hold your mouth just right. The water is alive with spray and whitecaps, leaping under a full moon in a clear sky. We are right opposite the narrowest part of Mexico. . . .
>
> This is the ideal way to travel. Accommodations are excellent and all the officers very friendly. The realism afforded by cargo freighting, the constant sight of cables, derrick booms and winches, the close contact with the crew—all make for fascinating travel. This was our sixth day out, and time has passed surprisingly fast. Most of our day is devoted to reading Spanish, and speaking it with what crew members we are able to find willing to talk to gringos.

His next letter home was written from Champerico, Guatemala, dated February 10:

> We are riding the hook here in the waters off Guatemala. There is no such thing as a harbour in this whole coast, so the loading problem takes on a little different aspect. We came to a halt opposite low-lying land, with only a steel-reinforced dock and a couple of red-faced buildings in sight. The stevedores came aboard bringing a large, tub-like barge to each side of the forward holds. They loaded into these, then took them to the dock to unload there. A slow process, but no one seems to be in the slightest hurry to speed it up. The captain and a couple of passengers are playing cards.

The journal, on the same day, adds this:

Strange that the other passengers get bored waiting around, and we hardly have enough time to get what we want done. Thank God for purpose in life. So many purposes come into existence when one works the will of God, that there is no excuse for laziness or wasted time. He is redeeming our lives, as well as our souls.

Another journal entry:

February 14. Rolling slightly in a strong breeze out of sight of land, but off Nicaragua. Tuesday afternoon we anchored off La Libertad, San Salvador, and went ashore with four other passengers. Hired a station wagon to take us all up to the capital. Eating tortillas in a restaurant we were approached by a pretty little harlot named Emilia. I will always wish I could have spoken clear Spanish. We tried to make plain our desire only to speak her language and she was willing for a while to walk and speak with us. She took us to the University Post Office, where we bought some cards. Then she became embarrassed somehow —curses on my Spanish—and bade us good-bye. My whole soul went out for her, so young, so sweet-faced, and yet so enmeshed in an evil net. How long, Lord, will the earth perpetrate its wrongs! Hurry the promise, Lord, that "the earth shall be full of the knowledge of the Lord".[7] She epitomises for me the wrong of earth and men. I could no more have slept with her than died at will. The whole idea violated all that I know and feel. But oh, I longed to speak about the Saviour of harlots, the Friend of genuine sinners. God help me in the language for just such cases as these. I am sure she thought us strange men, such as fit no pattern she has seen. But will she ever really know why we refused to have her go find her "amiga" for us?

From Buenaventura, Colombia, I received a letter from Jim:

The captain and steward invited Pete and me to go with them to net shrimp. The captain was high on martinis and went to sleep on the deck of the snub-nosed power launch, but the rest of us stayed sober enough to bring back about a hundred and fifty pounds of big, beautiful shrimp. Netting is great sport here, as you haul in about two hundred fifty pounds of everything imaginable at every lift—we found several squid, some hammerhead sharks, sharp-toothed corbina, sea cat, sting rays, big-headed blowfish, every possible shape and colour of jellyfish, besides dozens of other species no one could name. Came back slightly sun-kissed, but not before God gave real opportunity to witness to the captain (before he went under) and one of the engineers who was along. Praise God for the time. He always leads us in triumph and makes manifest the savour of His knowledge in every place.

February 24, 1952. Thursday, about 9 am, we dropped anchor off the ramshackle shore of the island of Puna. Our crew members were not allowed shore leave, by order of a bewhiskered and portly islander called "The Captain of the Port". By noon we were officially received, and Customs men all came aboard for their carton of Luckies. The islanders floated around our big hull in their little dugouts with banana stalks, beer, coconuts, and balsa-wood models of Grace Line ships like our *Juana*. By one o'clock the stevedores arrived with their bawling and bickering. Some of them brought leather goods—most of it pretty stuff of unborn calf—shoes, handbags, and what-nots. By 2.30 the beautiful little yacht *Santa Rosita* came alongside with the barges and called out for the passengers. We said our good-byes and had our stuff packed from the stateroom to the *Rosita*.

Glimpses of river life, and pleasant conversation with the Grace agent's wife and a friend of hers helped us forget the oppressive heat while we sailed the thirty miles from Puna. By six our eyes were checking the docks along the Guayaquil waterfront for a look at Tidmarsh. But no one was there to meet us. A stevedore escorted me pronto to an "evangelista" he knew of, and she recommended a German pension. I went back to the Customs dock to get Pete, and found they had passed all our hand baggage, twelve pieces, without even opening it. Praise

God. Off we went with it in a wheelbarrow to the pension.

It was a hot night and mosquitoes were treacherous. I heard the town clock every quarter of an hour from one till 3.45. I'm still scratching. Next morning we hit it off for the Grace office to ask about Tidmarsh. Learned that our baggage would not be up-river till afternoon, so walked over to the waterfront, and lo, along comes Tidmarsh. The office had not been informed of our arrival, so he had come a day late.

God gave us great deliverance at the Customs house. Our combined freight of 2,300 pounds was all passed without a cent of duty. "O Lord, Jehovah, Thou hast begun to show Thy servant Thy greatness and Thy strong hand, for what God is there in heaven or in earth than can do according to Thy works?"[8]

Notes

1. Mark 10:29,30, JBP.
2. Psalm 121:2, para.
3. Luke 2:29, para.
4. Genesis 45:28.
5. Matthew 6:8.
6. From 'Rutherford's Hymn'.
7. Isaiah 11:9.
8. Deuteronomy 3:24, ASV.

— 19 —

Dreams Are Tawdry

And God Almighty bless thee, and make thee fruitful . . . that thou mayest inherit the land wherein thou art a stranger.[1]

The first journal entry in Quito—dated February 27, 1952, began:

CAUGHT THE Panagra flight out of Guayaquil yesterday afternoon about 1.30. Clear view of the coastal plain as we came north, but began hitting clouds as we moved toward the mountains. Scudded over the mountains suddenly, catching sight of high ridges not far below. Then, as the clouds cleared again, we saw the great quilt of the plateau, beautiful and quiet with terraced hillsides and occasional buildings. Quito was in sight immediately and our DC-3 bounced down onto the runway at about 2.45.

Jim and Pete were taken to the Tidmarsh home at first, until they should be able to secure rooms with an Ecuadorian family. The study of Spanish began immediately. Jim wrote to his parents on February 29:

There is a real problem connected with this moving into a new language. One sees at once the terrific need of speaking for the Lord, and speaking clearly, pointedly, so as to be well under-

213

stood, and then one feels the utter helplessness of the situation in being unable to speak even one word without an accent so that he is detected the moment he speaks. The tendency is to throw up one's hands and say "what is the use?" But the necessity of speaking for the Lord drives us to get this language perfectly. Pray that for us it will be the latter. We started classes yesterday. I have four a week.

The city is beautiful, old, and picturesque, lying between two high mountain ranges. To the west, the volcano Pichincha, active and with traces of smoke the last few days, rises green and gullied, cultivated most of the way to the top.

The market is quite interesting. There one sees an aristocratic Latin in a fur coat shopping beside a beggarman in rags. There is a wide selection of vegetables and a fair show of fruit, though one cannot afford to eat much of either raw. Rhubarb was on our menu yesterday, cauliflower, Swiss chard, carrots, celery—and all cooked. But I miss our raw "rabbit food", and apples. Bananas, in all their forms, I am getting on to. We have had banana-meal mush for breakfast, fried bananas, and raw ones so far. A great "head" of green ones is on the garage floor.

Another letter to his parents is dated March 9:

I have made contact with a young Ecuadorian up here studying English. We are together about an hour every day, exchanging English and Spanish expressions. Nice fellow, twenty-three, named Abdon. Pray that I might be able to help him in the Word while I am here. It becomes increasingly obvious that our job here is to train Ecuadorians. We will never be able to speak as they speak nor get next to their own people in the way they are next to them.

More and more we feel the burden of the Auca and Cofan off in the Oriente, but feel that our first experience, if not our permanent one, should be with the jungle Quichua. Do pray that we might find out His work for us and do it for the greater glory of His name.

The diary continues on March 11:

Felt a strange bitterness this evening, tending to sullenness and dissatisfaction with everyone. Coming outside and feeling my barrenness, the beautiful night lured me on a walk. The moon has powers to wash a man inside and I experienced it tonight, the laving of the spirit by chill air, old mud walls, the smell of eucalyptus, night birds, and moon-burnished clouds. It's a different world over the walls here and up beyond the hill.

March 14. My first night under mosquito netting. Came down from Quito with Dee Short and family, and slept here in their rented house in Santo Domingo de los Colorados. Saw my first Colorado in the plaza this morning. Leaving Quito on cobblestone you climb awhile in view of all three peaks of Pichincha—swallowed in cloud yesterday at least the top third. Suddenly you see the valleys dropping away below, sunk in mist. Watching, you can see the mist part and the utter green denseness break clear, shot here and there with whites: a dead tree, a flash of waterfall, or a show of smoke. Down, down, down, twisting into canyon heads, past the cascades and smoking *carboneros*, squeezing past upcoming trucks, down through the chill mist until it is not chill, but steamy. Above, shouldering mountains swim into cloud now, and still you go down. The total drop is something around 9,000 feet from the highest point en route. Took us six hours in the pick-up truck. Here in Santo Domingo—a fast-growing agricultural centre with Negroes, Indians, and mestizos in the population—there is no other missionary for a radius of one hundred kilometres.

March 17. Living with Shorts these days, trying to be of some help around as well as sizing up the work and keeping Spanish before me. Most of the time it amounts to plenty of little things—washing dishes, helping with the kids, playing the harmonica in the open-air meeting, helping drive the truck. Yesterday we had a good meeting in the room off the plaza; lots of interested men.

March 18–22. Spent these days in San Miguel de los Colorados with the two English girls, Doreen Clifford and Barbara Edwards. First real time in the forests, and first contacts with Indians. The road is almost impassable, with all manner of mud-holes. We went on horseback, arriving in four hours. In the afternoon the girls and Don Gustavo took me to the house of the two albinos. Found the mouth-harp of good use in making friends, accompanying Doreen on her autoharp. Discussed location of a school for the Indians.

March 27. Returned to Quito in a fruit-truck with Abdon on Monday. Enjoying Christ and counsel with the Father these days, though since I have taken to pure Spanish reading of the Scriptures I feel that I have forfeited some of the freshness I once enjoyed from the Word. But it must be, and I have the hope that soon I shall be getting things from the Spirit in still another language.

April 6. Lord's Day. More inner joy today than for several days. Enjoyed the breaking of bread, simply remembering Him. One sees clearly the necessity for it here, not to speak of its honour to God, but for one's soul, to keep one pressing after Christ, pursuing fresh realities, purifying old ones.

Betty should be in Ecuador a week from today, God willing. Strange that we are led so close together so soon, wonderfully strange! There will be talk, especially in the US, but I tend not to care a bit for it here. Let them talk—and God shall lead us on! Faith makes life so even, gives one such confidence in his movements, that the words of men are as wind.

Jim's urgent desire to learn Spanish found further expression in a letter to his parents, dated April 19:

We are quite concerned at the slow progress we are making in the language. But these are problems. We would like to go somewhere and live where we are not given the opportunity to speak English. Here it is too easy for us. The only contact we have with Ecuadorians is that which we make ourselves, and one hour a day with the Spanish teacher. Not sufficient for real progress.

Jim wanted to share as much as possible in the life of the people of Ecuador, and found that mountain-climbing, sight-seeing, even bull-fights, contributed to this end:

Watched our first *corrida de toros* today. This is Ecuadorian "Labour Day", and they had a six-bull fight. Betty and I went with a group of missionaries and nationals. It was wonderful! The picador action is especially thrilling, while the ballet grace of the cape-wielders is beautiful.

I don't know why I love bulls. Nothing has quite the fitness to act *bravo*, it seems to me, as a well-built bull. They do nicely with their front feet, striking straight, stiff from the shoulders. The head-feint just before the lunge is clever technique, and although they hardly have a chance to vindicate themselves, they do well for all the confusion they are put to. One feels it a little unjust that the matador has done it so many times before, while the bull is at it for the first time. It is not as spectacular as a good western rodeo, and, of course, somewhat bloodier, but the whole thing seems to fit the Latin mind...gold braid and blood...exultation at death...paper ribbons and "picks"... gracefulness and brutishness...a bull and a pair of ballet shoes. These people are extremists.

Despite the freedom and ease of living which Jim wrote of in outward things, there were struggles of soul. My presence in Quito, a thing for which Jim was glad, as it was the first time we had ever lived in proximity since college days, opened for him again the issue of engagement. He was not yet in jungle work, and could not know the conditions it might impose. Yet God had led us one step further since our last discussion of these issues — we were now in Ecuador, by His clear direction. Once again principles, rather than impulse, were his guide. He wrote in the journal:

You understand, Lord. It is not easy, but we've had it out lots of times. I stick by what I've told You. So long as I can do a work in reaching a primitive people *better* as a single man, I will stay single. And that brings me to the other things we've been digging around: *Aucas*. My God, who is sufficient for them?

May 2. Oh for a heart like David's. For all his obvious powers of leadership he never goes out to lead the people in battle without consultation with Jehovah. "Shall I go up?" [2] This lack of self-confidence marks him as God's man for guiding others. He allowed God to press His cause, and the kingdom was established in his hand. Good lessons for the basing of our thoughts about moving to the Aucas.

May 5. Gave myself for Auca work more definitely than ever asking for spiritual valour, good Spanish, plain and miraculous guidance, among other things.

Consolidated my thinking about Betty. Reading of David's sin against Uriah the Hittite, I got to thinking over Uriah's attitude. David, obviously thinking he could make Uriah think himself the father of Bathsheba's child, brought him home from war, made him drunk and all but forced him to his wife's bed. But Uriah stayed with the king's servants and his reason for so doing is: "The ark, and Israel, and Judah abide in booths; and my lord Joab, and the servants of my lord are encamped in the open field; shall I then go into my house to eat and drink and to lie with my wife? As thou livest, and as thy soul liveth, I will not do this thing!" [3] It was not *time* to return to his house—though he had the right to do so, and the encouragement. It was the *time* for battle, and Uriah was a warrior; there could be no mixing of home-goodness and the business of his life. So it came to me. Marriage is not for me now. It simply is not the *time*. (I do not say, and never did say, it is not the *thing* for me.) With tribes unreached which I now believe reachable only by unattached men, "I will not do this thing".

May 7. Near full moon found Betty and me in the open fields, under a sparse stand of eucalyptus after heavy rain. The sky was broken with clouds, and flashed stars, but the horizon was sufficiently clear to see Cayambe, Antisana, and Cotopaxi by moonlight. No night like it so far here in Ecuador. It was one of those "asked-for" times, with her, depending on the weather, which God openly controlled for us. He seems to do much "for us" these days. I have not lost one nameable thing by putting her and our whole affair in the simplest way possible into His hands. There has been no careful planning, no worrying over details in the matter. I have simply recognised love in me, declared it to her, and to Him, and as frankly as I could told

Him I wanted His way in it. There has been no leading thus far to engagement, but the symptoms of a beautiful courtship prevail—not, perhaps, a routine one, or a "normal" one, but a good one, nevertheless, and, withal, a deep sense that it is God-directed.

May 9. I am now aware that my reasons for not being engaged are hidden in the counsels of God's Spirit. I simply know it is not for now—that knowledge is inward, God-given, and to be obeyed at whatever cost. There are no explanations except that God leads, and He does not let a man know why He leads. Faith binds a man to what he knows inside, like my coming to Ecuador. The world could not shake the persuasion. "The just shall live by faith."[4] Faith—not alone in facts and a rational apologetic—but in the reality of the inward work of the anointing which he possesses through the gift of the Holy Spirit. I must maintain a surer belief in the Spirit of God. It is no mere tenet of faith that He indwells the believer. He does indwell, and there He accomplishes His work of informing the spirit of man.

Dr Tidmarsh began a brief course in homeopathy for the several new missionaries in the group. This Jim found very interesting, as his letter home on May 15 demonstrates:

Right in the middle of tropical disease this week. Finished leprosy this morning. Most interesting, and I confess that I can hardly wait to start medical work—pilling, pulling, and puncturing! Had a chance to adjust Pete's neck last night. He gets occipital headaches and a neck rub fixes him up, we find, so I'll not lose my technique! Of course, yesterday he had reason to be a little tense. As you know, there was a full moon on Friday, and the moon just after waning is the best time for climbing mountains around here. So—Tuesday, about 9 pm, we decided to climb Pichincha. After a few hours in the sack I heard the alarm ring at 2.30. I woke Abdon (my right-hand Ecuadorian buddy), who was sleeping on an air-mattress here in my room. We looked up at a misty sky with a breaking moon. Rob Gill, Bill, Pete, Abdon, and I walked out into the night with three meals and rainwear on our backs in packs. We hailed a taxi, picked up Betty, and rode as far as the taxi could go up the trail. As soon as we got away above Quito we lost all trace of mist and the moon broke clear over the inter-Andean plain, exposing three of our most beautiful snow caps off toward the Oriente. At dawn we were back in a valley that cut off all but 19,170-foot-high Cayambe, blowing with three sharp clouds, tinted rose and deep purple. Turning, we could see ourselves standing in moonlight, shining on our side of the ridge, while across the valley dawn-light cast an entirely different sheen on the long mountain grasses. Nearly wept with the beauty of it. Up, up, up, with cascading water on all sides, exotic mountain flowers, broad-backed, rolling hills running up to the jutting peaks. Treeless, of course, but with the sense of habitation still, because of flies, birds, butterflies, toads, and even some horses grazing. Our final altitude at reaching the mist-washed peak (snowless except for dashes a few feet across) was 15,500 feet, the highest I've ever been on foot. Because we could use "Keds" for climbing and needed no crampons for ice hiking, the trip was much easier than climbing the peaks around home, and it didn't make me nearly as stiff or tired, despite the altitude. In all, a beautiful trip, well worth the effort and time, if only for the sweetening and enlarging it accomplished in one's spirit. The Lord made mountains to climb, not just to look at, and up there one understands why—seeing the vista that most folks never see, with the sense of farness that most never feel.

The same letter goes on to speak of the thing that yet remained a problem:

One doesn't learn to speak a language in a couple of months. It will be plugging for a good while yet. Seems that I'll never get through "preparing" for the mission field. But I've been comforted this week thinking of our Lord's thirty silent years of readying Himself at home with His family and bending over a carpenter's bench. Were those days any less of a fragrance to God than His later work before the eyes of the people? I think not. A well-made piece of furniture and a healed blind man represented the same thing to the Father—a job well done; mission accomplished. So with us here. Nothing great, but what is that to Him with whom there is no great or small?

The journal continues:

May 27. Moved to Dr Hugo Cevallos' home today, a pure Spanish context at last. Thank God! Taking midday meal with Sr Arias and morning and evening here. Great provision from God to have this place. I want to make the best of it, Lord.

The situation is described in a letter to his parents:

As I write, Pete is out in the *sala* reading the paper. The five Cevallos kids are engaged in various diversions. Doña Bacha is at work in the kitchen. The doctor, a fairly conscientious, but terribly conventional medic, has gone off on a call. He cannot support himself in a regular practice. His schedule runs something like this: first thing in the morning he has a class or two in biology in one of the big secondary schools. Then he goes to his office to wait on calling patients. Home at noon for lunch and siesta. Then until 6.30 or later he is at the Sanidad (Public Health Service) clinic. Any hour of the night he is obliged to run on calls, and he can't afford financially to turn them down. To supplement his funds he has rented the biggest bedroom of the house to us two gringos; the rest of the family sleep in two rooms. Not so soft, but he is a happier man than dozens of much wealthier, less busy, successful businessmen I have met in the States. The most modern thing in the home is a telephone. He has a radio, but no car. His wife cooks on kerosene, without electric beater, refrigerator, or oven of any sort. And they are supremely happy. I haven't heard a cross word pass between them or any of the children since I moved in. Just who is civilised, anyhow? "A man's life does not consist in the abundance of things that he possesses."

In June Jim accepted an invitation to make a quick trip to the Oriente, the eastern jungle, which would include some survey flying in search of Auca houses.

He wrote to his sister Jane, then a student at Wheaton College:

Mission work by airplane is different from what you imagine. First, there is the thrill of it. What I've said about "missionary thrills" is true—you get over them. But that doesn't mean you don't *have* them at first! The sense of lift, just as the wheels leave the ground, the "gasp" of dropping in a wind current 5,000 feet up, the tilt of swinging on a wing-tip to take a look at a tiny group of houses hidden in the forest, the shiver of dropping below trees to get a good look and the back-throw of pulling out over the trees—these are terrific thrills that I've had these last two days. I may get over them, or I may get sick, as Pete did, but at least I've had them.

We've been here in Missionary Aviation Fellowship head-quarters in Shell Mera making jungle surveys. We were interested to know about the Quichua population of the southern Oriente, and have discovered what we wanted to know. We also wanted to find out if there was any truth to the possible friendly contact southern Quichuas might have with Aucas, the one really savage tribe down here. There isn't. They have just killed five in the area. We were looking for Auca homes as well, but found nothing. Evidently they are hiding out or have moved east. More and more that tribe is brought before me as a possible field of labour for my life. They are utterly untouched, and so far they are inaccessible. It would take a miracle to open the way to them, and we are praying for that miracle. They may be only a few hundred in number, but they are a part of the whole creation, and we have orders for such.

Can't seem to get any news of the Portland gang. Mom wrote about A.'s death. Seems far away and hard to believe. One can't imagine death as a look on the face or the stiff position of a body, when he hasn't seen the person that way. You always bring up the living face in thinking about him. Another instance of what death really is—not just a coldness or a silence or a horror, but a removal, a separation. For those who are near it may be the former things, but for us who have not been closer than thousands of miles, it is always, "I can't imagine so and so without *her*." We don't think of her as she died, but in relation to what she left, and the idea of separation is constant with her death. Sad thing it was, and tragic. But it is very easy to mouth clear, flat platitudes about it and to draw old morals again for re-etching.

It is a warning to any of us who love. We should love hard, and not casually; fervently, playfully, and simply, never heavily or slowly. Slovenly loving makes for wearisome living. I think A. just got weary. If you ever love, Jane, love like a schoolgirl with giggles and sighs, and keep love alive by consciously keeping wonder and surprise at the core of it. For many "young-marrieds" get used to it after a year or two, because they think they have to. For me, I can't afford to with Betty. I've got to make it last and last. I have not found it hard, but I have found that love is not effortless. It needs control and direction.

I can't quite figure out how this got started, but there it is. Only know that I love you, Sis, and think of and pray for you often several times a day. We as a family have loved without saying so, just by enjoying and missing each other.

When Jim returned from the jungle he wrote to Eleanor Vandevort in Africa:

The Lord has brought Betty and me over some happy ground since last we had any contact with you. We are living right across the street from one another. Living in Ecuadorian homes is the only real way to learn Spanish, and we are enjoying it immensely. Oh Van, I couldn't have asked for more than God in deliberate grace has surprised me with! We didn't ask to be sent to the field together. We didn't ask to be sent to live in such close proximity. We hardly asked for each other. It seemed unreasonable to ask such things, six months ago. Dreams are tawdry when compared with the leading of God, and not worthy of the aura of wonder we usually surround them with. God only doeth wonders. He does nothing else. His hand can work nothing less. Praise to the Guiding God of Israel, and that Great Shepherd of the wayward sheep. When He directs a path, no way can seem bleak, no instance dull.

Betty and I are agreed that the Will of God for some time is to be undeclared to one another, though our feelings are clear, and I think known to you. So we go on, waiting and willing to do the Will of Him who sent us, and working away at the language, wondering sometimes at His ways.

We have found great joy in coming to the field as God's free folk. Answering to nobody but Himself, and with nobody's support or promise but His very own. It is a very inofficious way to work—without so much as a letterhead to make a man feel that he "belongs" to something. But it is most gratifying to look aloft to the God who keeps promises and is sufficient.

The days of Spanish study in Quito seemed golden. On July 11 Jim wrote in his journal:

I wonder sometimes if it is right to be so happy. Day follows day in an easy succession of wonders and joys—simple, good things like food well prepared, or play with children, or conversation with Pete, or supply of money for rent or board within hours of its being due. Grace upon grace in the outside sphere of living. But, simply because I am not really studying the English Bible, fresh truth for inner soul-refreshment is rare. I am supposed to speak at an English-language gathering again on Lord's Day, and find that I must go back to old truths, learned in the work-free days in Portland in 1949, to get solid material for peaching. I was reading my diary notes and noting the contrasting soul-soreness of those days with the freedom and joy of these. Those were certainly more productive from a point of view of getting things from the Word; these are more casual and less fruitful, but for reasons—Spanish *must* be gotten. I want God to speak as He did then, but I want Him to begin speaking Spanish, and I am not yet used to that, perhaps not ready for it. So I go on in these days, glad-hearted and simple in my thanks, lacking the profundity of material for depth of worship. But I have not left off seeking His depths and I believe He will take me back to those days of struggling and discovering in the Word.

How well I see now that He is wanting to do something in

me! So many missionaries, intent on doing something, forget that His main work is to make something of them, not just to do a work by their stiff and bungling fingers. Teach me, Lord Jesus, to live simply and love purely, like a child, and to know that You are unchanged in Your attitudes and actions toward me. Give me not to be hungering for the "strange, rare, and peculiar" when the common, ordinary, and regular—rightly taken—will suffice to feed and satisfy the soul. Bring struggle when I need it; take away ease at Your pleasure.

July 26. Oh, for a faith that sings! Thought of Jehoshaphat in II Chronicles 20. Threatened with defeat by a multitude that far outreached his powers of war he set his face toward Jehovah. He called a fast for the people, then publicly reminded God of His covenant with Abraham and Solomon. Stating the problem thus put God in a position of responsibility: "O our God, wilt Thou not judge them? for we have no might against this great company that cometh against us; neither know we what to do, but our eyes are upon Thee."[5]

Then, after an answer from a prophet, Jehoshaphat, himself humbled and believing, charges his people: "Believe in the Lord Your God!"[6] And then they broke out singing! Singing, in the face of such a problem! Lord God, give me a faith that will take sufficient quiver out of me so that I can sing! *Over the Aucas, Father, I want to sing.*

Jim's prayer for help in Spanish was obviously answered. Many Ecuadorians commented on Jim's excellent pronunciation, and looked suspicious when told that he'd been in Ecuador just five months. On July 27 Jim wrote to his parents:

Last Lord's Day morning and also today we went with Dr Tidmarsh to Sangolquí. Got my first crack at preaching in Spanish. Great joy in it, but not really fluent yet. Never felt more apostolic in my life than this morning, when I was actually "disputing in the marketplace"[7] with two or three interested questioners in the crowd of perhaps forty people. One feels all alone, but the joy of seeing people who do not know of the

225

evangel asking sensible questions about faith and works or our belief in the virgin is something I have not known before. Oh, to be able in their language! I look forward with great pleasure to this time of witnessing. It is true that we get a couple of hundred tracts torn up every week, and there are hecklers who throw an occasional jibe or orange peel, but in all we feel that we are making friends, and destroying the traditional prejudice. We believe God is supporting His Word and following it to the consciences of some. Pray for this work, won't you?

The next letter is dated August 9:

Next Wednesday or so Pete and I will be going down to Shell Mera to help in a boys' camp, and from there on in to Shandia. We've been trying to get a little studying done in Spanish for that, as we both have two messages to give to the boys each week. We spent two days at our *bodega* (learn this word—it means storeroom, but is just a little room where some of us keep our barrels and crates, etc.) going through all our things and sorting out what we want to take first to the jungle. We used those big black rubber bags to pack in, Dad. Filled four of them, and left some things, like our aluminium chairs and a buck-saw and an axe, unpacked. Every ounce of packing means extra weight in the little plane. This morning Pete and I have to go down to the market and get some things we were unable to bring with us—machetes, pots, some oil for the .22 and other such.

As Jim contemplated leaving Quito, after five of the happiest months of his life, he thought again of engagement, feeling it would be easier for us to part if God would give us His word of assent. But again the answer was clear, as Jim wrote in the journal on August 12, two days before he said good-bye to me:

Oh, for a heartiness in the will of God, "doing it from the heart".[8] I must confess that, though I am sure that engagement is not for us this summer, the acceptance of that as the Will of the Father is no gladdening thing. It is not that my wants (1. for her, 2. for the work, perhaps among the Aucas) conflict. They are not contradictory, but they do not seem to mesh. They have come at the same time, so that instead of fitting into one another, as cogs would, they grind against one another, sometimes with awful concentration. It is too soon for me, not having seen the Oriente, to believe that God may not want me there entirely unattached. But all the while I'm mad for her, wanting to be with her night and day, the haunting hunger of body, the loneliness of mind—making book-study a farce at times, and making life itself seem useless without her.

Notes

1. Genesis 28:3,4.
2. 2 Samuel 5:19.
3. 2 Samuel 11:11, ASV.
4. Galatians 3:11.
5. 2 Chronicles 20:12.
6. 2 Chronicles 20:10.
7. Acts 17:17, para.
8. Ephesians 6:6, para.

— 20 —

The Realised Will

*And he brought us out from thence that He might bring us in, to
give us the land. . . . Know therefore that the Lord thy God, He is
God, the faithful God, which keepeth covenant.*[1]

N AUGUST 17, 1952, Jim wrote to me from Shell
Mera, where the boys' camp was held on Bible
Institute property:

In the dark of Friday morning I walked across the street to your
wall, and stalked the length of it while Pete checked the room
for the last time. Almost called your name to your dark windows,
thinking you might be awake. Then I dropped into silence,
knowing I was leaving you and ending the happiest weeks of my
life. We were first to reach the church, waiting twenty minutes
for the HCJB[2] sound-truck to roll up to pile in our gear and
crowd ourselves into the noise of eighteen kids. The bus didn't
leave until six am and I shared a seat with a boy, Segundo, who
was, thankfully, a little strange to the group and not too
talkative. Drawing past the railroad station I felt the weepiness
coming on, but stayed it—I don't know with what. But
dawn—with its quiet rose glint on Mt Cotopaxi, making a
black silhouette of Antisana and melting Cayambe against the
cold grey of clouds to the north—teased the sadness out of me
(still not the silence), but making me thankful for the work of
the Master-hand and reminding me that

The Realized Will

*"A Father's hand will never cause
His child a needless tear."*[3]

Rising up into the paramo that runs to the slopes of Cotopaxi we came into fog and I slept fitfully until we reached Latacunga, where town activity roused me to watching things. We bought mandarins and bananas in Ambato and ate them all the way down here, killing a bottle of carbon water for lunch at Baños. Below Baños the trip was beautiful with a clear view of the Pastaza. Orchids are in season and flashed along the road cuts. I cut one yesterday while we were out on a hike, and brought it to the camp building, but you weren't here, so had to stick it in a tin cup with another bright red flower I found. The orchids thinned out as we moved out of the gorge and followed the Pastaza from its hurtling out into the semi-level where it begins to braid among the gravel beds.

The mountains are blue just now as it turns dusk and there is the far-off drumming of thunder. Husky clouds hide El Altar and Sangay, which were visible this morning. Sangay is like Cotopaxi in shape; I have never seen anything quite like Altar— it seems to be a whole range in itself with a half dozen peaks, at least, all snow-capped. They were beautiful last evening. They say you can see Sangay spewing fire at night, for with all its snow it is still active. A parrot is whining like a frightened dog perched on one of the store fronts across the street and field, a block away.

Now I must finish—the campers will be coming soon, and my group must walk the three blocks to the Institute to carry up the food tonight.

A week later Jim wrote to his parents of the results of the camp:

In all I believe it has been a profitable week. Certainly we have had God's help in the language. He blessed in our morning Bible studies evidently—we had two each week. Wednesday the Lord gave us a happy break. I had just finished a half-hour Bible study on the LORD, JESUS CHRIST, defining the words

229

from the Scripture and having the boys look up the references. Afterward four of my dear little kids went crying to their rooms. We prayed and talked with them, all of them shaking with that body-jolting sob of children, and all confessing faith in Jesus and sorrow for sin. A very simple thing, and very "sweetly moving", as Brainerd would say, and it has changed the whole face of the discipline problem.

We got up at six and had "café", their term for breakfast, which consisted of a cup of chocolate and two small bread rolls. After a brief break, we began with choruses and Scripture memorisation, then morning Bible studies, forty-five minutes of searching for passages to discover what the Bible itself says about us, the Lord Jesus, and so on. Usually a banana for mid-morning snack, or sugar-cane, or even "tostados", roasted corn kernels which, with salt, serve nicely in place of crackers. Then it was play, either teaching them American games or their own soccer, if not too wet outside. Lunch was followed by siesta and then more play or swim in a beautiful stream ten minutes' drive up the valley of the Pastaza.

Jim's journal says:

But the week was too short to train sons. One must live with them. Wanting sons these days, wanting to feed them, lift them, have them hound me, beg me in the name of a father. And for me, it looks like no sons are in sight. Still, as I read Job 12:10 again, "In His hand is the life of every living thing."[4] I recognised that all I am and have is the Almighty's. He could in one instant change the whole course of my life—with accident, tragedy, or any event unforeseen. Job is a lesson in acceptance, not of blind resignation, but of believing acceptance, that what God does is well done. So, Father, with happy commital I give you my life again this morning—not for anything special, simply to let you know that I regard it as yours. Do with it as it pleases you, only give me great grace to do for the glory of Christ Jesus whatever comes to me, "in sickness and in health."

On August 25 he wrote to me:

You won't know how glad I was to hear of the hardly believed-for peace you describe. May the Spirit who gave, maintain. More than once I have wondered at the way of God, a wonder that shaded into resentment. And it is easier to know that He who led, gave grace, lustring with love the sorrow once again. He knows better that you do, Bett, why and how intensely and how long I have desired you, and the struggle it has been to commit you to Him alone to comfort when I wanted devilishly hard to have you committed—insofar as engagement would make this possible—to me. But now I know that His loving-kindness, forever better than life, is better, too, than further human loving, for I doubt that even engagement could have wrought the impossible peace you speak of. Praise, then, praise for peace.

When camp was over, Pete and Dr Tidmarsh went into Shandia first, while Jim remained in Shell Mera to await a second flight. He busied himself collecting things for a garden in Shandia, as he wrote to me:

Saturday I went orchid-hunting down behind the house. Found two more of those waxy "shoe orchids", white with brown-spotted centre, growing on a fallen tree over the creek. They are now in a small packsack with other orchid roots, roses, naranjilla, coffee, hibiscus, geranium starts, and a poinsettia shoot. I hope things grow like folk say they do in the jungle. I've got the flower craze worse than I get it some springs in the yard at Portland!

The afternoon has cleared so that the big pillars of cloud, rising in a haze over the jungle, stand pure white against a blue sky. Silhouettes of distant birds are sharp against them, going east. And tomorrow, happily, and in the will of God, I follow. Only too well I know again the inner weakness to return, to go back to you, but I feel that I have set my hand, and to look back now would be dishonour. He knows the inner part, and He knows how much of me I really leave with you. And He knows why I leave, and for how long.

The journal continues on September 3:

Shandia. As I write my praise mingles with the steady rush of the Atun Yaku, running like pure silver into the jungle under a full moon. Left Shell Mera at three this afternoon in a sky of scattered clouds. Landed at Pano around three-thirty and made the walk to beautiful Shandia in just two and a half hours. The moon rose as I stepped into the clearing with Eladio, the school-teacher and two carriers, prognostically telling me of the faithfulness of God. Surely life is full in His Will and brings promise of good things yet for us here. In spite of my wait since Friday, first for the teacher and then for the plane, the thought kept recurring as I came along the trail, "right on time, right on time—God's time". So with much joy we have arrived at last at the destination decided on in the Will when at Wycliffe in 1950, and my joy is full, full, full. Oh, how blind it would have been to reject the leading of those days! How it has changed the course of life for me and added such a host of joys. As I looked up over the notched horizon of hills, the grandeur of the jungle was on me, and gave me again the sense of rugged solidarity, the sense of living alone and feeling satisfied within.

The forest is not unlike the west jungle, bigger, and emptier, but not much different. The trees with concave bark, and the roots ribboning down to the ground—the straight hanging vines—the clear, warm creeks—all beautiful, simply beautiful.

He wrote to his parents on September 7:

I am seated at the table with the Coleman double-burner lantern. We had supper a couple of hours ago of boiled bananas and manioc-banana soup, topped off with a cup of "hierba luisa", a sweet green forest tea that is supposed to have powers to make a man return to the Oriente, once he has drunk it, though he cross the world. Food has been most interesting these first few days, and I have eaten things fixed by our cook boy that I never dreamt existed. Ate chonta palm heart yesterday when the men clearing the airstrip cut down a big palm. It is the tender leaves deep in the trunk, soft and white and with a taste not at all unlike our chestnut. Always there is fresh fruit, papaya, sweet bananas (called "sedas"); then, too, I had my first chonta palm, although I confess I did not relish them as did the doctor, with his jungle-perverted palate! Since we have few other fats here, I suppose I'll get accustomed to them. The pineapples are luscious and the avocado, of which I eat maybe one and a half daily, are huge. We are supplementing our vegetable-lack with those great bottles of vitamins that we have carried half-way across the world. We have also started a small garden, experimenting with chard, cabbage, spuds, and other vegetables. Yesterday the Indians discovered a herd of wild pigs and we had genuine boar soup today.

Shandia is beautiful. We are high on a sheer cliff right above a big green river called the Atun Yaku, the "big water", in Indian parlance. Right here the small warm Shandia River runs into the bigger and much colder upper Napo, which comes down from the great snow caps of Antisana and Cotopaxi. We take daily afternoon baths down the fifty-five mud steps, though it is not deep enough to swim in the Shandia, and too swift to swim in the Atun Yaku. Mornings we employ thirty-five to forty men in clearing the jungle for our airstrip, and while they work, we study their language here in the house.

We have a board floor and bamboo ceiling, and impermeable paper on top to hold out excessive bat-droppings. The roof is thatch. Long screened windows let us look, from our bedroom, right out to the river and the airstrip and ball-field, and from the dining-room table, out to the garden and the uncleared forest fifty feet away. Our bedroom is exceedingly pleasant—a huge window looks out on a beautiful view. Door is a monk's cloth curtain between our room and the living-room; we have two throw-rugs, and the two aluminium chairs make the place look very civilised. The Indian Venancio, or his son Luis, sweeps it daily to clean out the mud and dead cockroaches (none under an inch long). The insect life here is fantastic. Right now there are half a dozen interesting beetles and moths crowding around the gas lamp, and we have several butterflies pinned daintily to our walls. Last week, as I was wearing blisters on my hand with my first machete practice, a little furry thing fell by my foot—

yellow and round like a baby bird, which I took it to be. My curiosity was satisfied that it was not when I drew back, a thumb stinging as if with nettles. It was a huge caterpillar with hair two inches long that had fallen from the tree I was hacking.

In a later letter Jim described for his parents the duties which occupied their days:

Last Lord's Day it was a boy to be splinted for a broken wrist. Wednesday a man with a machete cut. Thursday and Friday a breech-baby case which Pete and the doctor attended. Saturday a man with a 104-degree fever who had walked miles to get here and was too badly off to receive an injection, but instead of taking our offer to stay until his fever subsided he slipped away with only two or three atabrine pills. Then a baby and mother for quinine injections. It sure makes for an interrupted life, and we find it very difficult to spend any consistent time in language study. We have the full responsibility now of keeping the men working in the forenoons, getting the school-teacher (who has turned out to be a lazy guy) to plane boards for blackboards and a bookcase for the school, buying eggs, plantains, and selling salt and matches—any of a hundred and one little things, to say nothing of swatting at the little mean biteflies that have been on us since the heat came. The airstrip should be done soon, though, and that will relieve us of a great deal of worrisome details and cut down expenses considerably. I never employed a man in my life and here I am with half a hundred to manage. Of course, I'm not alone. I would be crazy now if Pete didn't share all the efforts.

Slight interruption. When the plane came into Pano, they left vegetables for us. I just went out to get the celery, green onions, cucumbers, and tomatoes to wash in potassium permanganate, so we can eat them for dinner raw, as a salad. They don't know anything about these vegetables here, and were wondering what to do with them. Usually everything goes into the soup, of which we have two bowls a meal. We eat it with sticks of steamed manioc. There is no type of bread here, so manioc and plantain are our staple starches. I just bought some forest potatoes—great, long, root-like affairs that grow in the dark jungle by means of a long vine that climbs the trees to sunlight. We eat off the plastic ware, and I notice it does scratch some, all advertising aside.

In spite of the difficulties of language study where interruptions were so frequent, Jim was gradually absorbing it, mostly by 'living it' with the Indians, swinging a machete, visiting in homes, with his pencil ever poised, slogging over the dim trails in company with these laughing, black-eyed brothers.

The Quichuas soon won his heart—indeed, they had done so years before he saw them. But now, living with them, he knew a greater love, just as Jesus, *'looking on* the multitudes',[5] was moved with compassion. They are short and stocky, with beautiful bronze-red skin, heavy black hair, and high cheekbones. They live in one-roomed, palm-thatched houses, walled with bamboo or split palm, if they are walled at all. There are no villages, a factor which greatly increases the difficulty of reaching them. Their houses are located, one here, one there, along the banks of rivers, and are connected by trails which vary from seas of mud, reaching often to the knees, to putty-like mud which soils only as far as one's shoe-tops. After the first six months in the forest, the six pairs of tennis shoes which Jim had brought from the States were rotted.

But the mud did not bog down his spirits more than momentarily, as snatches from his journal will verify:

September 21. Using Luis as an interpreter makes language study too easy, so that I don't feel the strong necessity of knowing the idiom. But I know all the same that I must get it, get it good, and get it rapidly. By Thy grace, Lord, I'm going to.

Just finished a sing out of the Inter-Varsity Hymnal, *Believers' Hymnal*, and *Little Flock*. Great joy in going over "At Even E'er the Sun was Set", "The Lord's My Shepherd", "And is it so, I shall be like Thy Son?", "O God, we adore Thee".

September 24. Full, happy, useful days. How I thank God for Pete and our present relation. Great sense of unity in attitudes with him. We were not vainly sent "two and two".[6]

September 25. Had my first chicha in the Indian homes today, made of mashed chonta. Also my first cooked chonta fruit. The latter was rich, though woody; the former flat and watery. Returning I stopped at a chagra-hut where a man with fever was lying under mountains of flies wrapped in a blanket, with boils on knee and shin. Ate my first ants yesterday—toasted "ukui".

To me Jim wrote:

The last minute before I left Shell Mera the pilot said the load had to be cut twenty pounds, so the bulbs and rose roots are still there. Our garden, too, that showed such high hopes before, has been root-eaten before the things got up an inch. Only a few cucumber shoots remain. We are going to have to change our methods, starting things in some sort of planting box so that they get a solid root before we set them out to the mercy of the Oriente insects. The only things that do well are the things I pick up on the trail and bring home to plant in the little sand stairway that leads to the river—lovely patterned leaves, an orchid or two, a wild snap-dragon, and a furry bluebell. Such things make the great forest somehow gracious and often sweet-smelling. Found a strange, single-petalled calla lily on the way to Pano, and brought home a root.

To his parents Jim wrote:

Hope you remember to pray for the multitudes of Indians around here. They are such children—wanting attention, running to the priest for insect repellent which he gives free to those who attend mass, and coming here for free medicines, bragging him up to us so that we will do some favour and avoid being called stingy, or sending their boys there to school and letting them come here to sleep and eat with our schoolboys. I have seen none who really seems concerned about his soul, the Scripture, or the gospel, and this I think is accounted for by our lack of concerned prayer for them.

September 30. An important day for the work here. Radio contacts all morning covering the first flight to Shandia. Easily a hundred and fifty Indians gathered for the event—the boys running about, the women hooting, the men crowding into the stopped Piper. Praised God for success and rapidity in getting the strip done. He supplied us with funds in time, kept the men working in a good spirit, sustained us with joy in the doing of it. "This God is our God *forever*; He will be our Guide until death."[7]

A letter I received, dated October 1, told more of the beauties of Jim's new home:

Bird songs in the forest are enchanting—long, low, almost sly whistles, clucking and knocking, sweet canary-like tunes, or a high mellow hoot—for all the world like a wood-wind instrument. And we hear the birds at night, as well as during the day, although their songs and whistles are not so frequent, and are often obscured by the rattling hubbub of crickets and other singing insects. I often think I would like to get a recording of night sounds as I lie in bed, from the squeaking of the bats in the thatch to the constant pounding of the rapids below. It is really a roar—only not rhythmic, like the oceanside, but constant, full, and interminable (that is, if one stops to think how long he's been hearing it). But it passes from the mind most of the time, only recurring when you look at the river consciously, or lie in the dark and listen. The river rose about four feet during the night, and canoes that were tied up on dry beach yesterday afternoon were rocking on a full current this morning, and the blank stretch of white boulders between the island and the opposite mainland was a turbid rush of slate when I woke. One thing that startles me with a shifting breath of wind is the orange tree in blossom just outside the door.

Some of the trees are veritable wonders for size and majesty. One, that we can see on the other side of the airstrip from the house, has roots which run away from the trunk like walls, bracing the height like structural triangles. I have seen one of these *uchu putus* with holes five feet across in the roots, where the Indians have hacked out a piece of wood for their huge trays, which they use for mashing chonta fruit, or for a butcher's block.

To his parents on October 18 Jim wrote:

Made my first coffin this morning, from pieces of crates that the radio equipment came in. A gorgeous dawn broke over our little place in the forest with the news that our cook's wife had lost a breech baby during the night. Dr Tidmarsh attended but they resented his interference, and refused to wrap the lower body in warm cloths while the head was still engaged. Dr Tidmarsh feared that cold on the body would make the breathing process start while the head be without air. The Indian attending simply said no, lifted the mother by the arm pits and shook the baby out, the mother hanging on to a rope on the wall. It took twenty minutes after the feet for the head to appear, and of course it was strangled. But it's got to be done that way; they have done it so for years and the wizards—the "knowing ones", as they call their witches—say it must so continue. It left Doc helpless. The mother cleaned up the mess. I saw her dumping it all over the cliff this morning as I washed out on the porch. We made the coffin this morning; the father condescended to dig the grave. Life isn't very important here, and death even less. Nobody cried, for they don't regard as human a thing that has not breathed.

The day was hot, and we had about a dozen men working on the foundation of the clinic building and clearing the forest directly behind. This afternoon a sudden tropical thunder-shower came up and blew the ridge of the roof right off the school. It also took the clothes off the line, turned the calendars over on the wall, and made a general mess of our shelves and papers with its wind. It only lasted about ten minutes, but it can give a man a lot to think about in that time. Screened windows leave one without anything to close when a storm comes.

Here we keep well. We eat loads, drink tea or lemonade

mid-morning and mid-afternoon. One sweats terribly and needs the liquid. Bathe daily in the river, go to bed around nine-thirty and get up at five-thiry. A good schedule, not at all heavy, if at times confused by everything coming at once. I'm not losing any weight, Mother, so I suppose you can let your fears perish for me here. We find the daily walk with God as always, a simple thing of faith, patience, and love, superabounding in the sheer joy of living. Only, we need the language to get over the first great hurdle of missionary jungle life. Then the war really begins in earnest, and we are eager for it.

Jim's journal was an outlet for thoughts which he shared with no one else at the time, and when he received word by short-wave radio that I was leaving Quito for the western jungle to begin analysis of the Colorado language, he wrote:

It quieted me almost to bitterness, making me feel as though I were saying good-bye all over again. Mail service will be slower, contact less frequent, the possibility of seeing her more remote. The Father was told all about it again, how I wanted her, needed her here, and, I must confess, the comforts of faith, at least my poor faith, are not always completely satisfying. But I believe, for all it's being poor believing, and know that I will not lose for having believed.... O God, having made me thus, and led me thus, enable me to endure Thy making and Thy leading.

To me on October 27 he wrote:

This I know. That if next year is as full of sweet surprises and things to be wondered at as has been this last one (and I have no reason now to expect anything less; the situations are analogous in their impossibilities) it will be but stronger evdience of the good hand of God upon and over us, keeping His promises and cofirming all we have hoped in Him. Is it not, for all its sting, a wonderful way to live, Betty? To dream, and want and pray, almost savagely; then to commit and wait and see Him quietly pile all dreams aside and replace them with what we could not dream, the *realised* Will?

Dawn was another delight this morning. Broken clouds, scattered as from the bright breaking dawn itself, vanished in the blue zenith. None shaped even similarly, the whole was hued as one, lavender shading upward into a brown ridge and brightening into a rich cream below with such a uniformity that it seemed to give the sky perspective, as though one could really feel that east was "down" the sky and north "across". The river twisted out of the mist, one colour and one movement with it up-stream, sheened from grey to green as it came into the light below the cliff, then turned and melted back into the grey below. I feel like running and shouting and throwing myself at it all as though it were possible to deliver oneself as wholly physically to it, as one feels with it spiritually.

And now the moon makes the clearing, the river, and the trees all shine, but not like the sun this morning. A quietness, a gentleness is moonlight, so quiet and so gentle that sometimes I feel fear to stand in it out here alone. One feels the emptiness more at night, and I must confess I have come into the house gladly, on simply beautiful nights, not knowing quite why, but knowing that I could never run and sing and give myself to the tropic nights as I am tempted to do to the tropic day. The night, for all its variety of noise, does not converse like sunlight, nor invite like day.

Along with language-learning, medical work, constuction of new buildings, and other daily chores, Jim and Pete shared the responsibility of the four-grade school. He wrote about the schoolboys on November 5:

We are in the middle of introducing a game of volleyball to the Indians. They love to play, but have neither patience nor aptness to co-operate with each other in team sports. They are beginning to catch on, and we hope that ultimately we will be able to bring in more complicated games like softball and basketball. They play soccer quite well, but are always kicking the ball over the cliff, or booting it into the forest where it gets punctured on a thorn. So we have a rule that nobody kicks the volleyball. This rule is observed only occasionally, when we are in sight, or in our room in full view of the playfield. The boys, still only about a dozen, are great pals with us, but each one is a strong individual, wilful, and even spoiled to do what he wants, so there are constant petty arguments to solve among them. We have devotions with them in Spanish at the beginning of every school day, taking the story of Elisha while Dr Tidmarsh is away. At night we may do any of several things—show them movies when the electricity is on twice a week, or slides with a gas lantern, or gather them in the radio room to listen to music from the radio or victrola, or show them colour slides of ours in the little viewer. (They think our homes and families are fine, and wonder why we don't like them, that we should come down here!) Usually it is a game of checkers, or looking at *National Geographic* magazine over in the school by gas light. We have also gone on a fish-poisoning spree and caught hundreds of little fingerlings to fry. It was a great privilege to have the boys with us, and we feel that even though our twelve seem few, it is a victory to have each one here. We think too, that while we are getting started at it, it is better to work with a few. We can do more with them as individuals. One is standing by me now as I write, and he said, as I paused to think of the next sentence, *ñuka kilkasha*, "I will write." And while I wrote that sentence, the whole room filled with men who are discussing the artifacts of our culture here—bedspreads, pictures, meat-cleaver, harmonica. Each holds a fascination for them, and I only wish I could explain to them what they are all for.

A letter of November 16 describes the death of a baby which Jim and Pete had treated, after the witch-doctor had tried all his methods of healing:

We had lent kerosene to the family so that they could watch all night, but the whole house had gone to sleep and woke when our schoolboys arrived with their lantern. They found the baby dead then, and sent for us. The mother and grandmother had started the weird three-pitched descending wail of the bereaved —an awful thing to have to work beside. We tried artificial respiration as the body was still warm. Sweating and crying to

God for life to be given back, kneeling on a dirt floor beside a sunken-eyed baby, wondering if the throbbing felt at my finger-tips were his heart or mine, trying to shut out of mind the death-wails and incessant sobbing of the family, I worked for more than half an hour. When we finished and looked up into the gas-lit faces it only served to increase the wailing, as it dashed any final hopes. And then the wake began, the chanting of the parents mingling with the laughter of the play of the guests. All the guests are expected to play and drink all night from a half-gourd, to keep the bereaved amused. We only stayed till eleven pm, and played a few games of checkers. One interesting diversion was a ball of wadded kapok soaked in kerosene and lighted, tossed among the guests to keep them awake and shouting. We tossed it, too—and a couple of days later treated a boy who was burned with it.

It was on this occasion that Jim was introduced to the game of 'flip-the-bowl'. A bowl of chicha was placed on the floor, and one of the guests spread his legs, leaned over, seized the edge of the bowl with his teeth, and then flipped the bowl over his head. The milky liquid drenched him. A second Indian escaped without a drop touching him. After a third had spattered himself and also several kibitzers, Jim stepped forward. Whoops of laughter woke some who had dozed off in the corners of the house, and all gathered to watch the inexperienced white man. Imitating the Indian stance, Jim clamped his teeth on the lip of the bowl, flung it over his head in a perfect arc, emerging unscathed. '*Pacha!*'—the Quichua equivalent of 'Wow!'— was all that the Indians could say.

Jim's letter continues:

Now, I can hear the rumbles—"What kind of missionary work is that?" Such questions rumbled in me, too. But it is a true fact that this is their death ceremony, and one who did not enter into it would be regarded as impolite and unsympathetic as someone in the USA who didn't go to the funeral and look sober. It is their way of forgetting how sad and cruel and hopeless a thing death is. We build beautiful coffins and send flowers and light candles, and put on our dark suits. They play games and sit up all night and sip *wayusa*.

They came on Saturday morning to ask if they could bury the baby under our school house; they would have had to abandon their house if they had buried it there. I was just about to nail the lid on the coffin when the mother told me to wait, and came with a bit of banana and manioc, a broken mirror, and some water to put in the rough little box. They buried it with its head toward sunset, so as to rise feet first on Judgment Morning to face the sun. And an hour later it was all over, forgotten in the excitement of the plane's coming in.

That wholesome weariness is on me now. As I sit down I can feel my legs warm and tingling-tired in the muscles. After the meeting this morning we went with two Indians upriver to the place they call The Valley. Several families have summer homes up there, where game is more plentiful. We had heard of sickness there, and, since no missionary has ever visited the place, so far as we know, we decided to take a look. It was altogether worth the looking. The Atun Yaku narrows and runs glassy below forest-capped two-hundred-foot cliffs, breaking in spewing rapids over outcrops of native granite bedrock, winding back into the uninhabited and mist-shrouded foothills of the Andes. We took our own lunch: lemons and sugar for lemonade, a few peices of *huriju* (a jungle partridge we bought yesterday), a bit of chocolate and cheese and a hard-boiled egg apiece. We ate that at the first house we visited in The Valley; the Indians had gone elsewhere. Then every succeeding visit brought us favours in food—milky chicha (yes, we drink the chewed stuff, and today even had some that was noticeably spiked), a tender bit of tapir shoulder (the best meat I've had while here), manioc, and steamed green bananas. Back home to bean soup after four river-crossings and a brief swim.

November 20. The work here is not going at a ripping pace. A couple of schoolboys have quit; the language suffers from the constant interruptions, correspondence lags, and visitation is not effective yet becasue we have only a smattering of Quichua. A visit from Arajune Indians yesterday made me long to travel in that area, and a visit last Lord's Day to Iluculin fanned the interest we had of a visit upriver to the gorge.

In a letter to me dated November 25:

You ask if I am speaking Quichua. No, I don't even understand it yet. The few words and phrases that I have memorised are a bare defence in any conversation. I can contribute nothing. But what can I do? This morning after devotions with the schoolboys I came in to study. Then it occurred to me that one of the men whom I had sent to cut bamboo for the clinic ought to be put on mowing the airstrip. By 9.10 or so, the grass is dry enough to cut, so I went out to break in a man on the lawn-mower. I hadn't been with him ten minutes when Pete shouted down the strip that someone had been bitten by a snake. The father took us upriver for twenty minutes; we found his twelve-year-old daughter lying quietly on a cane bed. The bite was already an hour or more old, and no blood had come out at all. I jammed a clean blade on to the scalpel and slit the fanged heel three times before the girl began to cry, "He's killing me", and I had to stop cutting because of public pressure. Pete read the snake-bite-kit instructions while I tried to work the suction syringe, but it made her scream, so I settled for pressure with one hand while keeping the slits open with wet cotton with the other. She bled slowly until about eleven-thirty, when there was nothing to do but give homeopathic *Crotalus horridus* and go home. We haven't heard how she is. But that cuts down a man's study time.

His next to me, of December 2, says:

I strongly sense the rightness of God's leading you and me as he has, Bett. I could not be doing now what I am doing and needing to do (such things as letting Indians invade the bedroom anytime we're here) if I were a family man. As it is, I feel we are making contacts and friends on such a level as is most advantageous for the future of our work here, playing and sharing with the Indians in a way I could not have time for if I were married. It is temporary. I, like you, don't feel a plastic tablecloth is for life, but in our present circumstances, there is nothing else, and we gain by having a table the Indians can touch with muddy hands. Newspapers line my three boxes of clothes, and I don't believe I would put up with boxes in a *home*, but would build some closeable shelf-and-drawer system. I was struck with the verse you wrote on the flyleaf of my gift copy of *Toward Jerusalem:* "Thy statutes have been my songs in the house of my pilgrimage."[8] That is what all houses are, and I feel it keenly about this one.

Thanksgiving passed with little more than a tremor of festivity. We had that can of salmon you sent for the evening meal, and a can of prunes for desert.

December 4. Somehow, this month especially with its rush of pressures, I have felt lost without you, Bett; felt like the world was going by in a whirl of wonder and I was dazedly letting it go by, in body participating, but somehow the "me" standing apart looking for something that didn't show in all the wonder, and aware that that something was you. It all goes over my head, it seems, and I go through the motions of keeping in the tide; however, if anyone were watching closely he would know, by the quiet sigh in a rowdy game of volleyball, the far-away glance upriver and over the tree-tops, from mid-current to the clouds away off to the west, and by the sudden creaking in our moonlit room as I roll to the other side of the narrow cot in an attempt to terminate a longing flight of imagination—he would know that I was not really all there where I seemed to be. Oh, what an ache wanting you can bring, when I know that the wanting itself is good, right, even God-granted, but realise that now it is wisely God-denied, and that He has not let me know all the wisdom of the denial. But I believe, and it is this that lets the living go on—the volley-ball, the swimming, and the sleeping, and keeps my arms moving and my lips making sounds while the most of me is with you.

Your picture has been a great help. It depicts you as I like to think of you—longly moulded, with clear, quiet eyes. It often speaks peace to a strong emotion in me, lending an antiquity to my thoughts, an old knowledge, a white-headed patience, as it brings back the dark oak chest of drawers in the dingy apartment in Chester where it stood, or the bird's-eye maple at home, the night stand at Cevallos' in Quito, the dozens of times, looking up sideways from a suitcase, it has surprised me. The picture makes it seem as if it has been forever with us, through everything—the way it is now, and seems to say: "Take it easy, Jim; we are not through the story yet, and you have no basis for believing it will turn out a tragedy." Still I do, Betty, I do fear sometimes, like a worrying mother, that something will happen to you and I will lose you, and then what would I do, where would I be when I wasn't where I seemed to be? Where would my imagination go when I went to sleep? There could be nothing else in life like this for me. Funny, but I never think of *my* having the accident and your losing me!

To his parents on December 18 Jim wrote:

Your day-dreaming about coming to South America is no joke. The rate on an Ecuadorian airline from Miami to Quito is something under a hundred dollars. So don't lose your daydreams. "Nothing is too good to be: so believe, believe to see."[9] In my own experience I have found that the most extravagant dreams of boyhood have not surpassed the great experience of being in the Will of God, and I believe that nothing could be better. That is not to say that I do not want other things, and other ways of living, and other places to see, but in my right mind I know that my hopes and plans for myself could not be any better than He has arranged and fulfilled them. Thus may we all find it, and know the truth of the Word which says, "He will be our guide even until death."[10]

That same afternoon Jim wrote in his journal:

The house is full of workmen. Pete is selling in the bodega, the doctor is sharpening a plane. I just stepped here into the bedroom to think a moment, about what we're doing here, about progress, about hopes and prospects. O God, life is slow, for all the action it holds. The clinic work lags, not half a wall finished this whole morning. The widening of the airstrip mouth moves so slackly with such a few men, the language hardly seems more intelligible today than it did three months ago, at least in the lips of many Indians. Betty seems so far away.

What shall I say, Lord? That I am dissatisfied, not pleased with the way You have led me? Almost I would say it. Why cannot I shout orders to the workmen, urge on the projects, press ahead with the language, hasten marriage? The pattern of life thus in the Will seems to drag, to wait for the nothing that happens, to push quietly up like trees, and to eat slowly away, and the clouds like slugs ooze over the fixed sky. It would not be happier otherwise, I suppose, but it seems discouraging this hot after-noon.

Notes

1. Deuteronomy 6:23, 7:9.
2. The missionary radio station in Quito, known as 'The Voice of the Andes'.
3. Source unknown.
4. RSV.
5. Matthew 9:36, para.
6. Mark 6:7.
7. Psalm 48:14, para.
8. Psalm 119:54.
9. From the poem 'Not in Vain' by Amy Carmichael, in *Made in the Pans* (London: Oliphants, Ltd., 1918), p. 130.
10. Psalm 48:14.

— 21 —

Three Challenges to Faith

This is no accident—it happens to prove your faith, which is infinitely more valuable than gold, and gold, as you know, even though it is ultimately perishable, must be purified by fire.[1]

ON THE NIGHT OF January 29, 1953, I was sitting as usual at a little card table in a thatch-roofed house in the western jungle, working over my Colorado language notes. Suddenly the sound of horse's hoofs broke through the clicking, singing, rattling, and buzzing of the night noises. I took the lantern outside, and was greeted by a friend from a village about eight miles away. He handed me a telegram. Jim was waiting for me in Quito.

The next day I went by horseback to Santo Domingo de los Colorados, and the following day, after ten hours in a banana truck, climbing the nine thousand feet to reach the Inter-Andean plain, arrived in Quito.

Jim's next letter to his parents was written from the Tidmarsh house in Quito on February 1:

I left the doctor with Peter in Shandia on Thursday afternoon and came up with Gwen in their Dodge on Friday. I am enjoying the change, and the time with Ed McCully (who had just arrived in Ecuador) and Betty immensely. You will understand this better when I tell you that I gave Betty an engagement

248

ring last night in front of a fireplace. It was a thing settled for me months ago, that I should become engaged, and only needed the opportunity for us to be together and her for to say yes. She did. I wanted to give her the ring for her birthday, the twenty-first of December, but, not wanting to leave Pete alone in Shandia since Dr Tidmarsh was here in Quito, I had to wait forty days and forty nights to pose the query. I think I have the Will of God in this. It has certainly not been done in a hurry, and the rest He has given in the matter since last fall has been a constant witness to the certainty of it.

It was only a week later that the first test of this 'certainty' came to Jim. We were informed that, according to X-rays, I had an active case of tuberculosis. Knowing as well as Jim did that he was called to the Indians of the jungle, I felt that this news spelled the cancellation of our marriage plans, for, even if I should recover, life in the jungle would not be recommended for me. Jim's attitude, however, was unchanged.

His journal records:

If I had any plans, they are not changed. I will marry her in God's time, and it will be the very best for us, even if it means waiting years. God has not led us this far to frustrate us or turn us back, and He knows all about how to handle TB. I don't know what this means. I only know that God is in the generation of the righteous, and guides their steps aright. Beyond His counsel and Will there is no going. I am there now, and want nothing more.

'According to your faith be it unto you.'[2] Jim's was rewarded—a week's further tests showed nothing whatever wrong with my lung.

Returning to the forest this time, Jim was accompanied by Ed McCully, who wanted a little preview of the life he looked forward to. On March 2, Jim's journal continues:

Ed left yesterday after our first ten happy days in the forest together. I am alone with Eladio now. Pete went out with malaria on Wednesday, putting me in close fellowship again with Ed. It is better than ever to be with him, and I almost stand in awe sometimes to think that God has really brought us together. Hurry the rest of our preparation now, Lord, and get us in the language preaching with one another again. With all of this planning and building going on, I will certainly enjoy our dreamed-of itineration in the forests.

Monday a week ago Betty came to the radio and said "It was all a mistake." The TB fears are gone. I wonder if God healed her in those ten days or simply proved our faith by a mistake. Whatever, He has done well, and I bless Him for her health and for my own.

Henri Andi died last Friday afternoon. He began vomiting great mouthfuls of red blood last Monday. Got along OK until Friday, when he vomited again and became exceedingly restless, dangerously so for one so weak. He tossed and wailed and we watched his pulse drop from 104 to 38 and then to nothing. The first man I ever watched die. And so, one day, it will come to me, I kept thinking. I wonder if that little phrase I used to use in preaching is something of a prophecy?—"Are you willing to lie in some native hut to die of a disease American doctors never heard of?" I am still willing, Lord God. Whatever You say shall stand at the time of my end. But oh, I want to live to teach Thy Word. Lord, let me live till I have declared Thy works to this generation.

The widow and mother of the dead man just passed, wailing. There is a desertedness about death here that I never felt elsewhere. It is an end of everything. They broke his flashlight to pieces and threw it in the grave. The wife broke up a big clay family cooking-pot while the mother untied the bamboo walls and let them fall away for burning. And always there is the wailing; half the women hereabouts are too hoarse for speech. Two full nights they played and cried, and they are still at it, though the crowd that followed us with the coffin from the mother's house to his own has mostly dispersed.

Two excerpts from letters to his parents tell of building progress:

March 5. I have been alone since Monday, when the little yellow plane lifted Ed off the brow of the cliff over the river and left me standing in a knot of Indians. He had come down to discuss the new house-site. Since he left I have laid out the foundation, and today lined up the first two forms for concrete posts. Since we are short of planks we will probably make two or three at a time and let them set and then re-use the forms. Slow, but so is everything here.

March 15. I have eight pillars poured for the new house, and intend to set up forms and pour again tomorrow. Sure could use some help on this building deal, Dad, but I suppose it would be all over by the time you could get papers straight to come. Well, I need and appreciate the experience, so the time is not all being lost.

To me he wrote:

I cannot see beyond concrete and nails and planks these days. I keep hoping some miracle will happen, something will upset our plans, even our hopes for the work, like a carpenter coming to do the building, and freeing me now to travel. Anything that would get me doing something besides building houses for other peole. But yet I feel, Betts, that no one else can do it who is now on the field, and that God has put me here for it—personal likes and dislikes aside. It's strange, but I both hope for and dread some cataclysmic upset that would bring you and me together. I feel now that it would have to be that, with things so well-formulated and going along so nicely.

I can hear the chariots of Thor rolling far away into the east, and the sound of rain is refreshing. It was hot today and I could hardly force myself to pour concrete into two pillar forms I did not get finished yesterday. I used up all the water in the rain-barrel, so I hope I get enough to mix concrete again day after tomorrow. I poured and mixed alone today as all the workmen were out in the forest dragging in the girders for the sub-floor. It is hard work, and now I am ready for bed.

Jim had been in a Quichua environment for just over six months when he wrote:

It is a great joy to be having little meetings in Quichua now, although admittedly, my Quichua is plenty poor. This morning I took the parable in Luke 14 of the folk who rejected the invitation to the feast, and it was a delight to see comprehension on the faces of some. Oh, pray that God would give us souls for Christ from this jungle, and that we may rejoice together in that day for men and women of this tribe who have believed through our word and your prayers. For we know now, if we knew only in theory before, that "except the Lord build the house, they labour in vain that build it".[3] Nothing can change the heart of this people but the Spirit of the Life-Giver Himself, and it is to Him we cry in our mute helplessness in this language.

The diary continues:

April 12. Struggling desperately with Quichua, and feel we gained ground in a solid week's listening and studying and trying to speak at the conference in Dos Rios. There was no real stirring. Illustration of the truth is no substitute for a statement of the truth; a story will not suffice where a sermon fails. Again it is the exhortation and stern warning to believe without sufficient statement of what is to be believed. But the statement of the truth is regarded as "too deep", too difficult to express in Quichua, which is such a simplified language. Still, it is better to try to make them understand, in order that they may know what they are rejecting, than it is, by pressing the acceptance more than the understanding, to allow them to accept something they do not understand.

Was touched at the Mishahaullí River after the conference, as the believing Indians came to the river's edge to say goodbye. I was startled to find two of the girls, the cripple Serafina and Christina, taking my two hands and leading me before the rest of the group to the river, and saying, "In every prayer we make we will pray for you."

On April 19, Jim's letter to his parents told of more building problems:

The Indians tell us that the rainy season has set in. It has held us up every day this past week, with rains every morning, and clearing only a little in the afternoon. This enables us to hoist around and notch one of the seven girders we have set on our concrete posts for the new house. Three remain for next week before we can level off and set in joists, for which, because of the young moon, we must wait. The cutters refuse to cut trees in the new moon and we won't have much hope of joists for a couple of weeks—more if the rains keep up steadily. The river is running brimful these days.

To me he wrote:

We poured a little more than half of the concrete slab for the breezeway this morning—arduous and patience-claiming work when done with Indians who have never seen a slab poured and do not take well to mixing sand with a shovel.

We have been very much encouraged—through reading a book that deals with examples of apostolic missionary methods—to believe again for some sort of New Testament pattern to be worked out among forest Quichuas. How false and fleshly to reason that God will do a work here "because Pete, Ed, and Jim are trained, capable, young, and strong"! I have been much impressed lately of the *absolute* necessity of God *Himself* rousing the conscience. I do not know how, nor even where, to begin to make a man think seriously about sin and judgment, and must look to the work of the Holy Spirit for the beginning move toward any hint of such a working. And pray that it will be so here, Betts, that God would take this work in hand, and do it ON HIS OWN LINES. To see Christ honoured and testified to publicly by one of these young Indian fellows we now know as friends would be something like seeing a miracle before my very eyes. Indeed, it would be a miracle, but I have never realised this fact so clearly as now. God must do His work, or it will not be done, and we stand waiting for Him here.

From the journal:

April 27. **Struggling** to maintain real faith for the genuine conversion of adult Indians and for confession on the part of schoolboys. Concerned lest my faith not be of the believing sort, for there are fears connected with it—fears of failure in our work here. Reasoning, "what if we don't get converts; what then of New Testament principles of church order? What then of teaching the Bible study method and memorisation, translation seminars and Book Study retreats with young men?" O Christ, I want this speaking-to-a-mountain faith, this faith that is bold, publicly, for God.

In May Jim went out to Quito to attend the Inter-Mission Fellowship conference and to see me again. We spent a happy two weeks shopping for materials for the buildings in Shandia, and visiting friends, and finally went down to the station in the west jungle where I was working. Of his trip back to Quito on a banana truck Jim wrote to me:

Of all trips I have made, it was the most difficult, and, for its length, way and above the most expensive. We hadn't gotten much past town when the gas-pump was full of water. At kilometre 106 we had a flat that held us up in repair until three o'clock. From there to Chiriboga the thing averaged the aching pace of five miles an hour. We arrived at the chain at nine pm and the guard refused to let us pass. Finally after a miserable snooze in the cab I persuaded him to lower the chain at five am. The *chofer* then encouraged me to take another truck because he was not sure his could make Quito. So I went to get my bag and discovered that it had been stolen. In the long, slow grind up to Chiriboga the conductor had come into the cab because of rain. Evidently someone had hopped on the cargo bed and thrown off my bag with other baskets belonging to passengers, while we were all huddled thoughtlessly in the front. Keep your eyes open for a green tarp, a seventy-dollar camera, light-meter, harmonica, all my coloured slides, boots, nylon shirts and wool slacks. Tell all the señoritas in San Miguel that their letters will have to be re-written and posted by someone more reliable than I. . . . The Lord gave me a victory in the loss, reminding me to be thankful for the abundance of possessions I have had. God knows, and I believe He sent this that I might be weaned more and more from things material—even good, legitimate things —and have my affections set more firmly on Him whom to possess is to have everything. Who could ask for more?

The journal continues:

June 14. This may become known as the season of the big flood. It started a week ago nearly, and has rained for five days and nights. Day before yesterday we noticed several large slides on the cliff wall downriver, and in anticipation of a possible sudden rise we tied the motor-house base and the generator to a rope and knotted it to the orange tree in front of this house. This morning at breakfast the Napo was plainly heading for a rampage. We went down to the coffee grove below the new house to watch the slides eat away the trail and the forest on the east bend. It crested between ten am and noon. The motor platform and generator are now dangling on the rope over a sheer wall. The new house, once thirty yards from the cliff, is now a bare fifteen. The trail is completely gone. The river was frantic and huge—gnawing off great chunks of earth and stone and forest, and growling deep in its guts as it churned up the stones. A fearful thing to see, especially when one is so close to it. I am about fifteen yards from the brink myself now as I write, and although the crest has passed for the present, the island is still far from the shore. Skinned flotsam lies crashed against the trees down low, and tons more are rolling by, on the mud-gone-greenish water. The problem is: shall we go on building the new house, with the expensive fixtures, aluminium and all, with the chance of a sudden repetition of today's show? The Indians intimate that it hasn't been like this for thirty years, but who knows when it will come again? Only God, whose voice is upon many waters. And He will show us His will and power.

To me, on June 17, Jim wrote of their decision:

Ed and Marilou have decided to move everything—taking

down all we have done; moving the cement pillars and all one hundred yards back. It was a terrific struggle for them to decide. Moving will probably hold us up another two months in the work schedule, but the discouraging part is tearing down all our work. Still, I have heard the voice of the Lord and am glad to do here as He is directing.

July 12 brought this word of progress:

We have been slowed considerably by the rains. All the postholes are full of water and working the posts into line is almost impossible in such mud. But we only have two more rows to go, and should have the girders up by the end of this week, if we get even three or four good days. But I can't get heart for this rebuilding job, somehow. It is not satisfying to me—such as finishing the steps was the first time—and I fear the workmanship is second-rate because of it; posts out of line, and not perfectly vertical, etc. And to think we must start a teacher's house next!

His letter to me a few days later says:

Tried to get some work done on the house this morning, but was rained in, and with all the stir this afternoon I don't suppose I'll get anything more done, either. It all seems so secondary, darling; so unimportant in comparison with what I want to be doing. Houses, exams, and all this has nothing to do with our love, and that is what possesses me these days.

That same afternoon, Jim wrote this prayer in his diary:

Lord God and Father, I call upon Thee to enter all the avenues of my life today, and to share every detail of it with me, even as Thou hast called me to share with Thee Thy life, and all the wonders of it. As I am to share the destiny, glory, and future affairs of Thy Son, so would I now have Him share this small destiny of earth which is mine, the joys of it, and all its small matters, that we should be one, Thou and I, even as we are in Christ.

The very night of this committal of heart, God brought about the 'cataclysmic event' which Jim had both hoped for and dreaded. Rains which had been more or less continual for a week became torrential, and fell relentlessly for thirty-six hours. The following afternoon, as I stood by the radio in Dos Rios, the jungle station six hours' walk from Shandia where I had begun the study of Quichua, I heard Jim's voice from Shandia:

> The brink of the cliff is only five yards from the house now. The river is still eating away the base of the cliff, and if you hear nothing from us at two o'clock you'll know we have had to abandon the house.

Two o'clock brought silence. So did the next two days. Though I tried to get an Indian runner to go to Shandia to find out what had happened, all said that the rivers would be impassable, and they would not attempt the journey. Finally an Indian consented to go, and brought back this letter from Jim:

August 1, Saturday. Shandia is no more. This is being written beside a fire outside with a dozen Indians looking on and telling me what to write. The first house went about 3.30 pm on Thursday, and we have spent the rest of the time moving our stuff away from the river, except for last night when we slept the whole night with about thirty Indians under one roof. Most of the stuff is here now, under temporary shelters, though the heavier items—barrels, motor, refrigerator, etc.—are at various points in the forest (we hope that they are out of the reach of the flood). Most of our stuff was saved, thanks to the invaluable help of all the Indians, though we have lost a little through thievery. We lost the boards we tore from the houses because the Indians were just too weary to pack them away from the river. The school went about midnight, and the school kitchen in early hours yesterday. Clinic and our Indian kitchen went late in the afternoon. Will you please send this telegram to Mr K. L.

Fleming, 1403 Tenth Avenue West, Seattle:

"FLOOD DESTROYED SHANDIA. SAVED STUFF. ALL WELL. INFORM PORTLAND. LOVE PETE."

We will try to get our tent up today and get housekeeping underway again soon. It was so thoughtful of you to send bread. We found some butter and honey and had chicken soup for supper—the first good meal in thirty-six hours—last night. Sorry I could not inform you sooner, but we were busy, carrying stuff the very moment your carrier arrived, and I had no idea where pen or paper were until last night. The new house is near the brink and we lost about one-eighth of the airstrip. I don't know if they will dare land or not. If they do, we need aerial wire for the radio. It was not well guarded by the Indians charged with taking care of it. Breakfast is on the fire and a beautiful dawn is breaking through the forest. We are both well and happy, and waiting on God to show us His Will for this station.

The waters have not quenched love. I do not know what this will mean for us. Housing here seems almost stupid now, and Ed and Marilou cannot come in for some time together. Still, in all the rain and mud and mess and sense of loss, I loved you strongly, and wished for some reason that you were here—I do not know why, for we could not have had a moment together. We have loads of invitations from Indians to stay in their homes, and our cookboy is doing well with what he can find in all the damp tangle of our possessions. We are doing very well, and should be getting settled, organised, stored, and dried out in the next few days. I see no hope for school here in October. We must use part of the foundation of Ed's house for smaller living quarters. The mush is cooked. All for now. Ever your own, Jim.

Upon receipt of this letter I left Dos Rios immediately with a group of Indians, to help in any way possible in Shandia. Arriving there the next day, Sunday, I was able to piece together more of the details in conversation with Indians who had been at the scene of the flood.

While I and others had been waiting at the radio on Thursday, hoping that Jim and Pete would manage to get their radio functioning again in another building, they were frantically throwing their possessions into kerosene-can boxes (which are the principal items of furniture in many a jungle home). These, in turn, were thrust into the arms of waiting Indians who had collected as they heard the thunder of the cliff's caving in. The loose stuff taken care of, they made a desperate effort to save some of the timbers of the house, which were of an imperishable wood, difficult to find in the forests. The entire inside of the house was dismantled, and Jim was just ripping the screens out of the kitchen windows when, with a wrench and a crack, the front porch dropped out of sight into the river. Jim decided it was time to get out.

The next thirty-six hours were spent in the kind of downpour that can be visualised only by one who knows tropical rainy-season rain. Ed and Marilou's steel barrels—eleven of them, which had been shipped into Shandia in advance of their coming—were rolled through trailless forest. (The trails had long since gone over the cliff along with the house.) An eight-cubic-foot refrigerator was dragged, with the aid of two boards acting as runners, through the mud and underbrush. Boxes of clothes, food, papers, valuable language materials, medical supplies—completely soaked through—and heavy tools, were hauled from place to place. It had hardly become dark when Jim—plunging through the jungle, trying to keep track of the things and the places where the Indians were dumping them—lost his shoes in the mud. There is a species of palm in this area which has, growing thickly up the length of its trunk, thorns two to four inches long. These lie scattered about in the forest, along with strong bamboo spikes which will pierce even shoe soles. The condition of Jim's feet, after twelve hours spent barefoot in this kind of terrain, in the dark, need not be described.

Each time that Jim and Pete felt that they had managed to get the equipment to spots where it would be beyond the reach of the disintegrating cliff, a cry of alarm would go up from someone stationed near the brink, and things would have to be moved again. In the morning the newest building which they had completed—the clinic—was in danger. In order to try to save the roof-leaf, which is scarce wherever Indians have been building houses, Jim tied a rope around the building, and, with the help of a number of Indians, pulled the clinic over. It lay on its side nearly on the edge of the cliff, and in order to release the rope Jim went around between the building and the cliff. Suddenly there was a roar, and all but the bit of earth on which he stood fell away behind him. The Indians, hidden from view by the thatched roof, shouted 'He dies!' But Jim yelled back 'I live! Pass me a machete *fast*.' They thrust one through the thatch and he chopped his way to safety before the rest of his foothold gave way.

Jim's next journal entry was August 15:

Two weeks have passed since I last wrote, and those two weeks have made me older. The day I wrote that prayer on the other page, the Atun Yaku wiped out Shandia. Week-end was a weary one, brightened only by Betty's coming here on Sunday. Then it was the job of collecting all the stuff, sorting it, drying it, storing it somewhere. Ed came on Tuesday, and we discussed the Will of God and talked, planned and discarded plans. Then, more sorting, saving, and throwing out. It rained that week-end and took some more off the cliff, leaving the newly-moved foundation useless, forcing us to alter our plans again. Tuesday we took off the girders of the foundation and in the night I got my first touch of malaria. Ed and Pete left Wednesday morning and I spent the day in chills, fever and utter weakness and quite a lot of pain. Managed to get the girders laid for the storage house half-way down the airstrip. That night I saw the luminous dial on my watch flash as I rolled over and read every hour from midnight to five. Dizziness and headache were constant, with total loss of appetite for everything but lemonade (which, in view of the gallons I have drunk to cool and fill and satisfy me these three days, I regard as a rich mercy from God; there is a teapot on the desk now about a third full).

Dr Tidmarsh left with Nate this afternoon. At supper the mental symptoms of malaria reached their pitch. With the cessation of any physical work (all I could do, anyhow, was sit and tell the men what to do) the mind works overtime. My thoughts were awful. I did not know I loved Betty. I could not sustain two sentences of prayer. I talked impatiently to the workmen. It was terrible. Slept from eight till midnight. Such a twisting serpentine mass of wretched and uncontrolled ideas I never thought the mind capable of, especially as I knelt in prayer. God forgive me. (Pardoned. Just took it in faith.)

Now it is cool and growing later than my recent early bedtimes. I may sleep tonight if I stay up a little longer. The wall studs, door, windows, and roof slats, with part of the aluminium, are on the storage house. By the great kindness of God I am feeling stronger and enjoying good food. Tonight it was raw carrots, tomatoes, lettuce, and cauliflower (a salad plate!) with a little home-made vinegar, vegetable soup and a snatch of chocolate cake from Shell Mera. God be praised. This is a good night in what used to be Shandia.

August 16. Not much better today. Had a meeting of some thirty Indians in the morning air (no buildings to have it in). Luis and Lucas preached. First time I ever heard an Indian preach the Resurrection the way it should be preached. Sickly and weak. Gave medical treatment to some folk, and folded laundry, in the kitchen. The tent was too hot to rest in this afternoon. Bathed leisurely and alone in the Talac river. First time I've felt I could walk that far in a while.

This came to me as I was sitting on the cliff after a light supper of manioc, raw carrots, and tea:

Because, O God, from Thee comes all, because from Thine own mouth has entered us the power to breathe, from Thee the sea of air in which we swim and the unknown nothingness that stays it over us with unseen bands; because Thou gavest us from heart of love so tender, mind so wise and hand so strong, Salvation; because Thou art Beginning, God, I worship Thee.

Because Thou art the end of every way, the goal of man; because to Thee shall come of every people respect and praise; their emissaries find Thy throne their destiny; because Ethiopia shall stretch out her hands to Thee, babes sing Thy praise; because Thine altar gives to sparrows shelter, sinners peace, and devils fury; because "to Thee shall all flesh come",[4] because Thou art Omega, praise.

Because Thou art surely set to justify that Son of Thine and wilt in time make known just who He is and soon will send Him back to show Himself; because the Name of Jesus has been laughingly nailed upon a cross and is even now on earth held very lightly and Thou wilt bring that Name to light; because, O God of Righteousness, Thou wilt do right by my Lord, Jesus Christ, I worship Thee.

Counsel with Pete, Ed, and Dr Tidmarsh led to a decision to make their first itinerary in the jungle, to spy out the southern area of the Quichua tribe in case God should be indicating, by the destruction of Shandia, that another location should be sought. I was asked to stay in the tent in Shandia while the men were away, in order to guard the stores of valuable equipment which were protected only by aluminium sheets set up on poles.

For three weeks the three men— Pete, Jim, Ed— travelled on foot and by canoe, visiting the Indians on the shores of the Bobonaza river, estimating the population and evaluating the possibilities for opening new stations.

Twenty-one days of scorching sun, of solid sheets of rain, and of sore muscles caused by the back-breaking position necessary in a dugout canoe gave the men a fair introduction to the itineration they had looked forward to. Jim and Ed soon got 'jungle rot', a softening and sloughing of the soles of the feet owing to prolonged wetness.

Despite what one finds in the adventure stories, the traveller on jungle rivers rarely sees anything exciting. Wildlife is extremely wary, and the knocking of the canoe poles and intermittent shouting of the *popero* (whose responsibility it is to choose the course) provides sufficient warning for any creature which might otherwise be visible from the river. The heavy growth of the jungle hangs out over the water, trailing lianas into its dark depths. Occasionally a fish flips on the surface and a flock of parrots flashes across the sky with strident screech. The odd *dumbiki*, or toucan, looking like a jet plane with its long beak and tail of equal length, flaps overhead, uttering its single-noted cry. However, for the most part the sameness of the river and its jungle borders is unbroken, and the one who sees a tapir or alligator is fortunate indeed.

Ten days of slow, arm-wrenching poling brought the canoes with their three 'gringos' back to Canelos, and from there they returned on foot to Shell Mera, confident that God had a purpose for the many Quichuas they had visited.

When Jim returned to Shandia he told me of the most promising spot that they had visited—the juncture of the Pastaza and Puyo rivers, where lived Atanasio, an Indian with fifteen children who had begged the men to come and live among them and establish a school. This plea, the first of its kind that the men had heard from Indians, was not to be lightly refused. Ordinarily the problems of winning friendship and establishing residence in a new location are great enough in themselves to require a long period of time. Here, these would be entirely obviated. The men agreed unanimously that they must accept Atanasio's invitation.

Ed felt that if they were to begin the study of Quichua then he and Marilou should not have the added responsibilities of opening a new work. So he decided to settle temporarily in Shandia, living in a simple split-bamboo house. The help of one of the unmarried men would be needed in the language as well as in the running of the station. Who, then, could enter Puyupungu? The answer seemed obvious to all three men.

'So,' said Jim to me as he told me of it, 'how soon will you marry me?'

Notes

1. 1 Peter 1:7, JBP.
2. Matthew 9:29.
3. Psalm 127:1.
4. Psalm 65:2.

— 22 —

Lo, This Is Our God

And it shall be said in that day, Lo, this is our God, we have waited for Him.[1]

ONE OF THE THINGS on which Jim and I had agreed years before was that a conventional wedding could never be for us. I, like most women, enjoyed attending them, but could not imagine myself in such a setting. Jim, on the other hand, held them in disdain, as a page from his journal of 1949 reveals:

Twentieth-century Christian weddings are the vainest, most meaningless forms. There is no vestige of reality. The witnesses dress for a show. The flesh is given all the place. The songs are absurd, if one paid any attention to the words, but no one does; they simply listen to *how* it is sung, not what it means. Candles are useless but expensive trifles. Ushers help no one, but appear very officious and the ceremony itself is the most meaningless hodge-podge of obsolete grammar and phraseology—sounds like a schoolboy's translation of something from Cicero. And the stupid form of asking who gives this bride in marriage. Who cares? Everyone knows it is her father or uncle or some such sweating pawn standing before the altar. Talk of Romanism! We Fundamentalists are a pack of mood-loving show-offs. I'm sure the minor prophets would have found subject for correction in this affair. I must read this to myself on my wedding day (if I have one!).

I do not think he remembered to read it. If he had, I am sure he would have smiled at his own vehemence, for he had matured in those four years. Maturity, however, had brought him no love for show. This is his comment on a newspaper account of a wedding which took place a few months before our own:

> For me, "heavy ivory satin... fitted bodice designed off-shoulder effect... embroidery, iridescent sequins... tiara of rhine-stones"... long aisles, tears and sniffling, waiters in white coats do not amount to a sublime event. It is no more than an expensive tedium with little remembrance value. There is something in me that resists the showy part of weddings with a passion I have against few other things in life, as I cannot abide a puny man who boasts of his achievements and cannot stand behind his words.

We decided on a civil ceremony on October 8, Jim's twenty-sixth birthday, and Jim wrote to his parents of our intention on October 3:

> Nobody can accuse us of rushing things just because we have decided to get married in less than three weeks—we have been in love for over five years and I think considered the Will of God in marriage as carefully as anyone could, except maybe Dad.... No one really understands our wanting only a civil wedding, but we are going ahead, believing that God is our leader and judge of our motives. Our wedding is not the first thing she and I have braved public opinion on. Few have really tried to understand our long waiting for engagement and my going to the jungle single. Few really thought we were the "perfect match" in the first place. To me the words and worries of the rest matter not at all. It has been a long lesson learning to live only before God, and letting Him teach the conscience and to fear nothing save missing His Will. But we are learning, and I would live no other way. I want always to say with the apostle, "God is my judge."[2]

It had been a 'long lesson' indeed—from the days of studying Thucydides together, through the months of silence, then correspondence; the days at Mt Hood and the Oregon coast; years of uncertainty about the mission field; subsequent guidance and assurance; then Ecuador; climbing Pichincha; noon meals at the Arias home; separation to the east and west jungles; Quito again, and engagement; separation again; the flood in July; the Bobonaza trip in August... and then October 8, 1953.

'They shall not be ashamed that wait for Me.' [3] We were married without fuss at the Registro Civil in Quito. It was a delightfully simple ten minutes—a dingy, high-ceilinged room in an antique colonial building; a suitably solemn official who read, in rapid monotone, several pages of Spanish, punctuated here and there by our 'si'. Dr and Mrs Tidmarsh, our official witnesses, were the only ones present beside the McCullys. We signed our names in an immense ledger, and were man and wife.

'Delight thyself also in the Lord, and He shall give thee the desire of thine heart.' [4] God had given us that desire, and perhaps in the sense in which Jim had interpreted it in a letter to me written in 1949:

> It does not say He will give you what you want. It does say He will give you *the want*. Delight in Christ brings desire for Christ. He gives the heart its desires—that is, He works in us the willing (Philippians 2:13). This is why He can say in John 15:7, "Ye shall ask what ye will... if ye abide." The branch takes its sap from the vine, the same surges the vine feels then become the surges of the branch. My will becomes His, and I can ask what I will, if I delight myself in Him. Only then can my desire be attained, when *it is His desire*.

After a honeymoon in Panama and Costa Rica we returned to Quito to pack equipment for the move into Puyupungu. Surrounded by boxes and barrels, Jim found a few minutes to write to his parents, the first letter following the wedding, dated October 28:

> Betty and I are extremely happy now, sharing all that we are and have. Just now we are staying in the *bodega*, a house that all of us rent to keep our things in, and half of our missionary staff is in Quito now, so we are having a fight getting things packed for going to Puyupungu. In Shandia we used only a very small part of the stuff I brought from the States, so that now, returning from the honeymoon and opening up the barrels and crates again is just like starting out with new wedding gifts. Together we really have a wonderful collection of stainless steel ware, pots and utensils. I am sitting beside a small drum which Betty is packing full of it now, really a lot of fun.
>
> We got back from Panama Sunday; each room in the hotel had its own balcony, and ours looked right out over the Pacific.

The employees of the hotel were mostly bilingual, and Jim and I had amused ourselves noticing how they seemed to know which language to speak to each patron. Jim decided that he would try to trip them up. Approaching the cigar counter one morning, he was greeted by a polite 'Good morning, sir.'

'Ay would laik wan rroll of teerty-fa-eeve meeleemeter feelm,' he said, in his nearly perfect imitation of a Latin speaking English.

'*Muy bien, señor*,' was the quick reply.

I of course was taken completely by surprise, but succeeded in maintaining my equilibrium till we were on the elevator. I realised that I was now the *wife* of this unpredictable man, and that I must identify with him.

The letter to Jim's parents continues:

> After a week there we took a plane to San José, Costa Rica, where we dropped in on Dave[5] and Phyl, right in the middle of Spanish classes. They had not even known we were married, let alone that we would be coming to see them.

We gaped and gawked at the store windows like a couple of palm-leaf savages, both in Panama and Costa Rica. They are both progressive countries.

With our things well packed in steel drums and boxes lined with waterproof paper, we left Quito at the end of October and flew to Shell Mera, where we spent the night with Nate and Marj Saint at the Missionary Aviation Fellowship headquarters. Next morning, Nate drove us to the last town on the road, Puyo by name, where Jim had arranged for canoes to meet us. Our gear was loaded in, and we started down the Puyo river toward our new home, Puyupungu.

In the late afternoon, as the sun slanted down behind our backs, a hoot was heard below us, and Atanasio, the head man from Puyupungu, hove into sight with several canoes full of friends. They hailed Jim heartily, and said,

'So you are a word-fulfiller!'

There was much back-slapping and laughter, and we proceeded on downriver together till we reached the mouth of the river, where it empties into the mighty Pastaza. High on the bank stood Atanasio's family—two wives, and a veritable battalion of children, peering shyly down through the trees. As the canoes scraped the sandy beach, all came running down the steep trail, and soon had our gear—a tiny iron stove, a steel trunk, folding bed, assorted boxes and drums, and a tent—carried up the cliff and deposited in a little thatched shack where we were to sleep that night. In short order we were supplied with wood, water, fresh eggs, papaya, smoked fish, and plantains. Our welcome was genuine.

We found that the thatched house, while it looked a haven for us that first evening, proved to be the same for the cockroaches. Moreover, neither Jim nor I could stand up straight under the low beams which supported the roof. Within two days Jim had the tent pitched—a sixteen-foot-square one which someone had given him at the last minute before he sailed from California. We did not imagine, when we pitched it, that this would be our home for five months.

Jim had just put up some poles for a tiny kitchen shack outside the tent, and was planning to lay an aluminium roof on it as well as to lay a bamboo floor in the tent, when he succumbed to a fever that we were not able to subdue with the usual malarial drugs. The short-wave radio set we had brought along had seemed rather a civilised luxury to us before this, but now became an essential as I tried to get into contact with a doctor to describe Jim's symptoms. The radio was powered by handcrank, which Jim was too weak to turn, so the difficulty of getting a willing Indian to turn it while I operated the transmitter was added to poor reception, and attempts to communicate were very frustrating experiences.

Jim lay in bed for three weeks, hardly able to lift his head, while the rain ran under the sides of the tent, making a slough of the mud floor, and poured into the wall-less kitchen.

Records in Jim's own words from the time of our marriage until his death are few and sketchy. There are several reasons for this, the first being an obvious one — that he no longer wrote letters to me. Then, other things which, for lack of any other means of expression he had formerly shared only with the journal, he was now able to share with me, thus 'delivering his soul'. Further reasons he wrote to his brother Bob:

Thanks, Bob, for your notes on the "Man" at God's right hand. I am sure my letters from the mission field have contained precious little of this sort of thing and I fear that it is representative of what goes on in my soul a good deal of the time. Some think the life of the jungles tranquil, and indeed if you ask an Ecuadorian why he likes the Oriente, he will tell you it is because of the quiet and easy life. I have not found it so. Occupation with affairs that I never had experience with before, and things arising any minute of the day or night have sapped my study programme of content, and I find myself wondering where passages are that once I had at my fingertips. It is a loss. I don't know how I will ever preach again in English. I have been using the Spanish Bible constantly for over a year, and most of the ministry I have done has been from what little there is of the Scripture in Quichua. It is a struggle even to get in a period of reading, to say nothing of meditation or study. Sometimes one is conscious of spiritual life only because he is still struggling to maintain it, not at all because he is purposefully living it. Pray for my soul. We need no funds here, really, nor more workers. What we need is spiritual power and vigour in the soul. Our enemy wields well his weapons, and his, no less than ours, are spiritual weapons, for the defence of those same strongholds which we are equipped to pull down.

Jim's journal was completely neglected until December 1, when he wrote:

It is not raining at the moment but the fresh-cut bamboo slats are chunked with fresh mud, and the other half of the tent, not yet floored, is slippery gum from an all-night rain on Sunday. We had to get this much of the floor in yesterday and they are supposed to be bringing more bamboo today so perhaps we will be fully floored this week. I am supposed to have had jaundice almost since the day we arrived, November 11, and am still a part-time bed-patient. Betty is out cooking in the kitchen shack while I sit at the card table, decked with an aster-flowered teacloth with a centre-piece of white candle and a graceful-leafed little forest flower set off beautifully in a tin can.

Married life is rich, as I have always known life to be, but richer in its complexity. We have known nothing but harmony. The marriage "adjustment" is something, which if it exists at all, I am going through effortlessly, unconsciously, even. Such is the love we know.

In December Jim and I walked from Puyupungu to Puyo, on our way to Shandia to spend Christmas with the McCullys. The trail was, even by jungle standards, a poor one, being little used by Indians, who had their own canoes for river travel. Densely overgrown in places where it was second-growth jungle, it was wide enough for only a single human foot in most sections. We travelled, of course, in single file. A young Indian boy went with us as guide. He set the quick, steady pace used by Indians, unvarying even on hills or while crossing unstable log bridges. Jim fell in behind him, and I took my place last, according to Indian custom. Women carry the loads (in this, however, we deviated from local practice!), and herd the children along, while the men, carrying nothing but a muzzle-loaded gun or a blow-gun, walk ahead, to watch for game or snakes. As I followed Jim, I noticed again the extraordinary lightness of his movements as he moved along the trail—occasionally leaping over especially deep mud, swinging himself down a bank by a vine, or springing over a fallen tree. There were places where we had to bend double to get through; others, where the guide had to hack a way through a tangle of vines and airplants which had broken a branch with their weight. We waded across rivers, went uphill and down—for the Indian builds a trail, by preference, on the highest ground to provide some drainage. There is little opportunity for enjoying the scenery while on the trail, but when we stopped to eat our lunch Jim commented on the gigantic trees, the delicate moss, the faintly sweet, cool smell of the forest. After some nine hours' walking, we broke out into the sugar-cane country surrounding the frontier town of Puyo, where Marj Saint was waiting in the pick-up truck with four iced 'cokes' and some cake. She drove us to Shell Mera and we flew from there to Shandia.

Jim's next journal entry is dated January 20, 1954:

Spent a holiday in Shandia from December 19 to January 5 with much joy. First young-men's conference went off with not enough prayer nor study, but albeit the blessing of God. Baptised Eugenia Cerda and Carmela Shiwangu in the Talac river on Lord's Day, with great joy and confidence in God. Began work on the airstrip and house site here in Puyupungu, but have been discouraged by rain and slowed by personnel problems. Still, God helps and progress is visible. Not happy altogether with

Lucas as a schoolteacher, but am encouraged with the attention some show to the Word of God. Last night in a little meeting we have on Tuesday, Atanasio said, "I will die in your words." I don't know how much he understands, but he does hear some. Praying for a work of God among the school-children, who now number ten. I may start a literacy class for some young fellows when the house is underway and the airstrip finished.

February 5. Finished the roof of the house and outhouse today. Men wearying some, and dropping off work. Only the Lord is constant and sure. It must be by His grace we have accomplished all that we have this past month, both on airstrip and in the house.

Praying especially for Pablo and Atanasio these days. Oh that God would bring light to their minds and life to their souls. Began literacy class daily with Tito and Benito this week. Tito does well. Perhaps God will give him to me to father in the faith.

April 1. Pause late on a rainy afternoon. Gratefully settled in our home in Puyupungu for a week now. Been a long, but not unendurable five months in the tent. God has been faithful, though Satan has fought us to discouragement through long weeks of rain. Men came from Pano to help, or I would never had gotten the airstrip done by now. Plane landed on three hundred yards of it yesterday, but this end is still too wet for take-off.

April 15 (letter to his brother). You apologise for sending stationery with roses, Bob, thinking we might be all orchidified by now. Wrong. I'd give plenty to get a rose-bush going here. True we have plenty of the lovely big orchids right over the cliff here, and I have made a small hobby out of collecting as many different species as I can find. They bloom only in season, but are a fascinating study. The big kind we get in the States are a developed brand. The one type of big orchid here grows out of the dirt like any wild flower. The last couple of weeks we have been cutting the forest back to lengthen the approach to the airstrip and have found that great, mossgrown trees when cut have an abundance of tiny true airplant orchids. There is a lovely small white one, maybe two inches across, blooming now on a tree growing near the house that we brought in from the forest, but the bloom only lasts a couple of days, even if left on the plant. Another green one a little larger abounds down near the river level on the cliff and has to be gotten at with a canoe. A delicate spider-orchid with long petals from a tiny blossom is one I found on the cut trees.

I bring in the plants and stick them on my orchid garden—a tree by the house here. In all I think I have eight varieties, although some have never bloomed. The bougainvillaea shoots we brought from Shell Mera are doing well and we have a couple dozen pineapple plants stuck in to keep the forest away from the house a bit. This kind of thing keeps a man from going entirely Indian out here. Of course they think it's crazy for anyone to plant flowers, but accept our doing it as one of the crazy things we do and get away with. Vegetable seeds rot in the ground, we find, but I have several vines of a nice wild squash started. It's about six inches long and has a very hard shall, but tastes very like Danish squash....

This is Holy Week and we find that the custom of having some religious festival is a convenient time for us to press home the gospel. We are having meetings every night here and Lucas and I are taking turns ministering on the Seven Words from the Cross, one each night. The Indians are most attentive and Atanasio told me the night before last, that even though he is old, his eyes are beginning to open and he is beginning to understand. He has a real desire to change his ways, but is a habitual drunkard and says he has lived like a burro and a savage till now. We pray earnestly for his conversion. His oldest daughter, who helps us by washing dishes, is not far from the kingdom, we feel. Pray that the family will wholeheartedly accept the kingship of Christ and that the work will spread to the other Indians who live one and two days away, too far for us to reach up until now.

Jim and I were looking forward eagerly to the arrival of his father, who was coming to help with the rebuilding of Shandia, and hoped and prayed that the airstrip would be usable before it was time to go out to meet him. On May 30 Jim wrote:

Both Dad and Pete are here with us now and their presence represents a great deal of answered prayer. Betty and I were able to fly out of Puyupungu on April 21. Met Dad with much thanksgiving at Puná six days later. One week took him and all the construction equipment he brought through Customs. We spent a week in Quito getting teeth fixed, attending the Inter-Mission Conference, and meeting people, coming down by truck to Shell Mera on May 14. Betty came here and I went to Shandia to choose a house site. O God, may it be the right one!

His next letter to Portland tells of progress begun on the new house in Shandia. It was the feeling of the men at that time that at least one of our stations should have a permanent-type house, while places like Puyupungu might serve as outstations. So they took advantage of the help of Jim's father to begin that project.

The boards are planing up fine, and although Dad was having trouble getting the big saw adjusted, I think the main work of preparing lumber ought to be over in a couple of weeks, barring breakdowns. Puyupungu is so nearly finished, and runs on so much smaller and simpler a scale than Shandia that it is a relief to come here after a stay up north. We are finishing the rail fence around the airstrip here now, so that the cows won't tear it to pieces at night, and there is furniture to make yet, but we are mostly finished with the physical plant at this outstation. We still eat from a card table and use folding chairs that I would like to replace with permanent things so we could use these for other outstations.

We said good-bye to Pete last week, as he leaves to go to the States to get married. Baptised six more Indian young people and had our first breaking of bread in Quichua on the previous Lord's Day.

The house site in Shandia is cleared now and we hope to get the cement a-pouring before long. Dad is a great help. . . .

Now my wife is playing on her organ some nice Sunday evening music, and I will try to get this finished. I don't know if I will or not, as the longer she plays the more things seem to go wrong with the organ—there are a total of three keys sticking since she began to play. Another instance of things that are nice to have but difficult to maintain in the jungle, and therefore of doubtful value.

A little girl just came in from Atanasio's house to ask if there would be a meeting tonight. I told her there would be. Pray that we might see the hand of God working among this small group of Indians and that the Lord would protect us from the work of the enemy here.

Notes

1. Isaiah 25:9.
2. Romans 1:9, para.
3. Isaiah 49:23.
4. Psalm 37:4.
5. My brother.

— 23 —

The Pattern at Work

According unto the patterns which the Lord had shewed Moses, so he made the candlestick. [1]

AT THE END OF June we had a little 'commencement' programme for the schoolchildren and their parents in Puyupungu, and, with a promise to visit them whenever we could, we closed up the house and went to Shandia so that Jim could put full time on the building programme while his father was still in Ecuador. Jim and I lived in a tiny bamboo house which Pete had built for himself, and ate our meals with Ed and Marilou.

Jim's days were spent in heavy, exhausting construction, in clearing jungle, in hauling sand and rocks, in building concrete forms, and in supervising workmen. When I took a pitcher of lemonade in mid-afternoon I would find him standing by the little cement mixer, stripped to the waist, bronzed and glistening with sweat as he heaved buckets of sand and directed the Indians who were working with him. He would return to the McCully house, which was a twelve-minute walk through the forest, near sundown, and bathe in the cool river before supper. Evenings were spent in letter writing, language discussion, preparation for Bible teaching, or talking with the McCullys. Working with Ed in the forest was another of Jim's dreams come true—which of course is what he fully expected dreams to do. For Marilou and me it was pure pleasure to watch Jim and Ed. Their minds met, it seemed, at nearly every point, and they found that the old fellowship of Wheaton and Chester days had lost none of its joy; in fact, the sharing of work together on the mission field had immeasurably strengthened the bond.

On October 8 he wrote to his mother and brother in Peru:

This is our wedding anniversary. It has been the happiest and busiest year of my life. I hope that by next week we'll move into our third house since we were married—first the tent, then the thatch roof in Puyupungu, and now, boards, concrete, and aluminium! Where does one go from there?

Ed is in Arajuno over the week-end. He went in there and built a shack and was there with his family for a couple of weeks. It will be like Puyupungu now, a preaching point to which we can "ride circuit" and teach and preach while basing our operations here in Shandia. We started school on Thursday with eleven boys and with promise of more coming on Monday. Some older fellows are coming along, too, so we are going to give some special attention to the school ourselves and not leave the teaching up to the poor, young Christian schoolteacher whom we have asked to come this year.

December 12. Ed and I are sweating out a warm afternoon in this little shack that Ed built in a Shell Oil "ghost town", Arajuno. It's a weird place—great cement slabs, steel girders, well-drilling heads, pipes, bricks, tumble-down buildings all grass-grown, rotten, and rusty. Had about twenty-five out to meeting yesterday in this place, and fifty out to a meeting in an Indian house this morning. There is genuine interest in the gospel here. They are not so jaded as those at Shandia. It is surely a thrill (even when you're hoarse, as I am) to announce the gospel to people who've never heard it, and I think it helps one get to the main point, leaving out the sidelines and details. When one gets out in these places one feels as though the Word is being fulfilled literally: "This gospel shall be preached throughout the whole world."[2]

We spent Christmas of 1954 alone in Shandia, because the McCullys had gone to Quito for the birth of their second son, Mike. We had moved into the new house at the end of October, and were greatly enjoying fixing up the inside. Jim spent Christmas week building a room-divider between the living-room and kitchen. This consisted of cupboards and drawers, made of a beautiful almost-black wood which he had selected from the forest.

On January 16, 1955, his journal reveals a spirit of heaviness:

> Cast down on this Lord's Day morning. Just came up from the meeting with twenty-five Indians, mostly schoolboys and young women. Felt as though I preached powerlessly, without unction, and resultant effect was evident. Restlessness, interruptions, playing. Almost no adults come. Vicente's wife, Kuwa's, and Upuchu's; no adult men. My first thought is that they have tired of preaching, and they do not enjoy it. I may be preaching too hard; I think that I am worried too much of the week with the finishing of the house—right up till Saturday supper. Translated and preached from Titus, but felt little life or even continuity in what I said. House and furnishing must take second place now. Getting the Indians out to meetings and individual witness to them has got to be my foremost concern. Elias Cerda wants to be baptised, but he did not come out to meetings today. I must speak personally with Gervacio, Venancio Grifia, and Abelardo as well as to Elias before the young men's conference which begins the fourth of February.
>
> I am sorry I have neglected writing here. Many times fresh thoughts come, and I have failed to record them, so that now they are gone.

The Flemings and McCullys were able to come to Shandia in February to help with the conference. Some seventy to a hundred Indians attended the sessions. On the final Sunday four young men were baptised and told the spectators of the power of Christ in their lives. One had been a notorious drinker—his life was now transformed. This was a great encouragement to Jim, for the young men, especially—since they were the ones to carry the spiritual responsibility of the little church—were the principal concern to him. He taught them carefully and patiently; always with a view to teaching *them* to teach. A Bible class on Mondays was for the instruction of believers only, and went far beyond the evangelistic preaching they received on Sunday mornings. With a small nucleus of baptised believers Jim began having a simple meeting for the breaking of bread, when Christ was exalted and worshipped. No one taught; the words of men were few. Hymns of adoration were sung, prayer was offered, and gradually the new believers began to understand the meaning of worship—offering to the Lord the love of their hearts, with simplicity and sincerity. Others began to observe this gathering from outside—some to scoff, some out of curiosity, some with a desire to understand. There was not much to watch. The room where we met was the schoolroom—bamboo walls and floors, thatched roof, backless benches. A small table stood in the centre of the circle with a loaf of bread and a cup of wine. The Indians gathered quietly, for once (with the dogs and babies outside), and sat barefooted and reverent around the symbols which spoke to them of the death of their Lord Jesus, whom they had so recently come to know and love. One by one, the young men would take part, suggesting a hymn, or praying, while all joined in lifting their hearts to Christ. Reminded of His death, they also thought of His coming again, and frequently ended the meeting singing '*kirikgunaga, kushiyanguichi—Cristo shamunmi!*' 'Be happy, believers—Christ is coming!'

At first Jim did most of the preaching, after Ed and Pete had left Shandia. This usually necessitated translating, first of all, the passage from which he meant to preach, for there were very few Scriptures in the lowland Quichua. All three men worked on this task continually, sharing their problems, and the results. The McCullys produced on their mimeograph in Arajuno an amazing variety of literary materials in a short time. Jim translated most of the Gospel of Luke—one of his last tasks—and also many isolated portions of Scripture, in the process of preparing his sermons.

Gradually, however, he felt that the responsibility of the preaching must go to the young Indians, and to that end he spent many hours with individuals, going over and over some portion of Scripture, helping them to study it for themselves, trying to lead them into a method of Bible study which they could follow when alone. Several young men exhibited a real gift in this, and it was not long before they were able to take charge of the entire Sunday morning gospel meeting—from leading the singing to preaching a sermon. It was something of a novelty for most of the Indians to see one of their own up front, and much patient teaching was required before they appreciated this. To them the gospel was for gringos, and for learned people only. An Indian preach? Absurd! But they came to see the fun.

Jim was able to show them that the Lord Jesus did not choose from among seminary graduates those whom He sent out to preach. They were common labourers in many cases, from the strata of society of their listeners. There was no dichotomy between clergy and laymen. Jim determined that in Shandia there would be none. The Bible was for all, and all could learn to read it if they would. He was planning to do all in his power to put it into their hands in their own tongue, and to teach them not only to read it, but to 'rightly handle' [3] it. If the Indians came to meetings only to hear a foreigner, they might as well not come. They must see that the written Word is the oracle of God—regardless of who is preaching it—or the missionary labours in vain.

In the United States there is usually respect for the Word of God—that is, outward respect, even where there is no thought of obedience to it. In the Ecuadorian jungle the

Indian has not reached that 'level of culture'—he has neither respect, manifested by apparent attention when it is being read, nor reverence, manifested in obedience to it. The women are the most difficult element in the meetings—they search their children's heads for lice, stand up in a body when anything passes outside, rush to the window if it promises to be interesting, thrust a foot up on the bench for the nearest person to examine for thorns, hustle in and out with children, and have discussions in a conversational tone of voice. The men will occasionally remonstrate with them from the back of the room, rise to rearrange the benches during the sermon, or stand up to talk with a passer-by through the window— but in general they pay much closer attention than the women. Pets are taken for granted, dogs going about through the rows, birds or monkeys perched atop the women's heads, puppies wrapped in carrying-cloths on backs. One is reminded of how the Lord Jesus was constantly trailed by a 'multitude'—the writers of the Gospels have left to our imagination all that meant to Him, but in spite of all, there were the few who came for more than loaves and fishes. These heard His word, and followed. And so it has been in Shandia. There have been the ones and twos, who, apparently seeing Him who is invisible, through all the distractions visible and audible, have believed, and have followed. These were the ones for whom Jim daily laid down his life. 'We ought to lay down our lives for the brethren.'[4]

His patience and wisdom in dealing with them was a source of wonder to me. The Indian reaction to a situation is as different from ours as his manner of sitting on the floor with a plate and spoon is different from our hugely complicated ritual of tables, chairs, cloths, napkins, assorted plates, and cutlery and flowers—to say nothing of the number of dishes served. If he makes a mistake, instead of registering embarrassment, frustration, regret, or fear, he usually laughs. This habit annoyed and baffled me. It must have been trying for Jim, too, though he had learned to love these people, and love has a way of showing what to do.

In February Jim and I went to Shell Mera, where he went to work helping on the construction of a hospital sponsored by the Quito missionary radio station HCJB, which was to serve all of the jungle stations. Two days after our arrival there, on February 27, our daughter was born. She had no sooner made her appearance than Jim stated simply, 'Her name is Valerie,' a decision he must have arrived at on the spur of the moment, for although we had discussed many names, Valerie included, we had agreed finally on no one of them.

Her birth took place in the home of the pilot and his wife who had done so much for us during our life together in the jungle. We stayed another week with Nate and Marj Saint, and found much to discuss with them, into the small hours, over cups of cocoa in their kitchen. On one occasion Jim held Valerie, looking into her face, and Nate, his own eyes shining with empathy (his own son was just two months old), said, 'Aren't they *terrific?*' Jim did not need to answer. It was evident that his daughter had captivated his heart. No rules of hospital asepsis or visiting hours for him. He picked her up within a few minutes of birth, and continued to do so whenever he pleased, be it her nap-time or whatever. He was not, however, one to change her diapers. Jim was a strong believer in a division of labour. There was man's work, and woman's work, and while the two met, they definitely did not overlap. This was something I had had to learn early in our Puyupungu days, for my months of jungle living had taught me to chop wood, nail up screens, or use a machete, while Jim in his bachelor days had had to see that the laundry was brought in when it rained and that a minimum standard of cleanliness was maintained in the kitchen. Jim made it clear that those days were gone forever. He was always ready, of course, to help me with my work if it became necessary, but I tried to see that it never did.

Jim's parents had come up from Peru, where they had been visiting his brother for several months, to be with us when Valerie arrived. Consequently, there are no letters to them until a month later, March 25, when Jim wrote:

> It's a frog-croaking Friday night in Shandia but we have put new mantles in the lamp and shined up the chimney and I feel full of noodles and desire to send a letter your way which I hope will beat you home. Spent the day painting a baby crib, and the kitchen side of the room-divider.
>
> We just learned of an Auca attack not far from Arajuno and even though the house is nearly ready to move into there, Ed is a little worried about going there with his family. The Aucas killed two children and their mother and were last seen heading up the Arajuno river in a stolen canoe. Pray for Ed as he wants to reach those Quichuas. . . .

This was followed on April 16 by another letter to his parents:

> The last two weeks have been ones of reaping. I have never seen so many Indians openly receptive to the Word. In Dos Rios at the conference last week there were over twenty, in Pano about the same, and here in Shandia about a dozen. Now to the job of readying them for life in Christ. Praise for this break, and continue to pray for these who have made the break. Many of their families are upriver and the real test has not yet come.
>
> I am trying to get the water system done now. I am standing the barrels upright on a platform above the baby's room window. Have to borrow pipe-threading tools from the hospital gang in Shell Mera. They are using our cement mixer. . . . We are tearing down the old wood-shed and the Indians have built a chicken-house for those noisy roosters on the north-west corner of the lot; next we'll have to have another wood-shed and then a motor-shed for the light plant.
>
> Dinner is over now. Eugenia and Camilo have gone down Talac to see her folks. So Betty and I did the dishes and have just

sung a hymn—my current favourite, "I cannot tell why He whom angels worship should set His love upon the sons of men"[5] to the tune of Londonderry Air. She is going to feed Val now, and I hope to get a little literacy material for our believers to read. They will read if they can get their hands on something they can understand. Then I have a pile of unanswered letters to do, so hope you will excuse me if I cut this short. We have all things and abound, so please do not be telling such sad stories to the home folks that they will begin to pity us. We are the happy ones and are feeling great joy in these days working with God here in the jungles. We long for both establishment and outreach in the work. Looks like we are to do the establishing this year while McCullys do the outreach as we did at Puyupungu last year.

From the diary:

May 16, 1955. This has been a busy morning and one of those that doesn't leave one with a great deal of satisfaction after it's all done. Morning reading was in 2 Thessalonians 3: "If any man will not work neither let him eat." Yesterday I had told three girls to come to work. *Six* came to clean two measly manioc-patches. Then I went down to put Urpi and son to work planting pasture. They achieved a morning's success of perhaps thirty yards, ten feet wide. The men were waiting for tools and to be sent for roof-leaf. I sent them. More than twenty women brought plantains and chicha to sell me, for the schoolboys' meals, and I outraged them by buying enough for only two weeks, as I had sufficient for one week already. And one package of chicha from each one, leaving much unbought along with a basket of unnecessary sugar cane. Then my change ran out. Then the workmen on the teacher's house needed two-by-fours planed. I planed two-by-fours for the school building. After that, the girls who had been cleaning the manioc-patch arrived; they wanted me to buy *their* plantains. Domingo wanted ink powder for marking boards. A boy came to buy five sucres' worth of snails for Señora Rosa downriver. The workmen had cut a two-by-four too short and needed a hand. Venancio's leg needed massaging and he wanted to sell me beans, though I had

had to give *him* some yesterday, because he said that he had nothing to eat. Had to tell the men to start weaving the roof and not to stand around doing nothing. Then they all wanted to work the whole day instead of just till noon. Yuyu wanted money for thirty pounds of peanuts, and his mother wanted a sack Ed had not given back to her. Protaco wanted his work-money and the gun that Pete sent down from Quito to sell. Pete had been on the radio in the morning, and it was urgent that I write Tidmarsh. Believers' meeting this afternoon. My snake-bite patient at Limon Chikta is in bad shape. I was there Friday and yesterday and must go again tomorrow, an hour or more each way. Betty and the baby both have colds. I have just eaten a good lunch.

A letter to his home assembly in Portland is dated June 2:

We've been fighting sickness again. I have been making three trips a week downriver, an hour's walk, to care for an Indian who was bitten by a snake something like our western rattler. The Indians fear to lance and suck the bite, so the poison is generally absorbed into the blood stream, where it damages cells and rots tissue. This fellow is improving and I am sure will walk again,[6] but at present he has no skin on the front of his leg from the toes to the knee, and sinews are visible at several points. The danger, now that I have taken out all the rotted matter, is secondary infection. In connection with this we have been having a meeting each week down there and are making contact with Indians who up until now have regarded us as devils. Tomorrow I will go again with some believers. They are helping in the singing and testimony and we can only pray that God will bring light to these sightless and hopeless souls. There is not even a word for *hope* in this language. Betty and I were on our way down there two weeks ago on a Sunday afternoon when our girl who helps us in the house, and who was carrying Valerie, was bitten on the foot by another type of snake. I slit the foot with a jackknife, sucked it, stuck it in cold water and, when we got home, applied ice and injected ten cc's of antivenin serum. She bled at the gums and the foot swelled some, but had little pain. This is snake season here. Don't leave the house without your razor blade!

June 10. I'm in Puyupungu again for a few days. Came back to give the final exams for the little school, visit, and let the Indians know we are still interested. Elena, Atanasio's wife, died last Sunday of smallpox, and I have had a couple of good long chats with Atanasio since arriving. Smallpox has gone right through the Indians here. That's why Betty decided not to come and bring Valerie, because she hasn't been vaccinated. Can't remember if I have or not, but will know for sure in ten days!

I planted dahlias by the palms at our front door in Shandia, and they are blooming nicely. We also have a wide path out to the river so that we have a nice long view of the big bend of the river. I'm planting coffee, palms, and some pasture grass for future millennial herds to keep the forest down. It makes a beautiful homesite now.

Valerie is a giggler already, as sweet and dainty as babies can be. Betty has started giving her banana and papaya and she loves both. We are very busy and very happy—desiring only a fuller experience of the power of Christ.

Jim's sister was married in June, and he wrote to her then:

This is a one-pager to let you know that I am very glad for you both and praying for you these days.

I have been thinking lately that life in the will of God is better in each phase that we enter, so I can say honestly today, "This is the best year of my life." Only now I don't *shout* it as I once did, but I don't despise the shouting, either. I am praying this for you both: that there will not be a sense of climax and then a fading such as I have observed in some young married people. But, rather, that the full experience of life, as it was meant to be lived from the beginning for adults, might be an increasing thing. God deliver us from lolling back and saying, "I've had it." We haven't had everything—only all we could take for the time being.

My warmest congratulations, my very highest hopes and

earnest prayers are for you!—Brother Jim.

Another answer to a prayer of Jim's—perhaps it was an unspoken prayer, but one of those 'desires of the heart'[7] that the Lord sees and answers before we get around to asking for them—came in July, with the visit of Jim's brother Bert and his wife Colleen from Peru. He wrote on July 3:

> It is surely nice to be with Bert and Colleen again. We share a good many things now that we did not before, having lived in the jungle. Their work is quite different and makes conversation very interesting. We haven't been getting to bed at our usual early hour these nights! Bert spoke this morning at meeting while I interpreted, but many didn't need the translation, because he speaks a very understandable Spanish, and some answered his questions without the Quichua translation.

During July Jim proposed a visit to the McCullys so that Bert and Colleen could see the work in Arajuno. I baulked at the suggestion, and said that I would remain at Shandia to take care of things while the rest went. Jim would not hear of this. He reasoned with me, and tried several means to persuade me, without success. Months before, we had agreed—though of course the civil ceremony contained no vows of obedience —that the Scriptural principle must be followed: 'The willing subjection of the Church to Christ should be reproduced in the submission of wives to their husbands. But remember, this means that the husband must give his wife the same sort of love that Christ gave the Church. . . .'[8] This was the only occasion when Jim found it necessary to use his prerogative. I went to Arajuno. Later it was evident to me that he was acting in accord with the principle—I was benefited by the trip. He had done rightly in insisting.

The work with the Quichuas was bearing fruit, and on July 17 Jim wrote to his parents:

Thursday some of the Indians who wanted to be baptised got the idea that we were to have a baptism after the school exams. Just where they got this idea I'll never know, but they were insistent that they had waited long enough, and it is hard to hinder such. So, even though I was alone, I called the believers together and we had a four-hour session Saturday afternoon examining eighteen of them. To my way of thinking, the older believers show a real interest and ability at discerning reality. They decided to hold back four of the young women who are silly and a little scared. There was a great victory in the case of Kupal Angu, a young fellow who left his wife in a huff more than a year ago, but now wants to be baptised. It was put squarely to him that he must fix it up with her, and although at first he did not want to at all, he finally said he would take her again. She was wanting to be baptised, too, so we called her in and settled the thing.

So with Venancio, the assistant schoolteacher, taking every alternate one, we baptised fourteen this morning in the Talac river, at the "Devil's Deep", as the unbelievers call it. They all gave good testimonies from the water, and we can only hope that the unbelievers will heed and soon follow in the way of obedience. Pray for Vicente, Dad; he is well again and working and we pray that God will speak to his soul. So far I have gotten nowhere in the things of God with the elder Venancio, who had the broken back.

That brings the number breaking bread to twenty-five at Shandia—a growth we would regard as phenomenal in any assembly at home but which appears to me to be normal where there is real application to evangelism by the believers and to sound teaching by the leaders. Remember—less than half of these are literate and must be fed and grow only on what they can hear and remember, so pray for them, won't you?

Jim's diary account of the baptism gives details not included in the letter:

My flesh often lacks the deep feeling that I should experience at such times and there was a certain dryness to the form this morning, but I cannot stay for feelings. So cold is my heart most of the time that I am almost always operating on the basis of pure commandments, forcing myself to do what I do not always feel, simply because I am a servant under orders. And there was enough of the physically distracting this morning to save me from walking in the clouds. A part of the cliff gave way and three girls sat down on the beach amid shrieks and laughter. The schoolboys threw stones into the water, Antonia's son fell headlong off the end of the airstrip onto the beach and set up a great wail just as his mother was being baptised. Venancio failed to get Carmela's face clear under, and a group of mockers came by and taunted the baptised ones about bathing with their clothes on. But God is my witness that I have fulfilled His word as I knew how.

In August Jim took the Shandia schoolboys on a hike with a group of Quichuas from the mountains, travelling on foot from Puyo to Papallacta, a journey of about five days. At one point a swift river had to be forded, and the mountain boys, having seen very little water of any kind in their lives, were terrified. Two of them were caught in the current, and it was only after he had lost his shirt with wallet and money in the pocket that Jim was able to rescue one of them, Ed McCully the other. Jim wrote to his parents:

> We were disappointed in the spiritual values of the trip, everyone being too tired to think after twenty miles or so of walking each day. However, I was glad to see the Indian boys get the enlarging experience of it—some had never ridden in a car, and none had climbed a mountain; they got their picture in a Quito newspaper and visited the government buildings.
>
> Valerie grows week by week. She is terrifically active, rolling about and bicycling and "rowing", as the Indians say—with her arms, lifting them first over her head and then whamming them down. She looks like Eisenhower at times with her wide grin and her fine, almost-invisible hair. She is getting over a cold and knocks herself out sneezing, as Dad always did. Nights

are some better—she has slept from five until five, but she usually wakes, cries a little, and goes back to sleep. Betty has started giving her plantain flour, which she makes herself, and the little squirt loves it.

On September 18 Jim's happiness in fixing up his home and garden were reflected in another letter to Portland:

I got some outside window casings on and varnished them and the barge boards on the house. Vicente and his son are clearing ground for a new school. I want to get at the upstairs flooring soon. I did some trimming on the coffee and avocado trees and have dahlias and white glads blooming in the front yard. Also got three rose bushes going and just planted three gardenias. The pineapples are ripening fast now and we eat papaya off the trees on the place, and have our own manioc. Planted corn beyond the clothes-lines and at the back of the house, so the site really looks nice. The pasture grass between here and the river is doing fine, so we thank God for the tropic growing-season. The rain has set in suddenly again and it is chilly at the moment.

Notes

1. Numbers 8:4.
2. Mark 14:9.
3. 2 Timothy 2:15, para.
4. 1 John 3:16.
5. Hymn by W. Y. Fullerton.
6. He died soon after of starvation, because of Indian taboos regarding food which a snake-bite victim may eat.
7. Psalm 37:4.
8. Ephesians 5:24,25, JBP.

— 24 —

Mission Accomplished

I tell you truly that unless a grain of wheat falls into the earth and dies, it remains a single grain of wheat; but if it dies, it brings a good harvest. The man who loves his own life will lose it, and the man who hates his life in this world will preserve it for eternal life. [1]

ONE DAY IN SEPTEMBER, 1955, the McCullys shared with us the most exciting news we could have hoped for — Ed and Nate, the missionary pilot, finally spotted some Auca houses not many minutes' flying time from Arajuno. From that moment on Jim had, as the Spanish say, 'one foot in the stirrup'. His prayer, his personal committal, his hopes for Auca work years before, had not been in vain. Perhaps God was going to give him a share in it with Ed.

Ed and Nate had begun a regular programme of dropping gifts to the houses, in hopes of winning friendship and later of approaching the savages on the ground. They well knew the failure of other attempts to reach these Indians. But they also knew Him who said, 'All power is given unto *Me* . . . . Go ye therefore.' [2]

The work in Shandia was being established. There was now a nucleus of believers, some of whom could read and understand the Bible. There were a few Scriptures in their hands.

Literary programmes for the boys and girls had been conducted. Material needs had been met—a permanent home, the cement base for a new school building, an adequate airstrip. A foundation for the future development of an indigenous work had been laid. The prayer that had been in Jim's heart for years was prayed with renewed energy now—that those who still had never heard, who had never even had the chance to reject the gospel message, might hear. Many Quichuas had heard; many had rejected, but their blood was now upon their own hands. The blood of the Aucas, however, Jim saw on his own.

He began immediately an even more concerted effort to get the young men to take over responsibilities of leadership in the church. He wrote to his parents on October 23:

> Had a great time teaching about patches on old clothes and sweet wine in old bottles this morning. In a culture where the basic drink in intoxicating, like chicha here, and wine in Italy, one gets the full force of such statements as the Lord Jesus' word about a man, who having drunk strong drink does not straight-away desire fresh-made brew. It is a never-failing source of amazement to me how the lofty teaching of our Lord—having been fitted to primitive situations—are frequently more readily understood by a jungle Indian than by a cultured person who is a product of twentieth-century civilisation.

> I am working on two of the ex-schoolboys to get them to take the Bible lessons on Tuesdays and Fridays. Venancio has the Wednesday class and Hector (the schoolteacher) the Monday one, so that I have Thursday only—but of course I sit in on all of them. A school is only worth while so long as the truth of God is being taught in it daily, but we have seen in Venancio that the one who teaches profits 100% more than the boys who hear, so we are trying to expand the blessing by giving others a chance. We have begun Friday afternoon meetings at the mouth of the Talac again, and we had twenty in an Indian house day before yesterday.

> There have been new Auca attacks recently at the mouth of

the Arajuno. Ed is alert and has an electric fence operating. Tuesday I want to go over and get some phrases in Auca from a captive Auca woman in Ila and I also intend to buy a pig there, for the schoolboys to raise.

October 29. Ed and I flew to Villano on Thursday to visit the Quichuas there for a couple of days. In the afternoon, while Ed and I were chatting downriver with the Indians, they came to tell us that a boy had drowned upriver right where we had bathed. We hurried back to find all the Indians sitting placidly at the beach, talking. They had searched the place for the body (none of it was over my head, and the boy who had drowned was a swimmer, about ten years old). They had found nothing. His mother took a canoe downriver to look for the body, wailing as she went. Two hours later we heard her scream and set off wailing anew. We went to the bathing hole just below where he disappeared and saw her paddling up with a stick, with the naked body in the bow of the canoe. It was too late for artificial respiration. The story is that he and his buddy were both going to bathe. He peeled his clothes off and dove in first, came up laughing, and then shouted, "What's got me by the legs?" At that he was dragged under. The Indians said it was a devil. To the rest of us it was pretty clear that a medium-sized boa, looking for food, had seen his feet, drowned him, and, finding him too big to swallow, had let him go.

That spoiled the afternoon for meeting, and their wake left them too tired to hear anymore, so we returned early Saturday morning. Pray for that group of Indians, for we would like to go there to preach the gospel often, but this may make a barrier in some of their minds.

We walked over to Ila last week and I bought two young pigs for the school to raise. A bunch of our boys are going to Tena today to vote, so our meeting will be smaller tomorrow. There has been a defiinite crystallising of lines between the Indians who are disposed to hear our message and those who are not. Pray that our testimony may be of God. Hope to go to Talac Pungu this afternoon to announce the good news there again. No real response from anyone there yet, though all seem friendly enough.

Since the Auca operation was kept secret from all but those directly involved at the time, Jim wrote nothing of it to his parents in the above letter. His journal account of the same trip gives also the sequel:

We flew together back to Arajuno, had a little talk about tactics and flew then with the battery-loudspeaker and the Auca phrases I had gotten from Dayuma, the escaped Auca girl in Ila. I repeated the phrases at the first circling of the houses at about two thousand feet: "Trade us a lance for a machete." "We are your friends." We saw perhaps eight Indians scurrying about the house, one crossed the river with something on his head and seemed to flash a new machete. I did not see him return even though it looked as though he only went to the manioc-patch. One rushed into the house and returned with a lance. I took this as evidence that one had gone to get food in exchange and another to get the lance I asked for. But when we dropped the machete on the string they tore off both the machete and the small basket we had tied on to receive some gift in exchange. One went about the house flailing the piece of canvas the machete was wrapped in. We hauled in the line (heavy work!), then dropped it again after several tries, thinking they might tie something on. It dropped into the water and they cut off a section of it, instead. It was old green line of other drops. We pulled it all the way in and set up the loudspeaker again this time, using the phrases "we like you: you will be given a pot". At this a group raced back into the trees behind the house and one lone man walked to the beach. He cupped his hands and seemed to shout. He flashed the new machete over his head. We dropped a small aluminium pot free with ribbons. It contained a yellow shirt and beads. The man on the beach pointed to the place of the fall. Those behind the house got it and one was soon flailing the yellow shirt. As we approached the drop houses two canoes, some distance below, going downstream turned and went upstream hurriedly. I noticed three people come running up through the water onto the beach at one time and a single man with a white cloth another time. Returned via the Curaray looking for possible landing beaches. Hopes not good. Decided to send for a Whittaker landing gear for the plane, and to plan a trip to make an airstrip whenever it arrives. Guide us, Lord God.

Jim carried the Auca phrases written on small cards in his pocket, whipping them out at odd moments to memorise them. At night he would take them to bed, for a last review before he went to sleep. Coming back from an Auca flight with Nate, Jim was so excited he could hardly eat—I am sure that if I had fed him hay he would not have given it a thought. I knew, then, that this was it. Those vows made to God years before, those declarations of willingness to go the whole way—here was the proving ground. I began to have vague, unsettling doubts. Was this truly the plan of God? Had Jim perhaps run ahead? Could God really mean for him to leave the work at Shandia so soon?

Vision is one thing, carrying it through is another. The tangible facts confronted us now. The men had seen the Aucas. They had known of them before, known of their killing apparently for sport, known of their disdain for the white man and all that he represented. But now they had seen them, shouted to them, watched the Aucas beckon and smile at them, and had received combs, feather crowns, and bracelets which Auca hands had made. And these people, these naked Aucas, were still total strangers to the message which the men held in their hands.

But there were other even more immediate facts for the men for face. For Jim, there was a school building just begun, some young Quichua men who needed nurturing in the Word of God, a house and garden which were only now getting into proper shape—to say nothing of a wife and nine-month-old baby who were dependent upon him.

Which way to go? As always, Jim acted on principle rather than on impulse. Had he acted on impulse, I do not know which way he would have chosen, for the impulse to go to the

Aucas immediately was certainly strong; his love for Shandia, for the Quichuas, and for his family was strong, too. But lessons learned in years of acquainting himself with God were applied. In 1948, after studying Numbers 32, where the sons of Reuben and Gad begged Moses to let them settle down in Jazer and Gilead, rather than go across the Jordan, he had written:

The reason they wanted "this side of Jordan" was that they had seen it and saw it fitted their case. How like many today who never having seen the mission field and, having talents and training usable in this country, stoutly declare "bring me not over Jordan".[3] This is a land of cattle (and I have cattle) or this is a place where teachers are sorely needed, and ably used, and I think I could be a teacher. "Shall your brethren go forth to war and shall ye sit here?"[4] This very thing brought forty years' wandering and left 603,550 carcasses in the wilderness. "Cursed be he that doeth the work of the Lord negligently and withholdeth his sword from blood."[5] The only way to be guiltless is to leave your possessions and little ones and go across to war.

On June 10, 1950, Jim had written:

Abraham was a slow learner. Commanded to leave his family he took Lot—probably as a kindly gesture, but disobedience all the same. This leaving of the family to God is common among the called, cp. James, John, and Zebedee. Any disobedience soon leads to doubt and dallying.

The question of relative population might also have been considered. Was it reasonable to leave a field of potential thousands of Quichuas in order to reach a tribe which in all probability did not number more than a few hundreds? Here again principles of Scripture gave the answer. Jim had written in 1951:

The argument of numbers does not hold entirely, since if my

call were to go where a great number are needy, I would not have chosen South America at all, but India. The Scriptures indicate that God intends some from every tribe and tongue and people and nation to be there in the glory, sounding out the praises of the Redeemer. This is specific indication that the gospel must be gotten to tribes who are not yet included in the singing hosts. Hence my burden for cultural groups as yet untouched.

The principles were plain. Jim was prepared to act on them. I was doubtful of my own willingness to let him go, however, until I challenged him with the question that burned in me.

'Jim,' I began, 'are you sure *you* are supposed to go?'

'I am called,' was the simple reply. So, it was all right. Scriptural principles, God-directed circumstances, and Jim's own inward assurance were consonant. I could share in it, then; I could happily help him plan.

I went to Ila myself a few weeks later, and gathered more linguistic data which Jim and I worked over together, comparing my material with his, filing it carefully, studying the constructions. It was a thrill to be starting on a new language again. We talked of the possibility of our moving into the tribe together, as soon as a friendly contact had been established. In fact, as the plan then stood, the men would go down the Curaray river by canoe first, spying out the land and perhaps preparing an airstrip near the river. Jim said I might go along, a suggestion I jumped at eagerly.

For him, the decision meant further heart-searching of his own motives for coming to Ecuador in the first place. He wrote on November 6:

> You wonder why people choose fields away from the States when young people at home are drifting because no one wants to take time to listen to their problems. I'll tell you why I left. Because those Stateside young people have every opportunity to study, hear, and understand the Word of God in their own language,

and these Indians have no opportunity whatsoever. I have had to make a cross of two logs, and lie down on it, to show the Indians what it means to crucify a man. When there is that much ignorance over here and so much knowledge and opportunity over there, I have no question in my mind why God sent me here. Those whimpering Stateside young people will wake up on the Day of Judgment condemned to worse fates than these demon-fearing Indians, because, having a Bible, they were bored with it—while these never heard of such a thing as writing.

Meanwhile, life in Shandia continued. The old school building of bamboo and thatch looked as though the next wind would demolish it, so Jim was working full speed on a new structure of boards. On November 9 he wrote:

Spent the whole day planing boards, so I'm pretty tired. I'm afraid to leave the Indians alone on the machinery, but they do fine pouring cement. We got seven pillars poured this week and now can't get cement.... I'm thinking of starting Vicente on digging that ditch from the Churu Yaku to the cliff, to get our hydro-electric plant going.

Monday, Lord willing, we'll have another work day and get all the Indains together to drag the girders to the school site. We can get more work done by mixing up a good soup for them than by paying them five sucres.

Valerie has taken to pulling herself up to a standing position in her playpen and letting herself down again. You'd love her now. She's a regular giggling doll. She got sore gums again and it looks as if two more teeth may be coming in soon. She laughs an awful lot, looks like an Elliot. She surely does leave us without any leisure for ourselves except after supper, and we love it. What in the world does one do with triplets?

It has begun to rain a little and I guess we deserve it. Weather has been terribly hot and we've had some really dangerous wind storms. A tree right above the spring, loosened at the roots some time ago, fell over in a small wind today. It's a fight to keep the jungle off your head. We've got to get our land papers settled one of these days, so I must open up the border trails again.

Late afternoons and evenings were spent in concentrated Bible study with young Indians. Jim would get one or two at a time, and go over and over a few verses with them, asking them questions, answering theirs, helping them to dig the meaning for themselves. This, he felt, was the foundation of any indigenous Church. It must be founded on the Word: the members must feed themselves on the Word. He had translated a large part of the Gospel of Luke, and I had a few passages of it translated. He said to me one day, 'We've *got* to get that done before I go to the Aucas.' So we worked over it together, putting our translations together, checking them with Indian informants, and correcting them as best we could. We finished the rough draft before he went.

November 20. A lot of Indians went upriver this week-end, so the number in the meeting was down to forty. Venancio Tapui, the assistant schoolteacher, led the singing, and Gervacio preached. He spoke on "Weep not for me, but for yourselves."[6] Rather good, I thought, though they still need a little poise to look the audience in the eye. Tomorrow Hector will have the Bible class, Tuesday Mariano, Wednesday Venancio, Thursday I give a summary, and Friday Asencio teaches. I am trying to get them all doing something, and they respond. Abelardo will preach this Sunday, God willing. Friday morning Betty and I go to Pano, so Venancio it to take the Talac Pungu meeting.

We have about half of the pillars poured for the new school now. The boys do all right, once they get the swing of the thing. We have all the girders cut, but we will have to have a work day next week to drag them to the site. Betty delivered an Indian woman's baby yesterday while I baby-sat here and made up some reading primers for the girls' school. I have spent some time on the trails this week to get our land-title papers settled. Not a lot of Indians around to work now, as many have gone to the coast and they found a gold-washing spot here this week and have all been panning gold.

Finished the upstairs in the house, using several sizes of flooring from six to nine inches. I couldn't see going to all the

work of ripping so much and I think I'll do the same with the
school, as there is much less waste that way. We tongue-and-
grooved it. I think I'll ship-lap the sides of the school.

I let Valerie go on her feet yesterday and she stood there
grinning and teetering for about five seconds alone. Betty is
weaning her now, and she is a little pestiferous at night again.
Has three upper teeth, and is drinking—a little sloppily—from
a cup.

The journal continues:

November 27. Nate and I made my second Auca flight. Flew
down their river to the grass shack where there are fenced
plantations but no people. Noted an increased amount of cutting
down the forest and land-clearing since my last visit. They seem
to know what to do with machetes and axes. On the way up we
dropped a pair of pants at the first house, where we saw a woman
wearing a grey slip that had been dropped on an earlier flight.
The second house has a model airplane carved on the house
ridge. There we dropped a machete, a pair of short pants, and I
saw a thing that thrilled me: it seemed an old man, who stood
beside his house, waved with both of his arms as if to signal us to
come down. Aucas waving to me to come! At the next house
they have made a large clearing and built a bamboo platform on
which one, a white-shirted one, stands and waves. Nate dropped
a roll of toilet paper and several streamered combs[7] into the trees
at the edge of the clearing to try to give them the idea that we
want those cut down, too. Dropped a machete there, too, with
streamer, which they got. Dropped a pot and an axe-head on the
string and they tied something with a red ribbon on, but we lost
it trailing it on the way back. Nate was in a hurry as it was late
afternoon and he stepped it up, so we lost it.

God, send me soon to the Aucas.

On the same day as the above diary entry, Jim's letter to his
parents told only of progress in Shandia:

I am very grateful to say that the Indian fellows are going great guns on the foundation pillars with only one more pouring left before we start on the girders....

The Indians are doing well in taking school devotions, too, and Abelardo had the meeting this morning. He spoke with a little previous help on the epileptic demon boy, the Lord's impatience with the mob who would not believe, His encouragement of the man who believed but needed help in believing, and the disciples, who even though they were believers were impotent because they had not been fervent in prayer and had lost their power.

Every afternoon and some evenings I have young fellows here in the house, and we go over and over the portion and then I listen to them say it, in Quichua much better than mine and with the great advantage that they make real progress in study and delivery. My ministry consists almost entirely in this now, and I am leaving the public presentation of the Word up to them, apart from the Monday afternoon class for all the believers, which I take myself. God help them. They are so desirous of learning and need no pushing at all, but lots of help in understanding the Word.

Thanks loads for sending the seeds. Sorry to hear you had a cold snap before the apples were picked. Are there any good trees left?

Keep praying for the men, Dad, especially those four: Vicente, Venancio, Chaucha, and Capitan. I felt a particular burden for them this week and I believe they may not be far, sometimes. Also do not forget that as the believers establish themselves here we are thinking of outreach with the gospel. If God sends us elsewhere for a couple of months I think it would be a good thing for the young church.

The hibiscus are blazing in the front yard, until some Indian comes along and strips them off. I got some varnish for the house this week and some tar for the roof, so we may get some finishing done on this place before long.

Guess that is all for now. It is after six and the crickets and frogs have begun their dusk-to-dawn concert. We have made a deal with friends to trade a big refrigerator for a good milk cow.

Our pasture is booming now. Thanks for all your love and prayers and care for us. We are constantly encouraged by the hand of God in the work.

I do not know whether Jim had any premonition that God was going to take him up on all he had promised Him—going to answer literally his prayer of April 18, 1948: 'Father, take my life, yea, my blood if Thou wilt, and consume it with Thine enveloping fire. I would not save it for it is not mine to save. Have it, Lord, have it all. Pour out my life as an oblation for the world. Blood is only of value as it flows before Thine altar.'

One of the last of many Quichua hymns he wrote was one describing what happens when a man dies, using a simile from Ecclesiastes 11:3 which was simple and understandable to the Indian:

> *If a man dies, he falls like a tree.*
> *Wherever he falls, there he lies.*
> *If he is not a believer, he goes to the fire-lake.*
>
> *But on the other hand, a believer,*
> *If death overtakes him,*
> *Will not fall, rather will rise*
> *that very moment, to God's house.*

This has become one of the favourites in Shandia, and several have spoken of its peculiar significance for them now.

But the Enemy of Souls is not easily persuaded to relinquish his hold in any territory. Seeing that his authority in the Auca region was going to be challenged, he soon launched an attack on the challengers. Jim was beset with temptation such as had never before assailed him, and that master-weapon, discouragement, which to my knowlege had held no power over him since his arrival in Ecuador, met him at every turn. A gloom seemed to settle over his spirit in December, and it seemed that battles were being fought which I could not share. During this time he wrote a little song to the tune of Balm in Gilead, lovely, plaintive words which lose their poignancy in translation:

> *Sometimes I say to myself,*
> *I am a believer for nothing.*
> *But in the hour when I say, I'm quitting,*
> *Jesus says to me again*
>
> *'Believe me, little son.*
> *Please follow me.*
> *To my Father's house*
> *I wish to lead you, little son,*
> *To a beautiful country.'*

When the beach was discovered on which Nate felt sure a landing would be possible, the plans of going down the Curaray river by canoe were discarded, and also the necessity of a woman's going. I knew that Jim would be leaving without me, and we began to discuss the possibilities of his not returning.

'If God wants it that way, darling,' he said, 'I am ready to die for the salvation of the Aucas.'

Just before Christmas, the Flemings, who had recently moved into Puyupungu, held a fiesta for the Indians there, inviting Jim and Ed to come down to help in the Bible teaching. Jim wrote of this on December 22:

There were about a hundred Indians there from up the Puyo river. Ten or so of our schoolboys and a couple of their sisters went from here on foot (three days!). There was excellent attention, after we took the gin away from them the first night, and there was no more drunkenness either. Pete gave the drink back to the owner on Monday morning. The older men gave very good attention, better than I have ever seen among Indians, and I can only hope that God will give them help to understand their responsibility to choose Christ and make an open stand for Him. Several of the younger fellows have already stopped drinking. Pray for Atanasio and his brother Isaac. Luis Capitan started out from here but got drunk on his way through Puyo and never made it any farther.

Friday morning on the radio contact Ed and I were standing by for Marilou in Arajuno and she sounded scared. An Indian who was staying with her had gotten up early and almost ran head-on into a naked Auca standing with a lance in his hand not fifty yards away from Ed's house. So Ed and Nate flew out there in a hurry, but nothing more was to be seen of him. The Indian had wanted to kill him on sight, but Marilou took his gun away from him and went out shouting a phrase that means "I like you" and tried to give him a machete, but he was gone. One lone wet footprint on a board and some mashed grass where he took off into the jungle were all she saw of him. We would like to reach this tribe. They have never had friendly contact either with whites or Indians, but we know where they live and will make a definite effort to reach them soon. This needs two things. The first is secrecy. There are some who, if they got wind of our plan, could wreck the whole deal, so don't tell this to anyone till I write you to do so. The second thing is prayer. These people are killers and have no idea of getting along with outsiders. Our Indians are deathly afraid of them, as are the whites, and we will be called fools for our pains, but we believe that God has brought Ed to Arajuno for this contact and we want to do his will in taking the gospel to them. They have no word for God in their language, let alone a word for Jesus. There is a "tamed" Auca woman at Ila whom Betty and I have visited and we are working on their language at present. It is much more difficult than Quichua and will need more work at analyzing, so pray for us. You will be hearing more of this in a month or so as plans develop.

Don't bother sending anything with Ruth Jordan, Mom. She already has a big box of stuff which Betty got her mother to buy, including pants and things for me. We don't need a thing but the power of God and that cannot be sent by anyone except via the throne of God.

We spent Christmas with the Flemings and McCullys at Arajuno. Marilou had set up a little bamboo Christmas tree, complete with lights and tinsel. Most of our conversations were taken up with the Aucas, with plans for the first contact on the ground, to take place the following week, and with the study of language data which we had gathered. Nate had succeeded in recruiting a fourth man to go along with Ed, Nate, and Jim—Roger Youderian, missionary to the Jívaros of the southern jungle. Pete Fleming took part in all of the discussion, but had not yet decided to go.

Christmas over, we all returned to Shandia for a New Year's conference for the young Indian believers.

Jim's last letter to his parents was written December 28:

By the time this reaches you, Ed and Pete and I and another fellow will have attempted with Nate a contact with the Aucas. We have prayed for this and prepared for several months, keeping the whole thing secret (not even our nearby missionary friends know of it yet). Some time ago on survey flights Nate located two groups of their houses, and ever since that time we have made weekly friendship flights, dropping gifts and shouting phrases from a loudspeaker in their language, which we got from the woman in Ila. Nate has used his drop-cord system to land things right at their doorstep and we have received several gifts back from them, pets and food and things they make tied onto this cord. Our plan is to go downriver and land on a beach we have surveyed not far from their place, build a tree house which I have prefabricated with our power-saw here, then invite them over by calling to them from the plane. The contact is planned for Friday or Saturday, January 6 or 7. We may have to wait longer. I don't have to remind you that these are completely naked savages (I saw the first sign of clothes last week—a G-string), who have never had any contact with white men other than killing. They do not have firearms, but kill with long chonta-wood lances. They do not have fire except what they make from rubbing sticks together on moss. They use bark cloth for carrying their babies, sleep in hammocks, steal machetes and axes when they kill our Indians. They have no word for God in their language, only for devils and spirits. I know you will pray. Our orders are "the gospel to every creature".[8]—Your loving son and brother, Jim.

The conference ended on New Year's Day. The guests were to leave on the second, and Jim planned to depart for Arajuno, where the men would assemble for the Auca expedition, on the third of January. But on the morning of January 2 Nate called in by radio to say that since the weather was good, they should take advantage of it for flying, and shuttle Jim to Arajuno along with the others. So we were not to have another day together, as anticipated.

Jim began to pack his things. I helped collect everything we could think of that might amuse the Aucas, things that would hold their interest and give more time for the establishment of friendly relations, since the men realised that sustained conversation with the Aucas, by means of the few phrases they knew, would be impossible.

Finally Jim's list was checked off. Everything was ready. We had the radio contact with the plane, Jim slung the carrying net across his forehead, and started for the front door. As he put his hand on the brass handle I almost said aloud:

'Do you realise you may never open that door again?'

He swung it open, followed me out and slammed it, striding down the bamboo trail in his usual firm, determined gait. As we reached the strip, the plane was circling to land, and it was only a matter of a few minutes before Jim kissed me, hopped in beside the pilot, and disappeared over the river. On Wednesday, January 4, 1956, he wrote me a pencilled note from 'Palm Beach':

Betts darling: Just worked up a sweat on the handcrank of the radio. Nobody is reading us but we read all the morning contact clearly. We had a good night with a coffee-and-sandwich break at 2.00 am. Didn't set a watch last night, as we really feel cozy and secure, thirty-five feet off the ground in our three little bunks. The beach is good for landing but too soft for take-offs. We have three alternatives: (1) Wait till the sun hardens it up and sit until a stiff breeze makes it possible to take off, (2) go make a strip in "Terminal City" [the code name of the Auca settlement] and (3) walk out.

We saw puma tracks on the beach and heard them last night. It is a beautiful jungle, open and full of palms. Much hotter than Shandia. Sweat with just a mosquito net over me last night.

Our hopes are up but no signs of the "neighbours" yet. Perhaps today is the day the Aucas will be reached. It was a fight getting this hut up, but it is sure worth the effort to be off the ground.

We're going down now, pistols, gifts, novelties in our pockets, prayer in our hearts. —All for now. Your lover, Jim.

As far as I know, these were the last words Jim wrote. He had yet four days to live. All that we know of those four days is told elsewhere.[9] Suffice to say that on Friday the thrill of Jim's lifetime was given. He took an Auca by the hand. At last the twain met. Five American men, three naked savages.

Two days later, on Sunday, January 8, 1956, the men for whom Jim Elliot had prayed for six years killed him and his four companions.

Notes

1. John 12:24,25, JBP.
2. Matthew 28:18,19.
3. Numbers 32:5.
4. Numbers 32:6.
5. Jeremiah 48:10, para.
6. Luke 23:28.
7. White-cloth streamers were attached to the combs to help the Aucas find them in the forest.
8. Mark 16:15.
9. *Through Gates of Splendour.*

EPILOGUE

W. SOMERSET MAUGHAM, in *Of Human Bondage*, wrote, 'These old folk had done nothing, and when they died it would be just as if they had never been.' Jim's comment on this was, 'God deliver me!'

When he died, Jim left little of value, as the world regards values. He and I had agreed long before that we wanted no insurance. We would store our goods in heaven, share what the Lord gave us as long as we had it, and trust Him literally for the future, in accord with the principles Paul set forth to the Corinthians:

It is a matter of share and share alike. At present your plenty should supply their need, and then at some future date their plenty may supply your need. In that way we share with each other, as the Scripture says,

"He that gathered much had nothing over,
And he that gathered little had no lack." [1]

When the children of Israel were given manna in the wilderness, they received enough for one day. They were not told to lay up for tomorrow.

So, of material things, there were few: a home in the jungle, a few well-worn clothes, books, and tools. The men who went to try to rescue the five brought back to me from Jim's body his wrist watch, and from the Curaray beach the blurred pages of his college prayer-notebook. There was no funeral, no tombstone for a memorial (news reports of 'five wooden crosses set up on the sand' were not true).

No legacy then? Was it 'just as if he had never been'? 'The world passeth away and the lust thereof, but he that doeth the will of God abideth forever.'[2] Jim left for me, in memory, and for us all, in these letters and diaries, the testimony of a man who sought nothing but the will of God, who prayed that his life would be 'an exhibit to the value of knowing God'.

The interest which accrues from this legacy is yet to be realised. It is hinted at in the lives of Quichua Indians who have determined to follow Christ, persuaded by Jim's example; in the lives of many who still write to tell me of a new desire to know God as Jim did.

When I was a student at Wheaton, I asked Jim to autograph my yearbook. Instead of the usual 'It's been nice knowing you', or some equally meaningless platitude, he wrote:

The dust of words would smother me. 2 Timothy 2:4.

The text cited says, 'No man that warreth entangleth himself with the affairs of this life, that he may please Him who hath chosen him to be a soldier.'

His death was the result of simple obedience to his Captain. Many thousands of men have died in obedience to their captains. The men at Gettysburg were among them. Abraham Lincoln's great words, spoken on that battlefield, apply as well to other soldiers whose obedience to commands is not the less to be imitated:

We cannot dedicate—we cannot consecrate—we cannot hallow—this ground. The brave men...who struggled here, have consecrated it, far above our poor power to add or detract.... It is rather for us to be here dedicated to the great task remaining before us—that...we take increased devotion to that cause for which they gave the last full measure of devotion.

Lincoln and those who were present at that ceremony viewed once again the ground whereon the men struggled—common green fields of Pennsylvania, but fraught with new significance. As I read again Jim's own words, put down in battered notebooks during the common routine of life, they become, for me, fraught with new meaning. To them I can add nothing.

He is no fool who gives what he cannot keep to gain what he cannot lose. (*1949*)

One treasure, a single eye, and a sole master. (*1948*)

God, I pray Thee, light these idle sticks of my life and may I burn for Thee. Consume my life, my God, for it is Thine. I seek not a long life, but a full one, like you, Lord Jesus. (*1948*)

Father, take my life, yea, my blood if Thou wilt, and consume it with Thine enveloping fire. I would not save it, for it is not mine to save. Have it Lord, have it all. Pour out my life as an oblation for the world. Blood is only of value as it flows before Thine altar. (*1948*)

Saturate me with the oil of the Spirit that I may be aflame. But flame is often short-lived. Canst thou bear this, my soul? Short life? In me there dwells the spirit of the Great Short-Lived, whose zeal for God's house consumed Him. "Make me Thy fuel, Flame of God." (*1948*)

Are we willing to build with a trowel in one hand, while the other grasps a sword? (*1948*)

Taking all, Thou givest full measure of Thyself,
With all things else eternal,
Things unlike the mouldy pelf by earth possessed.... (*1948*)

Father, if Thou wilt let me go to South America to labour

with Thee and to die, I pray that Thou wilt let me go soon. Nevertheless, not my will. (*1948*)

How few, how short these hours my heart must beat—then on, into the real world where the unseen becomes important. (*1948*)

Of the coffin: a swallowing up by Life. For this I am most anxious. (*1948*)

Ah, how many Marahs have been sweetened by a simple, satisfying glimpse of the Tree and the Love which underwent its worst conflict there. Yes, the Cross is the tree that sweetens the waters. "Love never faileth." (*1949*)

As your life is in His hands, so are the days of your life. But don't let the sands of time get into the eye of your vision to reach those who sit in darkness. *They simply must hear.* Wives, houses, practices, education, must learn to be disciplined by this rule: "let the dead attend to the affairs of the already dead, go thou and attend the affairs of the dying". (*1948*)

Overcome anything in the confidence of your union with Him, so that contemplating trial, enduring persecution or loneliness, you may know the blessedness of the "joy set before", for "We are the sheep of His pasture. Enter into His gates with thanksgiving and into His courts with praise." And what are sheep doing going into the gate? What is their purpose inside those courts? To bleat melodies and enjoy the company of the flock? No. Those sheep were headed for the *altar*. Their pasture feeding had been for one purpose: to test them and fatten them for bloody sacrifice. Give Him thanks, then, that you have been counted worthy of His altars. Enter into the work with praise. (*1949*)

To his mother when his brother Bert sailed for Peru:

Remember—and I don't mean to sound pedantic or impudent as if I knew all the costs—remember that we have bargained with Him who bore a Cross, and in His ministry to those disciples His emphasis was upon sacrifice, not of worldly goods so much as upon *family ties*. Let nothing turn us from the truth that God has determined that we become strong under fire, after the pattern of the Son. Nothing else will do.

*"O Prince of Glory, who dost bring
Thy sons to glory through the Cross,
Let us not shrink from suffering
Reproach or loss." (1949)*

I must not think it strange if God takes in youth those whom I would have kept on earth till they were older. God is peopling Eternity, and I must not restrict Him to old men and women. (*1950*)

Granted, fate and tragedy, aimlessness and just-missing-by-a-hair are part of human experience, but they are not all, and I'm not sure they are a major part, even in the lives of men who know no Designer or design. For me, I have seen a Keener Force yet, the force of Ultimate Good working through seeming ill. Not that there is rosiness, ever; there is genuine ill, struggle, dark-handed, unreasoning fate, mistakes, "if-onlys" and all the Hardyisms you can muster. But in them I am beginning to discover a Plan greater than any could imagine. (*1951*)

The principle of getting by spending is illustrated by the actions of God:

> *"He had yet one, a Beloved Son."*
> *"He giveth not the Spirit by measure."*
> *"He spared not His own Son."*
> *"He emptied Himself."*

Is heaven the poorer for this spending? Nay, both heaven and earth are enriched by it. Who dare not follow God's example? (*1951*)

Only I know that my own life is full. It is time to die, for I have had all that a young man can have, at least all that this young man can have. I am ready to meet Jesus. (*December, 1951*)

Gave myself for Auca work more definitely than ever, asking for spiritual valour, plain and miraculous guidance.... (*May, 1952*)

The will of God is always a bigger thing than we bargain for. (*1952*)

Give me a faith that will take sufficient quiver out of me so that I may sing. Over the Aucas, Father, I want to sing! (*July, 1952*)

I know that my hopes and plans for myself could not be any better than He has arranged and fulfilled them. Thus may we all find it, and know the truth of the Word which says, "He will be our Guide even until death."

Notes

1. 2 Corinthians 8:15, JBP.
2. 1 John 2:17.

Notes

E VERY EFFORT has been made to find the sources of
quotations in this book. The author will be grateful
for information regarding errors or omissions.

Jim's writings are full of allusions to Scripture which he
did not put in quotation marks. These are not included in
end-of-chapter *Notes*. I have also omitted any references to
quotations for which a reference is given in the main text,
even if the reference is only a partial one.

Owing to the fact that Jim usually quoted from memory,
there is sometimes a difference of a word or two between his
quotation and the original text. In other cases, he made his
own translation from a Hebrew or Greek text. Some references
which Jim put in quotation marks are allusions to Scripture
texts. In all three of these cases, I have listed the reference
with the word *para.* (paraphrase) following.

Abbreviations used in end-of-chapter Notes.

JBP J. B. Phillips' translations of the New Testament
ASV American Standard Version of the Bible
RSV Revised Standard Version
JND J. N. Darby's translation of the Bible

All other Biblical references are from the Authorized
Version.

Through Gates of Splendour

by Elisabeth Elliot

. . . Marg was standing with her head against the radio, her eyes closed. After a while she spoke: 'They found one body . . .'

Missionary history will never let us forget the five young American men savagely martyred by Auca Indians in the jungles of Ecuador as they attempted to reach them with the Word of God.

Elisabeth Elliot, widow of one of those men, records the story of their courage and devotion to Christ in the face of danger and difficulty.

The challenge of their expendability for God continues as strong today as it was at the time of their deaths in 1956.

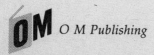 O M Publishing

Until the Day Breaks

The life and work of Lilias Trotter—pioneer missionary to Muslim North Africa

by Patricia St John

As a young woman who had just turned down the prospect of a brilliant career as an artist to serve Christ, Lilias Trotter's missionary call started as 'a strange, yearning love for those who were in the land of the shadow of death'. Despite being refused by a missionary society on health grounds, she was soon sailing into the port of Algiers to begin an evangelistic work that was totally unconventional for a European woman of the day.

The story of her 40 years of dedication to the task of building Christ's church in North Africa is told in this new biography by well-loved author Patricia St John, who herself worked for 27 years in the same area.

 OM Publishing